The *Made Simple* Series

Written by leaders and researchers in their fields, the *Made Simple* series offers accessible, step-by-step guides for understanding and implementing a number of evidence-based modalities in clinical practice, such as acceptance and commitment therapy (ACT), dialectical behavior therapy (DBT), compassion-focused therapy (CFT), functional analytic psychotherapy (FAP), and other proven-effective therapies.

For use by mental health professionals of any theoretical background, these easy-to-use books break down complex therapeutic methods and put them into simple steps—giving clinicians everything they need to put theory into practice to best benefit clients and create successful treatment outcomes.

Visit www.newharbinger.com for
more books in this series.

CFT
made simple

A Clinician's Guide to Practicing
Compassion-Focused Therapy

RUSSELL L. KOLTS, PhD

New Harbinger Publications, Inc.

Publisher's Note

Copyright © 2016 by Russell L. Kolts

New Harbinger Publications, Inc.
5674 Shattuck Avenue
Oakland, CA 94609
www.newharbinger.com

Cover design by Sara Christian; Acquired by Melissa Kirk;
Edited by Gretel Hakanson; Indexed by James Minkin

Library of Congress Cataloging-in-Publication Data on file

Printed in the United States of America

18		17		16							
10	9	8	7	6	5	4	3	2	1	

First printing

For my dear friend, colleague, and mentor Paul Gilbert. Paul, your brilliant work, inspiration, nurturance, and tutelage have made this book possible, and have given me a professional life that is more meaningful and rewarding than I had ever dared to dream.

Contents

Foreword

In this beautifully and skillfully written book, Russell Kolts uses his experience to outline the key themes in compassion-focused therapy (CFT). It's very easy to think that compassion approaches to psychological therapies are just about helping people be kind to themselves and others. In reality, the center of compassion—particularly in the therapeutic arena—is *courage*. Russell himself has worked with anger problems in prison inmates and has developed a CFT approach that he calls the *True Strength* program, highlighting compassion as the strength and courage to turn toward our suffering, and that of others.

I must confess that I was dubious about "making therapies simple" because this can easily be seen as dumbing them down. It's important to note that compassion-focused therapy is in some ways very complex: based in consideration of basic scientifically established psychological processes; the ways in which emotions, motives, and cognitions operate; and the manner in which humans are deeply socially embedded and organized through their social relationships. So when you read this in terms of "made simple," don't think that Russell is saying the therapy is "simple." Rather, he is outlining some of the crucial concepts of CFT in the hope that they will be useful to you, and perhaps excite you to learn more.

I'm delighted to say that Russell achieves his goal brilliantly and in a way I never could. I am one of those people who tend to see complexity rather than simplicity. So here is a wonderful guide to introduce you to the realities of the toughness, difficulties, and complexities of CFT—but, as Russell says, creating the layers and building blocks in relatively straightforward and simple ways.

As explained in this book, CFT began in a relatively simple and straightforward way in the 1980s. It started with just noticing the importance of understanding the *emotional tone* people created in their heads when they tried to be helpful to themselves. For example, imagine you are trying to generate helpful thoughts when you're feeling depressed. But imagine "hearing" and experiencing these thoughts in a very hostile way, as if you are irritated and contemptuous even as you say them in your mind. How will that be? Even an encouraging phrase like *You can do it* becomes venomous when communicated in a hostile mental "tone of voice." You might try saying that to yourself in a contemptuous, sort of hostile way and notice how that feels. Notice whether you feel encouraged. Then imagine that you can really focus on warmth and empathic understanding in the words, focusing on the feeling—maybe as if you were hearing somebody who really cared about you say it with a heart that wishes for you to be free of your depression, or maybe as if hearing your own voice as supportive, kind, and validating with the same intention. Actually doing exercises like this is helpful, because in CFT getting personal experience by doing the practices yourself is key to the development of your therapeutic skills.

What I found all those years ago was that while people could "cognitively" learn to generate new perspectives and coping thoughts, they often did so with a contemptuous or hostile, irritable tone. Indeed, they often found it very difficult to experience coping thoughts that involved two important aspects that are now recognized as being core to our understanding of compassion. First, they struggled to direct these thoughts toward themselves with a *heartfelt motivation* that is based on empathic concern to address the deeper causes of the difficulties (compassionate motivation). Many patients actually blamed themselves, or thought they did not deserve compassion, or that compassion was weakness in some way—just too soft! Sometimes they were very avoidant of the causes of their suffering—for example, not wanting to address the traumatic experiences underpinning their depression, or the fact that they needed to make life changes. It takes courage to begin working on these difficult issues. Second, they tended to struggle with generating supportive, kind, understanding, and validating *emotions* when they actually created those thoughts in their mind (compassionate action).

So CFT began with trying to think about how to help clients generate *compassionate motivation* and care-orientated emotions, and also within that motivation, to create certain kinds of emotional balancing within the mind. As Russell says, we use a standard definition of compassion—one that captures the heartfelt wish for suffering to cease, a preparedness to develop "sensitivity to suffering of the self and others with a commitment to try to alleviate and prevent it." The prevention part is important, because the training that we do is aimed at reducing suffering both in the present and in the future. So the first psychology of compassion is about how we begin to address our suffering and really start to understand it. As Russell outlines here, there are many competencies that we are going to need, such as how we pay attention, how we experience being in contact with distress, how we tolerate our distress, and how we empathically understand it without being judgmental or critical.

The second psychology of compassion is really about developing the wisdom of knowing how to be genuinely helpful. True helpfulness requires the development of wisdom—we must understand the nature of suffering before we are well equipped to work with it. Minds are very tricky and are full of conflicted motives and emotions. Also, although warmth and gentleness can be part of compassion, compassion requires a certain toughness, assertiveness, and a great deal of courage as well. Parents are prepared to argue with their children over their diets or going out late at night because they want to protect them, even though this may cause conflicts. In some therapy encounters, clients are frightened of their anger or anxiety or grief. Therapists may then need to encourage these clients to experience such emotions, even when a client is reluctant to do so, and even when doing so may not be pleasant at the time, because that is what's required to help this client learn to experience and work with these difficult feelings. It's a therapeutic skill and wisdom that allows the therapist to know how and when to do this. Indeed, some years ago, studies showed that some of the warmest therapists were behaviorists! That makes sense, because behavior therapy often has to encourage clients to engage with things they'd rather not connect with.

CFT also uses evolutionary functional analysis to help us understand how our emotions work. As Russ clearly outlines, we consider emotions in terms of three functionally distinct types of emotion-regulation system: there are emotions for dealing with threats and trying to protect us, emotions that are stimulating us to go out and achieve and acquire resources, and emotions that give rise to feelings of contentment, safeness, and slowing down—which are sometimes linked to the parasympathetic functions of rest and digestion. Many of our clients are very out of balance with these emotions, and the capacity for contentedness and peaceful feelings can be almost impossible for them to access. Studies of the parasympathetic nervous system have shown that this system is out of balance in many people with mental health problems, with the major emotion-balancing and regulating systems not operating appropriately. In such cases, we have to help them get these feelings of safeness online. In this way, building and cultivating the capacity for slowing down, grounding, and experiencing safeness, connectedness, and affiliation are central treatment targets for CFT. This creates the competencies and strengths for people to then engage with feared material—be these things they need to do in the outside world, or in the internal one.

Given that CFT is an evolutionary-based therapy, it will not be surprising to hear that it draws from attachment theory and its extensive research base. Attachment theory tells us that relationships with caring others can provide a secure base (which can be the platform to enable us to go out and try things, take risks) and a safe haven (a safe and secure base where we can be soothed, helped, and supported when we've gotten into difficulties). CFT helps clients begin to experience and develop this internalized secure base and safe haven.

Once a person understands the nature of those three different types of emotion we visited earlier, then a lot of things fall into place. For example, when soldiers are trained, their secure base and safe haven can shift away from their families and toward their combat buddies—because that is indeed the source of their safeness in combat. When they go out on sorties they will be in high-stakes arousal, and when they come back they will calm down and find that safe haven within the company of their buddies. So the soothing systems have been rewired to respond in connection with these combat buddies. When they come home, they can then lose the secure base and safe haven that their brains have gotten wired up for, and there will be fewer intense "dopamine rushes." Even though they are now at home with their families in a physically safe environment, it can be very difficult and even stressful, because those families are not now the source of the secure base and safe haven.

CFT outlines these kinds of processes clearly because it contains an emotional model capable of dealing with that degree of complexity. This example is reflective of a common aspect of CFT: the CFT therapist is very interested in how patients are able to calm and ground themselves, feel connected to a secure base and safe haven, and then develop the courage necessary to engage with feared and avoided experiences. Key too is the development of the internal affiliative relationship; that is, one learns to relate to oneself in a friendly, supportive way rather than in a critical manner that will continue to stimulate the threat system.

Good therapists want to know the evidence behind the therapies they utilize. Given the purpose of this book, Russell has not overwhelmed it with evidence, but makes clear that a lot of the evidence for CFT is *process* evidence. That is, we don't have many theoretical concepts, but rather try to understand and draw upon what the science tells us about things like motivation and emotion—for example, what we know about the importance of the frontal cortex and how that develops during childhood or is affected by trauma. We know that the affiliative motives (such as attachment or group belonging) and emotions played a very major role in mammalian evolution and in particular the evolution of human intelligence. We also know that affiliative relationships are very powerful regulators of motives and emotions. It follows, therefore, that these would be targets for therapeutic intervention.

The backbone of CFT is found in detailed knowledge of how our brains have become the way they are, understanding the evolutionary function of emotions, understanding core regulating processes of motives and how motives are linked to self-identity, and understanding how self-identity can be cultivated in the therapeutic process. All over the world now, we are beginning to recognize that the human mind is full of complex emotions and conflicts partly because of its evolved design—an awareness that is increasingly reflected even in popular culture, such as the Disney movie *Inside Out* (2015). The human brain is very tricky, easily pushed into doing bad things to others and harmful things to ourselves. Compassionate motives, however, help to bring harmony and reduce the risks of both.

CFT is an integrative therapy, which makes use of many evidence-based intervention strategies. These include Socratic dialogue, guided discovery, identification of safety behaviors, focus on avoidance and exposure, inference chaining, reappraisal, behavioral experiments, mindfulness, body/emotion awareness and breath training, imagery practices, supporting maturation—and more besides. However, CFT also features a number of unique features:

- Psychoeducation about our evolved "tricky" brains

- Models of affect regulation with special focus on affiliation and the parasympathetic nervous system

- A specific focus on the complex functions and forms of self-criticism and self-conscious emotions, highlighting distinctions between different types of shame and guilt

- Building compassion-focused motives, competencies, and identities as inner organizing systems

- Utilizing self-identity as the means for organizing and developing compassionate motives and competencies

- Working with fears, blocks and resistances to compassion, positive feelings, and especially affiliative emotions

One of the key aspects of CFT is the idea that motives are major organizers of our minds. They are linked to phenotypes in complex ways that are beyond the scope of the current discussion. But for example, imagine that you are invited to a party and you are motivated by *competitive social rank*. You want to impress the people there, and avoid making mistakes or being rejected, and you want to take any opportunity you can to identify the more dominant members of the group and impress them. Now let's change that motivation and imagine you have a motivation that's focused on *caring or friendship*. Now your attention is not on who is dominant or whom you can impress (or how you can impress them), but on finding out more about them. You are interested in sharing values, and perhaps developing friendships. You will be considering people in terms of whether you like them and want to spend time with them or not. The ways we think, pay attention, and act are guided by *motivations*. Of course, beliefs and things like organizing schemas come into it—in fact, these are linked to motives—but the crucial issue is motivation. When we see how powerful these motives can be in organizing our minds, it becomes clear why compassion and prosocial motivations are central in CFT.

Research has revealed that many people with mental health problems are motivated primarily through *competitive social rank systems* which play out in terms of harsh self-judgments, self-criticizing, and worries of being seen as inferior or incompetent in some way and rejected, often with intense feelings of loneliness. These individuals may often feel they are stuck in low-rank, low-status, or undesirable positions. Of course, there are others who are hyper-focused on attaining dominance; focused on getting ahead and taking control regardless of the impact it has on others. Switching to caring-focused or compassionate motivations can be a revelation to such clients, but can also be quite frightening. Different types of clients can experience resistance toward cultivating compassionate and prosocial motives rather than competitive social rank–focused ones. CFT teaches people how to think about different motivational and emotional states and to practice switching between them. When we learn how to create within us a wise, strong, compassionate motivation and then to anchor that motivation at the center of our sense of self, we discover that it brings with it a wisdom for how to deal with life crises, orienting us to our own suffering and those of others in very different ways. We discover that it's a way of liberating ourselves from suffering and learning how to tolerate that which can't be changed. A very simple depiction of the essence of why developing a compassionate sense of self is important can be seen in "Compassion for Voices," a very short film about how people who hear voices can develop a compassionate self: https://www.youtube.com/watch?v=VRqI4lxuXAw.

Russell guides readers through the processes by which we need to pay attention to our bodies, learn how to identify which emotion motivational systems are operating through us (motives which can be activated quite automatically and exert considerable control over our thoughts and behaviors unless we develop more mindful awareness), and cultivate care-focused motives, emotions, and self-identity using a range of techniques drawn from standard therapies, contemplative traditions, and acting traditions. As Russell makes clear, the details of CFT can indeed be complex, but the layered approach presented here helps to organize these complexities in a straightforward, understandable way. I'm delighted to see Russell write this book in such a clear and easy-to-understand, step-by-step way. I hope it will entice you to learn more—perhaps to get more training, and perhaps even motivate you to cultivate an ever-deepening compassionate motivation within yourself. As Russell points out, there's nothing like personal practice and insight to see how these processes work.

All that I can do now is to leave you in the talented and capable hands of your author and hope this inspires you to learn more about the nature of compassion and how we can bring it into therapy, and of course, into all aspects of our lives.

—Paul Gilbert, PhD, FBPsS, OBE

Introduction

And a woman spoke, saying, "Tell us of Pain."

And he said: Your pain is the breaking of the shell that encloses your understanding.

Even as the stone of the fruit must break, that its heart may stand in the sun, so must you know pain.

And could you keep your heart in wonder at the daily miracles of your life, your pain would not seem less wondrous than your joy;

And you would accept the seasons of your heart, even as you have always accepted the seasons that pass over your fields.

And you would watch with serenity through the winters of your grief.

From *The Prophet*, by Kahlil Gibran

Compassion involves allowing ourselves to be moved by suffering, and experiencing the motivation to help alleviate and prevent it. Compassion is born of the recognition that deep down, we all just want to be happy and don't want to suffer. In this book, you'll learn about compassion-focused therapy (CFT), a therapy that focuses on the purposeful cultivation of compassion, the skills and strengths that flow from it, and how to use these to work effectively with human suffering. When we see what we're up against—the situation we're all in together, just by the virtue of having human lives—there's a deep realization that can arise: *With all the potential suffering and struggle that we and all humans will face, compassion is the only response that makes sense.*

Why do we need compassion? We need compassion because life is hard. Even if we're born into a relatively advantaged existence, with ready access to food, a comfortable place to live, people who love us, education, and opportunities to pursue our goals—even if we have all of this—we will all face tremendous pain in our lives. We'll all get sick, grow old, and die. We'll all lose people we love. We'll all sometimes do our very best in pursuit of goals we desperately desire, and fail. Most of us will have our hearts broken, if not once, then several times. To have a human life means we will face pain. It's the price of admission. Life is hard, for everyone.

But we can forget this. We can forget that all of us hurt, and that these feelings are universal—part of what binds us together as human beings. Many of us, and many of those we seek to help, can instead experience these struggles and emotions as isolating, as signs that there is *something wrong with me*. Instead of reaching out for help, we may pull back from others. Instead of supporting, encouraging, and reassuring ourselves, we may meet our struggles with criticism, attacks, and shame. And even when we know better, it can be hard for us to *feel* reassured. This business of being human can be tricky indeed. And for some people—such as the psychotherapy clients we seek to help—things are exponentially *more* difficult.

COMPASSION-FOCUSED THERAPY

It was observations like these that inspired my dear friend and colleague Paul Gilbert to develop compassion-focused therapy. CFT was designed to assist therapists in helping clients understand their mental suffering in nonshaming ways, and to give them effective ways to work with this suffering. Over the last few years, CFT has been increasingly used by mental health providers—first in the United Kingdom where it was developed, and increasingly in other parts of the world as well. It's also been the focus of a growing body of empirical work.

What Is CFT and How Is It Useful?

CFT represents the integration of various science-based approaches for understanding the human condition with mind-training practices that are literally thousands of years old. Finding its scientific footing in evolutionary psychology, affective neuroscience (particularly the neuroscience of affiliation), the science of attachment, behaviorism and cognitive behavioral therapy (CBT), and the growing body of literature supporting the efficacy of mindfulness and compassion practices, CFT is focused on helping clients relate to their difficulties in compassionate ways and on giving them effective methods for working with challenging emotions and situations.

CFT was originally developed for use with patients who have a tendency toward shame and self-criticism, who may struggle in treatment even while engaging in evidence-based therapeutic protocols such as CBT (Gilbert, 2009a; Rector et al., 2000). For example, such patients may be able to generate thoughts such as *I know that what happened wasn't my fault*, but struggle to feel reassured by such thoughts. A focus of CFT is to create an emotional congruence between what clients think (for example, helpful thoughts) and what they feel (for example, reassured). CFT helps patients learn to engage with their struggles and those of others in warm, accepting, and encouraging ways, to help themselves feel safe and confident in working with challenging affects and life difficulties. CFT has been applied to a growing list of problems including depression (Gilbert, 2009a; Gilbert, 2009b), psychosis (Braehler et al., 2013), binge-eating disorder (Kelly & Carter, 2014; Goss, 2011), anxiety (Tirch, 2012), anger (Kolts, 2012), trauma (Lee & James, 2011), social anxiety (Henderson, 2010), and personality disorders (Lucre & Corten, 2013).

The CFT Approach

A growing body of empirical research supports the potential use of compassion interventions in psychotherapy (Hofmann, Grossman, & Hinton, 2011). One thing that distinguishes CFT from other therapies that incorporate compassion is our focus on helping clients understand their challenges in the context of evolution (how our brains evolved to produce basic motives and emotions), the dynamics of how emotions play out in the brain, and the social factors that shape the self, particularly early in life. None of these factors are chosen or designed by our clients, but they play a huge role in their struggles. In this book, you'll learn to help clients apply these understandings to their problems, so that they can stop shaming and attacking themselves for things that aren't their fault, and focus on taking responsibility for building better lives. Whereas shame is linked with avoidance that can contribute to our clients' struggles (Carvalho, Dinis, Pinto-Gouveia, & Estanqueiro, 2013), compassion can give them a way to approach their difficulties with acceptance and warmth, to face them and work with them.

In CFT, clients learn about how different emotions and basic motives evolved to serve certain functions, exploring how these emotions play out in ways that can create interesting challenges when combined with modern environments and new-brain capacities for imagery, meaning-making, and symbolic thought. For example, clients learn how the confusing dynamics of threat emotions like anxiety and anger make complete sense when viewed through the lens of evolution. Such understanding reveals why it's so easy to get "stuck" in such emotions, which can help lessen clients' tendencies to shame themselves for their feelings. CFT also explores how social contexts and attachment relationships can serve to transform our underlying genetic potential into challenging behaviors and emotions. This exploration creates a context for self-compassion to take root, as patients begin to realize how many of the factors that create and maintain their problems were not of their choice or design, and hence, not their fault.

In CFT, this de-shaming process is accompanied by a simultaneous building of responsibility and emotional courage through the cultivation of compassion. Patients learn to work with evolved emotion-regulation systems to help themselves feel safe and confident as they approach and actively engage with life challenges. They are guided in developing adaptive, compassionate strategies for working with emotions, relationships, and difficult life situations. In CFT, the emphasis is on helping clients learn to stop blaming themselves for things they didn't get to choose or design, and to skillfully work with the factors they *can* impact to build a repertoire of skills for working with life challenges and building fulfilling, meaningful lives. As we will explore, this is done through both implicit aspects of the therapy, such as the therapeutic relationship and the therapeutic emphasis upon guided discovery, as well as specific techniques such as imagery, compassion cultivation practices, and the development of compassionate reasoning.

The Evidence Base for CFT

One of the most important movements in the field of mental health over the past century or so is the emphasis on having our treatments grounded in solid science. The evidence base in support of CFT is twofold: First, there is the growing body of research supporting the efficacy of CFT interventions. Second, there are several underlying bodies of literature that provide the scientific basis for the theory behind CFT as well as the process-level components of the therapy. While the focus of this book is on learning the therapy, I wanted to take a moment to briefly introduce you to the science underlying CFT.

EVIDENCE FOR CFT INTERVENTIONS

Of course, the first question to consider is *Does CFT work?* There is a relatively small but rapidly growing body of research documenting the efficacy of CFT interventions. Research has shown that CFT can help to reduce self-criticism, shame, stress, depression, and anxiety (Gilbert & Proctor, 2006; Judge, Cleghorn, McEwan, & Gilbert, 2012). Other studies have documented positive outcomes using CFT with people suffering from psychotic disorders (Braehler et al., 2013; Laithwaite et al., 2009), eating disorders (Kelly & Carter, 2014; Gale, Gilbert, Read, & Goss, 2014), personality disorders (Lucre & Corten, 2013), problematic anger (Kolts, 2013), and traumatic brain injury (Ashworth, Gracey, & Gilbert, 2011), and in conjunction with eye movement desensitization and reprocessing for the treatment of trauma (Beaumont & Hollins Martin, 2013).

The primary limitation of the current literature supporting the efficacy of CFT is the relative lack of randomized controlled trials (RCTs) documenting its effectiveness. At the time of this writing, there are two such RCTs in print. One of these (Kelly & Carter, 2014) showed significant impacts of CFT in reducing binges, global eating disorder pathology, and eating and weight concerns, and increasing self-compassion in individuals with binge-eating disorder. The second (Braehler et al., 2013), documented the impact of CFT upon clinical improvement in patients suffering from psychosis relative to controls, along with increases in compassion that were associated with reductions in depression and perceived social marginalization. A recent systematic review of the literature on CFT (Leaviss & Uttley, 2014) concluded that CFT shows promise in treating psychological disorders, particularly for highly self-critical individuals, but notes that more high-quality clinical trials are needed before definitive statements can be made about CFT being an evidence-based treatment approach. We in the CFT community agree with this assessment, believing that a therapy model is only as good as the science behind it, and are committed to the growing production of rigorous research examining CFT's effectiveness.

THE SCIENCE UNDERLYING THE CFT MODEL

A second question to ask in considering the science behind CFT is *Where does CFT come from?* In developing CFT, Paul Gilbert's goal was not to create an entirely new model of psychotherapy in competition with other therapy models, but to integrate and build upon what existing science tells us about how humans get to be the way they are, and how we can best help them work with suffering when things go wrong (personal communication, 2009). As such, CFT finds its roots in a large and varied body of scientific research, including the neuroscience of emotion and affiliation (e.g. Depue & Morrone-Strupinsky, 2005; Cozolino, 2010), the existence and dynamics of basic evolved emotion-regulation systems (e.g. Panksepp, 1998; Panksepp & Riven, 2012), and the social shaping of the self through attachment relationships (e.g. Schore, 1999; Siegel, 2012).

In its approach to understanding the dynamics of emotion, CFT also draws heavily on behaviorism (e.g. Ramnerö & Törneke, 2008) and upon cognitive science regarding things like the working of our implicit and explicit memory and emotion systems (e.g. Teasdale & Barnard, 1993). Likewise, in structuring our approach to treatment, CFT draws upon science documenting the social regulation of emotion (e.g. Cozolino, 2010; Porges, 2011) and growing evidence supporting the use of compassion practices (Hofmann, Grossman, & Hinton, 2011) and related therapeutic strategies in the treatment of psychological disturbances—strategies such as mindfulness, mentalization, and other interventions we'll explore in this book. We won't dive too much more deeply into the scientific basis of the therapy here, as the focus of this book is on the *application* of CFT, and there are existing resources that provide a detailed articulation of both the theoretical basis of CFT and the science that underlies it (see Gilbert, 2009a; 2010; 2014).

The Practice of CFT

My goal in writing this book is to give you an accessible guide to learning and applying CFT. *CFT Made Simple* is primarily designed to be an entry point for mental health professionals who want to learn the CFT model and begin applying it in their clinical practice. It may also be useful for clients, or anyone who is interested in CFT and wants to learn more about it and how it is used in therapy.

LAYERED PROCESSES AND PRACTICES

My hope is that after reading this book, you will understand CFT not as a collection of techniques, but as a set of *layered processes and practices* that interact and strengthen one another. These layered processes and practices are aimed at helping clients to establish and elaborate upon two common themes: developing compassion for themselves and others, and cultivating a repertoire of compassionate capacities for working courageously with suffering. This book will be loosely organized to mirror this layered approach to CFT. Many of our clients will enter therapy with deeply seated shame and self-criticism, or with lives that are defined by experiences of threat and emotional distance, volatility, and ambivalence. In the beginning, such clients may not be ready to benefit from diving into traditional self-compassion practices. As with the practice of master gardeners, the first few layers of CFT are designed to prepare the soil, so that when planted, the seeds of compassion will flourish. Let's explore this layering:

Figure 1: Layered Processes and Practices in CFT

After a brief orientation to the origins and basic concepts of CFT in chapter 1, chapter 2 will provide an introduction to compassion and how it is operationalized in CFT, giving us a context for what is to come. In chapter 3 we'll focus on the first layer in our approach: the therapeutic relationship. In the context of an unconditionally warm therapeutic relationship designed to help clients learn to feel *safe*, we'll orient ourselves to the process of the therapy. We'll explore the presence and roles served by the CFT therapist, and the general therapeutic approach used in CFT—one of guided discovery. This relationship forms the first layer of compassion in CFT, as clients gradually learn to feel safe in relationship to the therapist, and to experience *compassion coming to them*, from this person who is committed to their well-being.

In chapters 4 through 6, we'll begin exploring the second layer of compassion in CFT: compassionate understanding. We'll learn how CFT helps clients to begin to understand their emotions and life experiences in nonblaming, compassionate ways. This work is done via the development of *understanding* about how their minds and lives have been shaped by forces that they neither chose nor designed—evolution, social shaping, and the ways these interact. We'll revisit this theme later in the book, introducing a CFT-based model of case formulation in chapter 13.

In chapter 7, we'll turn our focus to compassionate, mindful awareness, which is the third layer of compassion in CFT. We'll explore strategies to rapidly help clients increase their awareness of their emotions, thoughts, and motives. We'll also consider ways to help our clients not get caught up in some of the common obstacles that often hamper beginners in their efforts to learn mindfulness.

In chapters 8 through 15 we'll formally turn our focus to the fourth layer: compassionate practices for working with suffering. In chapter 8, we'll explore how to help clients develop motivation to shift from a self-critical to a compassionate perspective in working with their challenges. In chapter 9, we'll explore how to help clients develop the *compassionate self*—a wise, kind, courageous, adaptive version of themselves that will serve as a reference point from which they can develop the courage to work with the things that terrify them, and the compassionate strengths to use in doing so. We'll then explore ways to help clients cultivate compassionate thinking and reasoning (chapter 10) and the ability to use compassionate imagery to self-soothe and deepen compassion for themselves and others (chapter 11), and introduce the use of chair work and perspective-taking exercises in helping clients strengthen the compassionate self, giving it a central role in their lives (chapter 12). In chapter 14, we'll explore the Multiple Selves exercise—a powerful method for bringing compassion to difficult emotions and situations—and in chapter 15, we'll explore how the compassionate perspective offered by a CFT approach can fit with and enhance the tools you already use in your therapy practice.

Together, these layers provide a framework for learning CFT, and for how CFT can be used in conjunction with empirically supported technologies of change such as behavior activation or exposure. Hopefully you're beginning to realize that CFT is not simply a recycled form of cognitive behavioral therapy with some compassion practices pulled from Buddhism added in for good measure. We're working to layer an interactive set of processes—nurturing relationships, powerful understandings, deepening awareness, and the purposeful cultivation of compassionate strengths—to help clients shift away from threat-focused ways of existing in the world and toward a perspective that is kind, wise, and confident, and which draws upon a body of effective skills for working directly and courageously with life challenges.

WHAT IF MY CLIENT DOESN'T BELIEVE IN EVOLUTION?

One factor distinguishing CFT from other therapy models is that we consider human emotions, motives, and behavior in an evolutionary context. This understanding helps facilitate compassion for ourselves and other people, because much about how these experiences play out in us *makes a lot of sense* given our evolutionary history. Given the current cultural environment in the West, I thought it might be useful to consider what to do if we find ourselves working with someone who doesn't agree with the theory of evolution. News articles indicate that approximately one-third of Americans don't believe in evolution theory, instead ascribing human origins to the action of a supreme being.

In fact, evidence suggests that rates of belief in evolution may be *declining* in some groups (Kaleem, 2013). So it's likely that at some point we'll encounter clients who simply don't subscribe to the theory of evolution. I certainly have.

Is this a problem for CFT? Well, yes and no. Certainly CFT therapists do not have an agenda around challenging clients' spiritual beliefs or religion, and there are plenty of CFT therapists who have religious beliefs of their own. Trying to change the mind of someone who is motivated to reject the idea of evolution is probably not going to be helpful, and may actively undermine the therapeutic relationship. There are a few ways we could work with this issue. We could refer such clients to clinicians who utilize approaches that don't emphasize evolution—which is pretty easy to do, as there are many therapies that don't speak to it at all. Alternatively, we could continue with CFT, leaving out the evolution pieces. I don't see either of these solutions as optimal. There are lots of people who may not believe in evolution, but who could still benefit from CFT. At the same time, evolution isn't a *small* facet of the therapy—it plays a significant role in how we conceptualize the brain, the mind, and the problems our clients bring us.

I'd suggest some middle ground, which can actually help us create a model for how to work with difficult issues that will come up in therapy: Honestly discuss the issue in a way that names the situation, and enlist the client in considering how to work with it. We can also soften or omit language around evolution across species, instead emphasizing adaptation *within* the human species—referring to how our challenging characteristics may have been quite useful for our human ancestors (who faced very different threats and demands than we do now), even as these qualities play out in ways that aren't very well suited to modern life. Here's an example of how that conversation might take shape:

Therapist: Evan, as we continue to explore our emotions and how they work, I wanted to mention that I'll be talking about evolution—specifically about how our emotions make sense when we look at them in an evolutionary context. I know that some people don't accept the theory of evolution, and I wanted to touch base about that.

Evan: (*stiffening a bit*) I don't believe in evolution. I believe that God created humans, just as we are.

Therapist: Good—that's what I wanted to clarify. I want to say at the outset that I don't have any agenda around challenging or changing anyone's religious beliefs. People have different beliefs, and there are different ways of understanding how we got here, and how we got to be the way we are. So I'm not going to try and push any beliefs on you.

Evan: (*visibly relaxing*) Good. Because that wouldn't have gone very well.

Therapist: (*smiling warmly*) I don't imagine it would have! So I want you to know that I respect your beliefs, but at the same time, the therapy we'll be doing is based on science, and so I'll sometimes be talking about things from a scientific perspective—because it can help us make sense of how our emotions work. You don't need to accept the theory of evolution for us to proceed. All I need you to accept is that we have brains and minds that sometimes work in tricky ways to produce emotions that can be hard for us to handle. How does that sound?

Evan: That's not hard to accept. I've definitely got some emotions that are hard to handle.

Therapist: Most of us do. Now, I'll probably still talk about evolution from time to time, because I come from a scientific perspective, and that's the way I make sense of things. How about when I do that, I'll talk about it as "from the scientific perspective," which you can choose to agree with or disregard—taking what is helpful and ignoring the rest. What do you think?

Evan: Sounds like it's worth a try.

Therapist: We can also focus on things as they played out for humans across the years, as our societies have changed. The idea is that our brains work in ways that may have helped our ancestors—say, humans who lived in isolated villages in a harsh world that included lots of very real physical threats—but which can be less useful in the modern world, in which most of the threats we face are very different. What do you think?

Evan: I don't have any problem with that. I know humans have lived in different ways over time. It's the "coming from monkeys" stuff that I don't believe.

Therapist: It sounds like we've got lots of room to work with, then. Also, if it *does* seem like this issue is getting in the way of our therapy, I'd appreciate it if you'd let me know. If that were to happen, we could explore it together and figure out a way to work with it. What I *don't* want to happen is for you to be uncomfortable or unhappy with the therapy and for me to be clueless about it.

Evan: Sounds good.

I've found that once clients understand that I respect their right to hold different beliefs and am not trying to change them, the evolutionary perspective becomes much less of an issue. I've also found that using the phrase "from a scientific perspective…" allows me to continue talking about things in the manner we'll explore in this book, and that clients can often accept it—because we're acknowledging that there are other, valid perspectives as well. I've even had clients come up with alternative explanations, such as "This tricky brain is a riddle that God gave me to figure out." Sometimes, I've found that as clients see how the information I'm presenting fits with their lived experience and helps explain how their emotions work, they tend to soften to the evolutionary perspective (without giving up any of their religious beliefs).

Even clients who generally reject the concept of evolution are often willing to consider adaptations occurring within the human race that fit better with some times in our history than others, and that's a good thing. The evolutionary piece isn't just about deshaming emotions by considering why we have them. It also helps us clarify and understand the ways that different emotions play out in us. When we consider that threat emotions like anger and anxiety evolved to help us identify threats and rapidly do what is needed to deal with them, it makes complete sense that when we perceive a threat, our attention, thoughts, and imagery would all be drawn to the threat until the situation is resolved—in the harsh world faced by our ancestors, ignoring sources of threat could mean injury or death. The problem is that these threat responses are better suited to the savannahs and forests faced by our ancestors than to the boardrooms and relationships that form most of our modern-day threats—and they are of no use at all in facing the multitude of threats dreamt up entirely via our "new-brain" capacities for thought, imagery, and fantasy.

CFT AND OTHER THERAPIES

One of the things I like best about CFT is that it is generally quite compatible with other therapy models. We'll explore this compatibility in the final chapter of the book, and will highlight it along the way. Regardless of whether you want to become a "CFT therapist" or simply want to use a compassion focus to enhance and deepen your work within your current therapeutic modality, I hope you'll find much here to draw upon.

CFT isn't intended to be an entirely new model of therapy, but rather a basis for compassionately understanding and working with psychological difficulties. Relative to other therapies, you may find that CFT is distinguished by its emphasis on compassion as well as on conceptualizing human problems in terms of evolution; how emotions and basic motives play out in our brains, or minds; and the ways we can learn to help ourselves feel safe as we confront and work with the things that scare us the most. At the technical level, you'll likely find a number of new therapeutic tools here, but there will be things you'll recognize from other therapies as well.

I think it's fair to say that CFT fits well into the "third wave" of behavioral and cognitive behavioral therapies, alongside acceptance and commitment therapy (ACT), dialectical behavior therapy (DBT), functional analytic psychotherapy (FAP), mindfulness-based cognitive therapy (MBCT), and emotion-focused therapy (EFT). As with these therapies, we rely on behavioral principles and don't seek to change the content of problematic cognitions and emotions so much as to change *our relationship to* these mental experiences (while cultivating more helpful ways of attending and thinking). As with many of these other approaches, mindfulness plays an important role in CFT. I think the experiential emphasis and perspective-taking practices used in CFT will resonate with practitioners of ACT, and as with DBT, we place a significant emphasis on things like distress tolerance and learning to work with acutely difficult emotional experiences.

Longstanding cognitive therapists may find new ways to approach thought work that can help to facilitate affective congruence in their clients—so that new, reassuring thoughts *feel* reassuring to them. You may also find that the ways compassion is brought into CFT therapy have the potential to "warm up" longstanding approaches such as exposure therapy, to make them more accessible for clients and more comfortable for therapists. I think practitioners will also discover aspects of CFT that can enhance and deepen their existing therapy practice—things like considering emotions and motives in an evolutionary context, helping clients work with evolved affective systems to create feelings of safeness, and applying the purposeful cultivation of compassion in facilitating one's willingness and ability to work directly with suffering.

Our Current Approach

Particularly in psychotherapy, I think it's nice when a learning process models, shapes, and reinforces the content that is being learned. That's what we're going to strive for here. The *process* of CFT—regardless of what we happen to be working on with our clients at the time—is one of warmth, guided discovery, courage, and commitment.

You'll find that this book features a fair number of experiential exercises. Occasionally, I'll ask you to do some of the same things that CFT therapists ask their clients to do, and I'd like to formally encourage you to practice all of the exercises yourself before trying them out with clients. We can learn *about* things like compassion, mindfulness, and safeness, but if we really want to understand them, we need to *experience* them. Personal practice can give us a depth of understanding with regard to these practices—the nuances, potential obstacles, and how to overcome them—that can be very difficult to get any other way.

With that in mind, I'd like to begin this book with a motivation-setting exercise drawn from my experiences learning from Buddhist teachers. These teachers believed that our motivation or intention, the *reason* we are engaging in a particular activity, is highly related to the outcome of the activity. As I've already mentioned, motivation is also a core component of compassion, and it's a component that we'll be working to help our clients cultivate. So let's do that now.

WORKING WITH MOTIVATION AND INTENTION

As we go through life, we'll do lots of different things, for lots of different reasons. Sometimes our activities will be driven by feelings of obligation, sometimes by excitement or ambition. We go through the day figuratively (and sometimes literally) checking off items on our list, doing things simply so that we can move on to the next thing that needs to be done. But motivation and intention are aspects of life we can *work with*.

So right now, I'd like you to consider your motivation for doing this activity. Why are you reading this book? Perhaps you've heard about CFT and were curious to learn more? Perhaps you've been looking for ways to deepen or enliven your existing therapy practice? Perhaps you're a psychotherapy client whose therapist uses CFT, and you wanted to learn more about it? Maybe something about the cover caught your eye, and you impulsively bought the book to see what it was about, as I often do.

Compassionate motivation is something we can choose to cultivate. Now that we've found ourselves here together, let's see if we can bring up a kind, committed sort of motivation as we go about exploring compassion-focused therapy.

- Consider the therapy situation. Our clients come to us at their most vulnerable, sharing their struggles and suffering, and asking, "Will you help me?" Could anyone ever pay us any greater honor than this? Open yourself to the feeling of wanting to help them work with this suffering.

- Is it possible that we can do this—me thinking, organizing, and writing; you reading, considering, and practicing—out of a deep commitment to help alleviate suffering in our clients, ourselves, and the world?

- What if we really *felt* that commitment to alleviate suffering—felt a deep wish to help those who are struggling?

- Don't worry about whether you do or don't feel it right now. Instead, simply try to *imagine* what it would be like if you really did feel it—this deep desire to further your ability to help those who suffer most.

- What if that were our motivation? How might it shape the way we engage in learning about and practicing CFT?

Let's see if we can carry that compassionate motivation with us as we proceed.

CHAPTER I

Origins and Basic Themes

In this chapter we'll briefly explore the origins of CFT, and how it developed out of the desire to better help individuals who suffer from shame and self-criticism. We'll also explore some of the basic ideas behind the CFT approach, with an emphasis on considering how the theoretical roots of CFT—found in evolutionary psychology, affective neuroscience, attachment theory, behaviorism, and the power of cultivating compassion—are translated into what we do in the therapy room.

THE ORIGINS OF CFT

The beginnings of CFT go back to the 1980s, in the form of observations by British psychologist Paul Gilbert. Paul approached psychotherapy from a diverse training background that included cognitive behavioral therapy, Jungian analysis, evolutionary psychology, neurophysiology, and attachment (Gilbert, 2009a). In his therapy work, Paul noticed that many of his clients seemed to have deep-seated self-criticism, shame, and self-loathing. He also noted that for these patients in particular, traditional cognitive therapy exercises like cognitive restructuring often didn't work terribly well. For example, these clients were able to identify their maladaptive thoughts, identify them as irrational, and perhaps even categorize them in terms of thinking errors they featured. They were able to look at the reality of their lives, and generate more rational, evidence-based alternative thoughts. But there was a problem: despite all of this work, *they didn't feel any better* (Gilbert, 2010). In these clients, Paul observed a lack of congruence between what they thought and what they felt—a cognition–emotion mismatch—that hampered their therapy. He found that reassuring thoughts were helpful only when they led clients to *feel* reassured. And in highly self-critical clients, they often didn't.

As a result of these observations, Paul set about finding ways to *warm up* the cognitive behavioral work he was doing with his clients, and began to notice dynamics that, although not often spoken to in his CBT training, very powerfully impacted his clients' experience. For example, looking more closely at their experiences, he noticed that while many clients could generate new, evidence-based thoughts that seemed like they should be helpful, the mental "tone of voice" in which these thoughts were expressed was often harsh and critical.

As a result of observations like these, Paul gradually developed what would become compassion-focused therapy. In doing so, he sought to help therapists make use of existing technologies of change while helping clients relate to their experiences in warmer, more compassionate ways. This developing approach focused on helping clients understand and work with their emotions to help themselves feel safe, and emphasized the cultivation of compassionate strengths that would help them approach and work effectively with their difficulties.

CFT: CORE IDEAS

There are a few basic ideas that form the core of CFT. Let's introduce some of these ideas now.

Shame and Self-Criticism Can Be Crippling

As I've mentioned, CFT was originally developed to assist individuals who struggle with shame and self-criticism (Gilbert, 2010). Shame can be defined as an acutely painful affective state related to negative evaluations of the self as bad, undesirable, defective, and worthless (Tangney, Wagner, & Gramzow, 1992; Gilbert, 1998). We can distinguish between internalized shame—in which we harbor negative personal judgments of ourselves—and external shame, in which we perceive that others see us as inferior, defective, and unattractive (Gilbert, 2002).

A growing body of literature has shown that shame and self-criticism isn't very good for us. Research shows that shameful memories can function in similar ways to traumatic memories, becoming central to individuals' identities in a manner that is linked with depression, anxiety, stress, and post-traumatic stress reactions (Pinto-Gouveia & Matos, 2011). Shame and self-criticism have been linked with a wide variety of mental health problems (Kim, Thibodeau, & Jorgenson, 2011; Kannan & Levitt, 2013), including depression (Andrews & Hunter, 1997; Andrews, Quian, & Valentine, 2002), anxiety (Gilbert & Irons, 2005), social anxiety (Gilbert, 2000), eating disorders (Goss & Allan, 2009), post-traumatic stress disorder (PTSD; Andrews, Brewin, Rose, & Kirk, 2000), borderline personality disorder (Rüsch et al., 2007), and overall psychological maladjustment (Tangney, Wagner, & Gramzow, 1992). In terms of psychological processes, shame has been linked to experiential avoidance—the unwillingness to be in contact with one's private experiences such as emotions—which has itself been associated with various emotional difficulties (Carvalho, Dinis, Pinto-Gouveia, & Estanqueiro, 2013).

These negative self-judgments also appear to impact the course of treatment. Self-stigma, a shame-related experience in which individuals apply negative judgments to themselves related to internalized negative group stereotypes (Luoma, Kulesza, Hayes, Kohlenberg, & Latimer, 2014), has been associated with higher levels of inpatient treatment utilization in individuals experiencing severe mental illness (Rüsch, et al., 2009), lower levels of treatment adherence in patients diagnosed with schizophrenia (Fung, Tsang, & Corrigan, 2008), poorer medication adherence (Sirey et al., 2001), and longer length of stay in residential treatment for addiction (Luoma, Kulesza, Hayes, Kohlenberg, & Latimer, 2014). These findings are particularly relevant, as the self-stigma experienced by the individuals in these studies was anchored to identification with group stereotypes about mental illness or addiction. This demonstrates the power of shame to magnify and exacerbate problems of mental health in clients who may criticize, shame, and stigmatize themselves upon observing their own psychological struggles. A fundamental goal of CFT is helping clients shift the perspective they take toward their challenging thoughts and emotions from condemnation and judgment to compassionate understanding and commitment to helpful action. In this way, self-attacking and avoidance can give way to warmth and responsibility-taking.

Let's consider an example of how shame can get in the way of working with challenging emotions. We can imagine a father who observes himself yelling at his children (perhaps prompted by his children's fear-filled faces) and experiences shame: acute emotional pain prompted by the thought, *I'm a terrible father.* That's a painful thought, and one that can set him up for more difficulty. First, from a CFT perspective, harsh self-criticism or shameful attributions are themselves powerful threat triggers. They keep us stuck in feeling threatened, which organizes the mind (we'll talk about this in future chapters) in ways that aren't conducive to making positive changes like improving one's parenting. Rather than focusing his efforts on learning more effective ways to cope so that he doesn't yell at his children anymore, this father is focused on his own inadequacy.

The emotional pain that accompanies shame can also foster avoidance—that is, the feelings that come up following shameful thoughts like *I'm a terrible father* can be so painful that the father might quickly move to avoid by distracting himself, rationalizing his behavior, blaming his children for his reaction, or doing just about anything else to escape the experience. CFT places a strong emphasis on helping clients overcome such avoidance by shifting from a shaming perspective to a compassionate perspective that helps them approach and work with their challenges.

It's also important that we don't shame or stigmatize the *experience* of shame and self-criticism—we don't want our clients to feel ashamed of feeling ashamed. It makes a lot of sense that they may have learned to cope in this way. Most of us don't set out to create problems for ourselves through self-attacking. However, we live in a culture filled with messages presenting us with idealized images of how people are supposed to look, feel, and perform—images we can easily internalize, and to which we have no hope of measuring up. These damning comparisons can be magnified by our ability to perceive our own internal experiences versus those of others. We have almost *unlimited access* to our own struggles—difficult emotions, struggles with tasks or motivation, or thoughts and behaviors that don't match our values. At the same time, we have *very limited access* to the internal experiences of other people—we mostly see what they choose to show us, and like us, they want to appear competent, intelligent, and attractive. We all tend to put on the "game faces." Seeing this turmoil and struggle inside of themselves, and seemingly surrounded by people who *look like* they have it all together, it's easy for clients to feel shamed and isolated, and to conclude, *there's something wrong with me*. And this is before we even consider the many specific factors that can contribute to experiences of shame in our clients, including histories of trauma or bullying, harsh rearing environments, learning history, and potentially belonging to stigmatized groups. Given all of this, it makes a ton of sense that our clients may have learned to shame and attack themselves.

CFT's perspective on shame and self-criticism doesn't mean there isn't room for helpful self-evaluation. There certainly is—sometimes our clients are doing things that are problematic, and they need to do things differently! It's just that such self-evaluation works a good deal better when it's presented in a warm manner that doesn't overwhelm the threat response. For example, compassionate self-correction involves noticing when one is doing something harmful or unhelpful, allowing oneself to feel guilty about it, and turning the focus toward doing better in the future. Instead of *I'm a terrible father*, compassionate correction would look more like this: *It makes sense that I would yell because of my own experience, but that's not the sort of father I want to be. It's time I committed to interacting with my kids in ways that model the things I'd like them to learn. What might help me do that?*

Compassion: The Strength to Move Toward the Pain

While shame can lead people to shut down and turn away from their struggles and suffering, we need ways to help clients move *toward* their pain, and work with it in helpful ways. In CFT, this is accomplished through the cultivation of mindfulness and particularly compassion. One question that may come up is *Why compassion?* There are lots of helpful virtues out there. Why are we choosing to make compassion the central focus of our therapy?

In CFT, we've spent a good deal of time working to define, operationalize, and apply compassion in working with our clients. A generally accepted definition of compassion reads something like this: sensitivity to suffering combined with the motivation to help alleviate (and prevent) it (Gilbert, 2010). This definition includes two separate but important components: *sensitivity* and *motivation*. CFT emphasizes compassion so greatly because we think that this is a particularly workable orientation to have in the face of pain, difficulty, and suffering.

There's a lot contained within this simple definition. First, it provides us with an *approach* orientation toward suffering—both in terms of being *sensitive* to its arising and in the emphasis on moving *toward* the suffering to help. This is very different from the avoidance that can drive so many of our clients' difficulties. Compassion also contains warmth—suffering is approached with the motivation to *help*. This warm motivation and affective tone can help us (and those we help) to feel safe in confronting difficulties, helping us shift from a threat-focused perspective to a mental state that is open, reflective, and flexible.

If we look even more deeply within the definition of compassion, we find that it contains other helpful capacities as well. If we're to maintain this warm, approach orientation toward suffering we have to be able to tolerate it, so CFT, like dialectical behavior therapy (DBT; Linehan, 1993), places an emphasis on distress tolerance and emotion regulation. If compassionate action is to truly be helpful, it must be *skillful*, and so CFT works to help clients cultivate capacities like empathy, mentalization, and perspective taking.

Finally, many clients, particularly those coming into therapy with lots of shame and self-criticism, may have a very negative experience of themselves. In CFT, we try to provide clients with a unifying framework for the various aspects of compassion we're helping them cultivate—which we call the *compassionate self*. The compassionate self is an adaptive version of the self that manifests the various aspects of compassion we work to cultivate in the therapy. In the beginning, this takes the form of imaginal perspective-taking exercises that are similar to method acting: the client imagines being at her very best—her most kind, compassionate, wise, and confident—considering what it would be like if she fully possessed these strengths. She then imagines how this compassionate version of herself would feel, pay attention, reason, be motivated, and behave.

As the therapy progresses, the compassionate self becomes a perspective that the client learns to shift into again and again, considering how she would understand and work with her difficulties from this compassionate perspective. All the while, she is working to cultivate compassionate strengths and establish them as habits, with the goal that over time, the space between the client's idea of *me* and *the compassionate self* gradually diminishes, as these capacities become more a natural part of her everyday life. In this way, CFT shares ground with ACT and the positive psychology movement. The focus of the therapy isn't simply on the alleviation of symptoms, but on the purposeful development of strengths—adaptive ways of living that are workable and which reflect the client's most positive aspirations and values.

Building Blocks of Compassion: Shifting from Judgment to Understanding

As we've discussed, highly self-critical and shame-prone clients attack themselves upon observing many aspects of their experience—their feelings and thoughts, their reactions, and their relationship difficulties. While compassion for oneself and others is a primary goal of CFT, we initially spend less time talking with clients about compassion, and more time setting the stage for it to arise. We do this by helping them understand the factors that lead to their challenging emotions, motives, and behaviors. Rather than try to *convince* our clients why they should have compassion for themselves and others, the idea is that when they really understand the challenges presented by having a human life, compassion will make sense to them, and will be likely to *arise* without the need for convincing. Of course, we will also talk about what compassion is, what it isn't, and why it is helpful—but we want to set the stage for this by creating a context of understanding.

In CFT, we think it's important to recognize that many of our struggles can be rooted in things we didn't get to choose or design. This is part of a larger shift we want to help our clients make—one in which they move from a threat-based perspective of blaming and shaming to a compassionate stance of understanding and figuring out what would be helpful. If we look closely at the human story, we find many unchosen factors that shape our experience and the sort of people we will become.

THE CHALLENGES OF OUR EVOLVED BRAINS

In CFT, human emotions and other cognitive functions are understood within the context of evolution. We group emotions into three types, according to evolutionary function: emotions and motives that center on identifying and responding to threats, those that are focused on pursuing and being rewarded for attaining goals, and emotional experiences of safeness, contentedness, and peace that are commonly linked with feeling connected with others. Emotions, motives, and behaviors that are initially perplexing can make a lot more sense when we consider them in terms of their evolutionary function and the survival value they granted our ancestors. One quick example is the tendency to crave and be comforted by sweet, salty, fatty foods. Lots of people struggle with emotional eating, and how many of us have wished that we could crave broccoli the way we crave pizza or sweets? But in the environment our ancestors faced—one in which calories and nutrients were relatively scarce—sugar, salt, and fats granted survival value, making it more likely that those who readily consumed them when available would live to pass their genes along to future generations. From this evolutionary perspective, these cravings (and so many of the emotions we may find ourselves struggling with) make complete sense, even as they're now a terrible fit with our current environment—one in which cheap, salty, sweet, fatty foods are to be found all around us.

The ways our brains and minds have evolved can create difficulties for us. From the tricky interplay of old-brain emotions and new-brain capacities for symbolic thought to the ease with which we automatically learn connections between different things, there is much about how our minds work that we didn't choose or design, but which can be quite difficult to manage. This awareness can help create a context for self-compassion by depathologizing emotions and experiences which in isolation may feel like *something that is wrong with me*, but which in reality are part and parcel of what it means to be human in this day and age.

THE SOCIAL SHAPING OF THE SELF

As we've discussed, having a human life means we'll experience powerful emotions and motivations that can sometimes be difficult to manage, particularly when we're faced with trauma or other life challenges. Early social experiences powerfully shape the ability to help ourselves feel safe and regulate our emotions, along with many other aspects of who we are. For example, early and ongoing attachment experiences powerfully impact our ability to feel safe in connection with others (versus feeling threatened), to expect support and nurturing from others (versus expecting harm or neglect), and to relate to ourselves as lovable and worthy of care (versus unlovable and isolated) (Wallin, 2007).

These environments, many of which we don't get to choose or design, interact powerfully with the way our brains learn, sometimes to devastating effect. Through processes like respondent/classical conditioning, operant conditioning, and social learning, as well as processes articulated through more modern elaborations of learning theory, such as relational frame theory (Hayes, Barnes-Holmes, & Roche, 2001; Törneke, 2010), our environments can teach us to fear the very interpersonal connections that should help us feel safe, and can systematically shape behaviors that will cripple us later in life.

In CFT, we want to help people begin to understand that much of what they feel and even how they've learned to respond was not of their choice or design—that these things are *not their fault*. This "not your fault" piece doesn't mean that we're letting anyone off of the hook or absolving people of their responsibility for their own behavior. It's about being honest with ourselves about which factors we control in our lives, and which ones we don't. In fact, it's precisely *because* of all these factors we can't control that we need to understand our minds and learn to work with the things we *can* affect. Our clients may not have chosen to have brains that were shaped by learning experiences to produce crippling fear and anxiety when faced with certain situations, but we can help them cultivate the ability to work effectively with these situations and affects, and to validate and support themselves in doing so.

There's a powerful scene in the movie *Good Will Hunting* in which Robin Williams, playing a psychologist, holds up his client's (Will, played by Matt Damon) file, thick with documentation of years of childhood abuse that Will had experienced. The dialogue went something like this: "I don't know much, Will, but I know this." He holds up the file. "You know all this shit? It's not your fault. *It's not your fault.*"

In the scene, he warmly repeats this phrase, again and again. Will is initially resistant to this idea, and fights back a bit, just like we and our clients might find ourselves doing. It's not always easy to admit to ourselves that there's a lot about our lives (and the way our minds work) that is not under our control. And like Will, if our clients' lives have been filled with trauma, struggle, and suffering, this realization can be as heartbreaking as it is enlightening. But if we can help our clients honestly recognize the things in their lives that aren't their fault—the experiences they didn't choose to have, the powerful emotions that arise unbidden, the spontaneous thoughts that may go against their values, the habits they've tried unsuccessfully to change—and help them stop attacking and blaming themselves for these experiences, it can create a context that makes change possible.

In CFT, we want to help our clients make realizations like those described above. However, going into long-winded explanations generally isn't helpful, and unlike the example from *Good Will Hunting*, we don't typically back our clients into a corner and say, "It's not your fault" over and over again. As we'll discuss, CFT aims to be a process of guided discovery, making extensive use of Socratic dialogue and experiential exercises such as thought experiments, perspective-taking, and chair work to help clients develop an understanding of their experiences and how to work with them.

The Importance of Learning to Feel Safe

As I've mentioned, CFT is heavily influenced by research in affective neuroscience. There is a wealth of scientific literature documenting the existence of evolved emotion-regulation systems that humans share with our ancestors, and the ways these basic emotions and motives play out in our brains and minds (Panksepp & Biven, 2012). This isn't just part of the theory underlying CFT—it's brought directly into the therapy session. Clients learn about different emotion-regulation systems and how basic motives and emotions can organize our minds and bodies through shaping patterns of attention, reasoning, physical responding, and so on, with a specific focus on learning to work with these systems to help balance emotions and cultivate the states of mind our clients want to have. This learning helps lay the groundwork for self-compassion, as clients' understanding about the "how and why" of their challenging emotional experiences allows them to *make sense* of them.

In chapter 5, we'll explore these basic emotion-regulation systems in detail, but it's worth noting at the outset that a big part of CFT involves helping clients find a balance between emotions that are focused on threats, those that are focused on the pursuit of goals, and those that are linked with feelings of safeness and peace. These emotions shape our mental experience in varied and powerful ways. For example, threat emotions such as the anxiety, anger, or fear that dominate so many of our clients' experiences are associated with a narrowing of attention, decreased cognitive flexibility, and tendencies to engage in strategies like rumination that fuel rather than soothe the state of feeling threatened (Gilbert, 2009a). Alternatively, when we feel safe, the mind is organized in entirely different ways—the scope of our attention and thinking opens, and we tend to become calm, peaceful, reflective, and prosocial (and, CFT would argue, better able to work with difficult emotions; Gilbert, 2009a). Unfortunately, many of our clients live in a world that can be almost entirely defined by experiences of threat. So a major therapeutic goal of CFT is helping our clients experience feelings of safeness and the mental shifts that come with them.

This can be a challenging therapeutic task. Humans evolved to feel safe primarily in contexts of affiliation—in connection with others (Gilbert, 2009a). Early social relationships and experiences of nurturing connections with others help shape both cognitive templates (Bowlby, 1982; Wallin, 2007) and the underlying neurological architecture (Siegel, 2012; Cozolino, 2010) that can help us to feel safe and successfully regulate our emotions (or not). Individuals who have experienced abuse, neglect, or other forms of insecure attachment environments (as exemplified in DBT's *invalidating environments*; Linehan, 1993) may have implicitly learned to associate interpersonal relationships with threat or disappointment rather than with soothing and safeness. This implicit association can present a primary challenge for therapists—how do we help our clients learn to feel safe when experience has taught them that the things that are *supposed* to help them feel safe (close relationships) don't work?

In CFT, we want to infuse safeness into both the content and the process of the therapy. We'll spend a fair bit of time exploring this idea in later chapters. One of the reasons we've placed compassion—a warm, sensitive, and helpful approach to working with suffering—at the center of CFT is that we want to help clients develop habits of relating to themselves and others in ways that can help foster felt experiences of safeness, as well as assist them to develop the underlying neurological systems that will support mental experiences of safeness in the future.

On the content level, our clients will learn numerous strategies for relating compassionately to their challenges and bringing about experiences of feeling safe. On the process level, the therapeutic relationship and therapy environment in CFT is designed to help create feelings of safeness and emotional balance in the client, as the therapist engages with the client in a compassionately collaborative, warm, nonshaming, and encouraging manner. We'll explore how this works when we look at the roles occupied by the CFT therapist, in chapter 3.

In this chapter, we've explored a number of themes that are core to the practice of CFT. Let's consider a case example of how these themes might be interwoven in the course of a therapy session:

Therapist: Jenny, we've spent some time talking about the fears you have that you'll do something embarrassing in front of others, and how these fears affect your social life. It sounds like you're feeling pretty ashamed about this. Have I got that right?

Jenny: That's right. I'm just such an idiot. I'm so scared that I'll do something stupid that I don't do anything. My friends invite me out, but I always bail at the last minute. I'm such a terrible friend. It's amazing I have any friends at all.

Therapist: So you make plans to go out and then cancel at the last minute?

Jenny: Yeah. I make plans thinking it'll be fun. But then I sit around thinking about how if I go out, I'll dress the wrong way, or say something stupid that will offend everyone. I get so scared that I can't bear the thought of going out, and so I cancel and just stay in. I'm just terrified and weak. Other people aren't afraid of this stuff. They just go out and have fun.

Therapist: Jenny, let me ask a question. When this fear of doing something embarrassing or offensive comes up for you, are you *choosing* to feel afraid? Are you *deciding* to feel that way?

Jenny: I'm not sure I understand what you mean.

Therapist: Well, let's imagine you have the thought, *I'll do something embarrassing and everyone will think I'm an idiot.* After that thought, are you thinking, *I think I'd better get really afraid of that happening,* or does the fear just arise in you?

Jenny: I get terrified at things like that, but it's not like I *want* to feel that way. Who would choose that?

Therapist: Exactly. It sounds like this thought, *I'll do something embarrassing,* is a very powerful threat cue for you—when you have thoughts like that, your brain registers: *Oh, here comes a threat!*—and then comes the fear. Does that make sense?

Jenny: I guess so.

Therapist: So if you're not *deciding* to feel all this fear that you're feeling so ashamed of, is the fear your fault?

Jenny: I guess not. But I'm the one sitting there thinking all that stuff that makes me afraid. That's my fault.

Therapist: (*smiling warmly*) Is it? So you sit there and decide, *Well, I could go out and have a happy evening with my friends, but instead I think I'd rather sit and think deeply about the inevitable humiliation I could face if I did that...*

Jenny: (*laughing a little bit*) I think I see what you mean. I guess I don't choose that stuff, either. But I still do it.

Therapist: As we've discussed, evolution has shaped our brains to be very sensitive to things we perceive as threatening us, and when that happens, they can produce really powerful emotions—to try and protect us. This is what kept our ancestors alive—they were *really good* at identifying and responding to threats. I mean, if your friends were asking you to go out and do something *really dangerous*, like swimming in a pond full of crocodiles or shooting heroin, would it make sense for you to be afraid?

Jenny: It sure would!

Therapist: It sounds like you've somehow learned that being embarrassed in public is *really dangerous*, so even being asked to go out triggers thoughts that you could do something embarrassing, which is terrifying.

Jenny: When I was young—like in sixth grade—my family moved. At my new school, there was a group of girls who hated me. I still don't know why. They made fun of me constantly. They spread rumors about me, called me names, told me over and over that no one liked me. It went on for *weeks*. I cried for hours every day, and started throwing up before school, just thinking about what I'd have to face when I got there. (*Pauses, sobbing.*) I couldn't figure out what I'd done wrong. I didn't know what was wrong with me, that they hated me so badly.

Therapist: (*pausing, then speaking kindly*) That sounds terrible, Jenny. I'm so sorry that happened to you.

Jenny: (*tearfully*) It *was* terrible. It was the worst experience of my life.

Therapist: So does it *make sense* that you would learn that social situations can be very dangerous? Does it make sense that even now, you might imagine this rejection could happen again—and that imagining this could be terrifying?

Jenny: (*looking up, as facial expression lightens a bit*) It does.

Therapist: Is that your fault?

Jenny: No. No, it's not my fault.

In the example above, we can see several of the themes we've discussed playing out. We see that Jenny is crippled by both internal shame (*there's something wrong with me*) and external shame (*others don't—or won't—like me*), which she relates to her experiences of social rejection that occurred many years before. This shame, and the fear related to it, results in Jenny avoiding social activities that would probably be very helpful for her.

In the example, the therapist quickly moves to explore and depathologize Jenny's emotions and the thoughts that prompt them, in two ways. First, the therapist helps her recognize the dynamics around how the emotions arise in her mind (that she isn't choosing to feel afraid). The evolutionary model is also referenced, helping anchor Jenny's understanding of her emotions not to personal flaws, but to valid reactions of her evolved brain in response to a perceived threat. Second, the therapist prompts exploration of how Jenny's fears are valid given her history of social rejection— how *it makes sense* that she would have learned to be very afraid of making social mistakes and the potential for others to quickly turn on her—and in doing this, begins introducing the concept that our social shaping can very powerfully influence our thoughts and feelings.

While the word "compassion" is never mentioned, we see evidence of it throughout—in terms of both implicit process and explicit content. It can be found in the kind recognition of how terrible Jenny's experience was for her, the willingness to look closely and courageously at the fears she's experiencing, the focus shift from a perspective that judges and labels these experiences to one that seeks to understand them, and the exploration of how Jenny's emotional reactions make sense when we understand them in context. Finally, we see that this unfolding process seems to help create feelings of both safeness and courage in Jenny, who spontaneously brings to mind and explores a traumatic socially shaming experience that she might have been inclined to avoid.

SUMMARY

In this chapter, we explored the origins of CFT and some of the core themes that guide the therapy. These themes—the importance of deshaming and depathologizing the client's experience, modeling compassion and the courage to approach and work with suffering, prompting shifts from judgment to understanding, and the facilitation of experiences of safeness—are deeply woven into both the content and process of CFT. In chapter 2, we'll dive more deeply into the topic of compassion, and how it is brought to life in the therapy session.

CHAPTER 2

Introducing Compassion

In CFT, we begin with a definition of compassion that is consistent with both the dictionary and the Dalai Lama: *sensitivity* to suffering with an accompanying *motivation* to alleviate or prevent it. In the context of CFT, compassion isn't simply one of any number of values our clients might seek to pursue—although it certainly can be chosen as a value to guide one's life pursuits (one which we would obviously encourage). First and foremost, compassion in CFT is an *orientation to suffering*—one that empowers us to *approach suffering* with the helpful motivation to work with it and alleviate it. Let's take a moment to unpack this definition.

In the context of compassion, we can consider sensitivity as referring to the *ability to become aware* of suffering, as well as the *willingness to be moved* by it. If our minds are unbalanced and powerfully caught up in experiences of threat or drive, we can find ourselves oblivious to suffering. It's not that we don't care, necessarily. It's that we can become so powerfully focused on perceived threats or caught up in pursuing our goals that the suffering of others (or even ourselves) just doesn't show up on the radar.

Additionally, if our clients are going through the world with mind and body dominated by experiences of threat, opening themselves to suffering can be overwhelming. In such a situation, we can understand why they might resort to avoidance strategies in the effort to alleviate intensely felt distress. On the other hand, if things are balanced, with threat and drive emotions tempered by the ability to experience safeness and the mindful capacity to observe emotions without pushing them away, our clients can learn to notice their suffering, and to be warmly moved by it without becoming overwhelmed. Avoidance can give way to a willing, mindful, compassionate awareness: *I'm really hurting right now. This argument with my spouse has really activated my fears of being abandoned. This is really hard for me.* In considering this possibility, we see that a primary aspect of compassion we'll be helping our clients develop is *emotional courage*—the willingness to approach and connect with very difficult feelings, in the service of helping themselves work with these experiences.

The second component of compassion involves the kind motivation to help alleviate and prevent suffering. While it may seem obvious that when presented with suffering, we'd want to help alleviate it, this isn't always the case, particularly for clients with extensive histories of shame and self-criticism. For such clients, observations of their struggles and pain may serve as antecedents not for helping but for self-attacking, as they interpret these experiences as more evidence that *there is something wrong with me*—that they are bad, flawed, or unworthy. Other clients may become fused with such experiences—so caught up in rumination and cycles of threat-based thinking and emotion that they are unable to disengage from the experience and consider what they might be able to *do* about their pain.

Here again, we see the importance of helping clients relate to their experience in nonshaming ways, to mindfully observe when threat responses begin to carry them away, and to connect with feelings of safeness. When this happens, it paves the way for compassionate reasoning to emerge, as ruminative thoughts like *I can't take this* give way to compassionate questions, such as *What would be helpful as I work with this difficult experience?* Additionally, If we're to help our clients maintain this helpful motivation to approach and work with suffering, we also need to help them develop confidence that they can engage in helpful action—confidence rooted in a repertoire of useful skills for working with the pain of life. We need to give them tools, strategies, and practices that *work*.

COMPASSIONATE ATTRIBUTES

Now that we've explored a working definition of compassion, let's spend a bit more time exploring how compassion is operationalized in CFT. This operationalization is depicted graphically in the *Circle of Compassion* in figure 9.1, below. In this figure, compassion is depicted as a collection of *attributes*, which are cultivated via the training of various compassionate *skills*, all of which occurs within a therapeutic context defined by *warmth*.

Compassion in CFT involves the cultivation of various attributes that facilitate a skillful, approach-based orientation toward pain, struggle, and suffering. Woven throughout these attributes is a focus on helping clients develop compassionate *courage*—so that they can approach and work with the really difficult things, particularly the challenging emotions they may be inclined to avoid. Let's briefly explore these attributes.

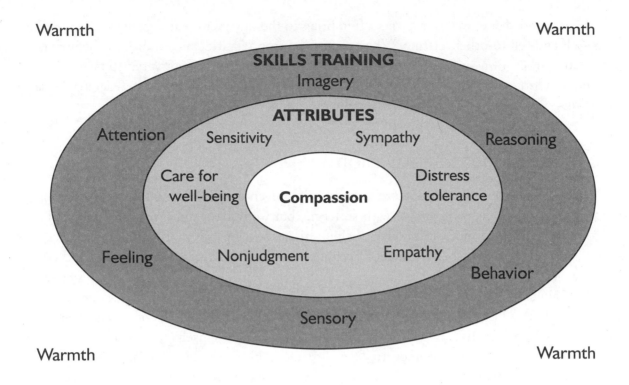

Figure 9.1: The Circle of Compassion—Compassionate Attributes and Skills. (From Gilbert, *The Compassionate Mind* [2009], reprinted with permission from Little, Brown Book Group.)

Sensitivity

As we've mentioned previously, sensitivity is a core component of our definition of compassion. In this context, sensitivity refers to helping clients open their awareness to experiences of pain, suffering, struggle, and difficulty. This openness may stand in stark contrast to the avoidance that may characterize their habitual coping methods. Sensitivity involves noticing these experiences, so that they show up on the radar. Rather than avoiding the difficult things in their lives, we help clients learn to actively and purposefully attend to them, which allows the possibility of being *moved* by them.

Sympathy

The sensitivity of compassion isn't a cold awareness that things aren't as we'd prefer them. It is infused with warmth—containing a felt connection to the being that suffers, whether that being is us or someone else. Sympathy involves feeling a bit of heartbreak for the being that is suffering—we are *moved* by their suffering. This sympathy is important, and it stands in stark contrast to the self-criticism and shame that our clients often bring to therapy. Sympathy involves a softening of self-to-self and self-to-other relating. When clients can stop self-attacking and allow themselves to be moved by their own suffering (or that of others), it helps them be motivated to face and work with this suffering, even knowing that doing so won't be easy. With compassion, *we are moved, and we want to help*—which brings us to the next attribute.

Compassionate Motivation

Compassion involves a sincere motivation to help prevent or alleviate suffering. With compassion, we accept and engage willingly with suffering, but we don't wallow in it. In helping clients develop compassionate motivation, we're helping them develop the motivation and courage to approach suffering with a specific intent—to understand the suffering and the causes and conditions that lead to it, so they can engage in helpful activity to help alleviate or prevent it. We're trying to help clients strengthen and learn to shift into a caregiving social mentality (we'll discuss social mentalities a bit later), so that rather than being consumed by feelings of threat, their attention, thinking, motivation, and behavior are focused on helping themselves and others. This motivation can give rise to the courage to face difficulties head-on. This caring motivation isn't something we're manufacturing from scratch—we're working to *awaken* our clients' natural capacity for caregiving and nurturance that evolved with our mammalian ancestors, enabling them to face tremendous hardship and danger to ensure the survival of their young.

Distress Tolerance

As we see in other therapy models, such as dialectical behavior therapy (Linehan, 1993), CFT incorporates distress tolerance as a capacity to be cultivated. In order to work directly and actively with suffering and the factors that lead to it, both clients and therapists need to be able to tolerate the discomfort that comes with doing so. Distress tolerance in CFT involves both the willingness to endure discomfort and the cultivation of the ability to self-soothe—to help ourselves feel safe and to make life a bit easier when there is pain that must be endured as we approach and work with suffering.

Nonjudgment

As we'll see, compassion in CFT also involves helping clients develop mindful awareness. In addition to the sensitivity—the *noticing*—described above, compassion involves the ability to relate to one's experience in accepting, nonjudgmental ways. In cultivating compassion, clients learn to replace the judging, labeling, and self-blame that may accompany difficult experiences with a compassionate awareness that seeks to understand these experiences. This leads us to the final compassionate attribute: empathy.

Empathy

Whereas sympathy involves being moved by suffering, empathy involves making efforts to understand the suffering as it exists from the perspective of the being that suffers. We want to help clients look deeply at the range of emotions arising within themselves and others. *What am I actually feeling? How does it make sense that I might be feeling this way?* Having suspended judgment, compassion seeks to understand the emotional landscape that is being traversed—in therapy, and in life.

Taken together, these compassionate attributes form a powerful orientation toward suffering, which unfolds from awareness to action. With compassion, *we notice suffering, we are moved by it, and we want to help.* In order to do this, we must work *to tolerate distress, and to nonjudgmentally and empathically understand the causes and conditions that contribute to the suffering and difficulty.* Armed with this motivation and understanding, clients and therapists are well equipped to draw upon a wide variety of powerful technologies to address psychological suffering—which is why CFT can potentially be a helpful adjunct for those whose therapeutic work is rooted primarily in other modalities.

COMPASSIONATE MIND TRAINING

In helping clients cultivate the compassionate attributes described above, CFT focuses on assisting them in developing a number of compassionate skills. Let's take a look at the skill-training domains we'll be targeting in helping our clients cultivate the compassionate attributes described above.

Compassionate Thinking and Reasoning

Compassionate thought work in CFT is twofold. First, it involves helping clients relate to thoughts mindfully—nonjudgmentally noticing and accepting their thoughts as mental activity without getting caught up in clinging to them or pushing them away. Second, it involves the purposeful cultivation of compassionate ways of thinking, reasoning, and understanding—ways of thinking that are validating, soothing, encouraging, and skillfully focused on working with suffering. In CFT, compassionate ways of thinking are defined by *helpfulness*. These ways of thinking will be represented in multiple areas of the layered approach we're taking in this book. First, we help clients develop compassionate understanding of their minds, emotions, and how things came to be the way they are in their lives. A bit later on, we focus on helping clients specifically cultivate compassionate ways of thinking.

Attention and Sensory Focusing

A primary goal in CFT involves helping clients to work with their attention in skillful ways. First, we'll help clients develop compassionate awareness through the cultivation of mindfulness, introduced in chapter 7. Mindfulness occupies a central role in CFT, both in increasing client awareness of how thoughts and emotions arise and play out in their minds, and in helping them relate to and work with these mental activities in accepting, nonjudgmental ways.

CFT therapists also utilize specific sensory-focusing exercises in training clients to focus their attention in ways that can help them soften the inertia of threat emotions, calm the body, and prepare the way for compassionate states of mind. One of the most common of these exercises is *soothing rhythm breathing*, introduced in chapter 4.

Imagery

CFT utilizes imagery extensively, both in helping clients work with difficult affective states and in developing and applying compassion in their lives. The latter is best exemplified by the Compassionate Self practice, introduced in chapter 9. This practice is an imagery-based method-acting practice aimed at helping clients cultivate a compassionate, adaptive version of the self that provides an organizational framework for the development of a repertoire of compassionate strengths. We'll also use imagery exercises to help clients learn to self-soothe and create feelings of safeness in themselves.

Feeling and Emotion

One factor that perhaps distinguishes CFT from other cognitive behavioral approaches is the high premium we place on working with affect. Like other therapies, much therapeutic work in CFT is anchored around helping clients work with difficult emotions. However, CFT also involves a very intentional focus on the purposeful *cultivation* of compassionate feelings—warmth, kindness, courage, affiliation (to self and others), and safeness. Both sides of this work cross many of the layers of therapy mentioned earlier—the therapeutic *relationship* as a basis for the development of relational safeness, compassionate *understanding* and mindful *awareness* of our affects and how they play out in us, and the cultivation of *compassionate skills* for emotional soothing and for working with difficult emotions and experiences via chair work, exposure exercises, and imagery.

Behavior

The second component of compassion—the motivation to help address and prevent suffering—is incomplete without *compassionate action*. In CFT, there is a strong focus on helping clients develop a repertoire of compassionate behaviors. Behavioral work in CFT is focused both on helping clients understand and work skillfully with sources of suffering and on building lives that are filled with meaning, fulfillment, and good relationships. In this work, CFT therapists draw upon behavioral theories of learning to understand the historical roots and conditions that maintain client difficulties, and to help clients relate to these challenges in compassionate ways—as *learned responses* and coping strategies that were shaped by social forces they didn't get to choose or control.

Additionally, CFT therapists make use of a wide range of empirically supported behavioral interventions—including behavior activation, exposure work, and social skills training—depending upon the needs of the client.

In CFT, all of these strategies are couched within an organizing framework of compassionate motivation and understanding. The idea is that we're *warming up* the techniques, with the goal of softening their threatening aspects and potentially increasing client motivation and utilization. We want clients to experience these behaviors and strategies not as *something I have to do (that I'd really rather not do)* but as compassionately motivated efforts to care for themselves and develop strengths and competencies in the service of having good lives.

SUMMARY

In this chapter, we've introduced a working definition of compassion, and have explored how CFT operationalizes compassion in terms of attributes we help clients cultivate and specific skills we'll be working to develop in therapy. As we saw in the introduction, *CFT Made Simple* takes an approach defined by *layers* of treatment: the therapeutic relationship, the development of compassionate understanding, the cultivation of mindful awareness, and the specific development and application of compassion. Each of these layers is centered around laying the groundwork for clients to manifest compassion in their lives: creating a therapeutic environment defined by *relational safeness*; facilitating our clients' *understanding* of the unchosen biological and social forces that have shaped their experience in ways that were not their fault; cultivating *accepting, nonjudgmental awareness* of their experiences; and purposefully working to develop a repertoire of compassionate strengths. In the next chapter, we'll explore the first of these layers: the therapeutic relationship in CFT.

CHAPTER 3

Compassionate Relating: Roles of the Therapist in CFT

It is well established that one of the most important predictors of therapy outcome is the relationship between the therapist and the client (Martin, Garske, & Davis, 2000). The process of therapy can be a scary and difficult one for many clients, as they confront, explore, and work with the parts of their lives that are most troubling, and the things they like least about themselves. A good therapeutic relationship can help clients have the courage to explore and work with difficult emotions and traumatic memories, support the self-acceptance and confidence needed to confront themselves when their behaviors don't fit with who they want to be, and provide them with a valuable template of how to have and maintain good relationships with other people, even when the going gets tough (Kohlenberg & Tsai, 1991; Tsai et al., 2009; Holman, Kanter, Kohlenberg, & Tsai, 2016).

Many of our clients will never have had such a trusting, safe relationship with anyone, and may even have learned to feel unsafe in connection with others. Additionally, there are a number of therapeutic tasks in CFT that require the therapist to serve a number of different but related roles within the context of the therapeutic relationship. In this chapter, we'll explore the various roles of the therapist in CFT, and how the CFT therapist can embody them.

DIFFERENT ROLES FOR DIFFERENT TASKS

In a typical course of CFT, there are a number of processes that the therapist seeks to facilitate. The overall process of CFT is one of guided discovery, in which clients learn about how and why their emotions work the way they do, and how to relate to and work compassionately with these experiences. Compassion and mindfulness are both taught and modeled, within the context of a safe therapeutic relationship that allows the client to explore and work with scary emotions and life situations. In this way, the process and content of CFT are consistent and serve to deepen and reinforce one another. In CFT, therapists function as teachers of the evolutionary model, as facilitators of a process of guided discovery, as a secure base for exploration, and as models of a compassionate self. Let's explore these roles.

Teacher of the CFT Model

As they go through CFT, our clients will do a lot of learning. One thing that distinguishes CFT from other therapy approaches is its firm rooting in the evolutionary model. As we'll see in chapters 4 and 5, an initial goal of the therapy involves helping clients understand their basic motives and emotions within the context of evolution. Looking through the lens of evolution, clients can make a lot more sense of confusing emotions and motives. Rather than seeing them as personal flaws, clients can see how these emotions had great survival value to our ancestors, allowing them to pass their genes on to us. They also learn about the evolutionary functions served by different emotions, and relatedly, how these emotions play out in terms of our attention, thinking and reasoning, mental imagery, bodily experience, motivation, and behavior. Clients also learn about the tricky ways our "old-brain" emotions and motivations can interact with "new-brain" capacities such as mental imagery, symbolic thought, and rumination, as well as how these dynamics are shaped by the social forces in our lives. These realizations set the stage for compassion for the self and others in CFT, as clients develop a growing awareness that many of the factors which powerfully shape our mental experience and development are not of our choosing or design (Gilbert, 2009a; 2010; 2014).

In helping our clients understand themselves and their minds better, we'll also touch on other things, which can include exploration of the client's learning history, attachment history, and other factors and experiences which can contribute to the social shaping of the self. At each stage, there will likely be some teaching involved, as we work to help our clients develop greater insight into the causes and conditions that have contributed to who they are, and how their minds work. We'll also be teaching our clients about compassion—what it is, what it isn't, and how we can apply it in working with challenging emotions and life situations.

So particularly in the beginning, CFT can feel a bit content-heavy in comparison to other therapy models, with the CFT therapist serving as the teacher, helping clients to make the realizations described above. As you might imagine, if done unskillfully, this teaching could come off as quite invalidating to our clients. Imagine anxiously making the courageous step to come into therapy, finally ready to share the most difficult aspects of your life with a therapist, only to find yourself receiving a lecture about evolution! So it's important that we find ways to do this teaching that not only help clients learn about their minds, but also validate their experience, convey compassion, and help to establish and strengthen the therapeutic relationship. Let's explore a few ways of doing this.

RELATING THE MODEL TO THE CLIENT'S LIVED EXPERIENCE

As is seen in other models such as functional analytic psychotherapy (FAP), perhaps the best way to teach the CFT model is via an interactive process in which we're helping clients relate it to lived experience of their emotions, motivations, and social history (Kohlenberg & Tsai, 1991; Tsai et al., 2009; Holman et al., 2016). This can involve conducting what we call an evolutionary functional analysis (Gilbert, 2014), helping clients to consider the evolutionary origins of their emotions in relation to how these emotions play out in their current lives. In this way, teaching clients the evolutionary model can be woven into the most foundational elements of the therapy, such as getting a thorough description of the client's presenting problem. We'll discuss this in more detail later, but to give one example, clients are guided to explore how the dynamics of the emotions they struggle with (such as fear or anger) *make sense* when considered in an evolutionary context. For example, threat emotions narrow one's attention and reasoning to the source of a perceived threat. This narrowing can be frustrating for us when the threat is a social interaction we had days earlier that we can't stop ruminating about, but we can see how such narrowing would have survival value to our ancestors who were faced with physical threats that needed to be immediately attended to if they were to survive to pass along their genes.

This process can be very powerful. Consistent with the research on therapist credibility, I've found that when the information I'm providing clients clearly reflects their experience of how emotions play out in their own minds (and deepens their understanding of why), my credibility as a therapist goes up rapidly, which increases my therapeutic influence (Hoyt, 1996). Clients are much more likely to walk with us along difficult emotional roads when what we're saying fits with their lived experience.

When it comes to teaching our clients about compassion, while CFT includes numerous imagery and perspective-taking practices, we can also use present-moment affective work in therapy. If we pay close attention, we'll sometimes observe our clients being moved *in the present* over suffering that they or others have experienced *in the past*. If we choose to look through the lens of compassion, we can see these emotions—sadness, grief, even anger—as wonderful examples of the first component of compassion, which involves being moved by suffering, and can point this out to the client.

> *Therapist:* You became emotional when describing how difficult it was for you growing up—how terrible it was to be bullied at school, and to face your father's rages at home.
>
> *Josh:* Yeah. It was awful. I just wanted to be a kid, you know. I just wanted to play and not be scared all of the time. To not have to worry about who's gonna kick the shit out of me. (*Makes pensive expression and shakes head slowly back and forth.*)
>
> *Therapist:* It's moving, isn't it, to imagine that childhood version of you…that little boy who only wanted to play, have friends, and be safe. It's heartbreaking to recognize how terrible that was for him—how terrible it was for that younger version of you.

Josh: *(going quiet)* I never thought about it like that. I guess it was terrible. No kid should have to go through that. *(Shakes head; becomes slightly teary.)*

Therapist: I guess I find myself wondering if there might be a whole lot of hurt and sadness behind this anger you've been struggling with. Sadness about what that younger version of you went through.

Josh: I guess it is sad, you know. Why couldn't I have had a dad who took care of me, and friends who played with me rather than bullies who beat me up? Every kid should have better than that.

Therapist: Do you hear that, Josh? What you just said? *That* is compassion. That's what it is. It's opening our hearts to the suffering of that little boy—to *your* suffering—and wishing that we could do something to help him. This anger, pain, and sadness that you feel—how much of that is rooted in knowing just how hard it was for that boy, and not wanting to ever feel vulnerable like that again?

Josh: Lots of it.

Therapist: So what if we could experience that pain and heartbreak—maybe even the anger—as a compassionate sensitivity to that pain you went through? Instead of attacking yourself for having those feelings, what if we could use them as a prompt to help us really commit ourselves to helping you work with this suffering—to help you feel safe and work on becoming the sort of man you want to be?

Josh: *(Makes considering expression and nods.)* That sounds good.

Helping clients see the links between their present emotional challenges and their previously experienced suffering can reinforce their understanding of what compassion is, and it can help depathologize their emotions—softening shame or negative reactions they may have in relation to these feelings. Clients can come to understand previously avoided emotions as reactions that are not only natural, but potentially useful prompts for the second part of compassion—helpful reasoning and action.

PROVIDING SUPPLEMENTARY MATERIALS

One way to ease the "teaching load" is to provide the client with materials they can read, listen to, or view outside of the session. Examples of patient handouts, guided audio practices, and other resources for clinicians can be found on the New Harbinger website for this book: http://www .newharbinger.com/33094. The international Compassionate Mind Foundation (http://www .compassionatemind.co.uk) website also includes instructions for joining the CFT e-mail list, through which numerous CFT clinicians will readily share resources they've developed. Many CFT therapists begin using materials developed by others, and then adapt their own to fit the needs of their clients—I'd recommend you consider doing the same, and then share what you've developed on the CFT mailing list, to contribute the growing set of resources we have to help our clients. Finally, the *Compassionate Mind* series of self-help books tailor the CFT model to specific client problems such as anxiety, social confidence, trauma, anger, and eating disorders, and can be readily used alongside individual psychotherapy. Such resources can help clients deepen their understanding of the model between sessions.

Ultimately, we need to keep in mind that the "teaching" in therapy is done via a process of guided discovery, which is a nice segue to the next role the therapist takes on in CFT—that of facilitator.

Facilitator of Guided Discovery

The overall process of CFT is one of guided discovery, in which clients learn to relate to themselves, their mental experiences, and other people from a perspective of compassion. As we explored in chapter 2, the development of compassion in CFT is a multifaceted process. The therapist acts as the facilitator of this process, working to create opportunities for experiential learning that will help clients develop capacities such as compassionate understanding and reasoning, empathy, mentalization, distress tolerance, and wisdom (Gilbert, 2009a; 2010). In this role as facilitator, the therapist operates from a perspective of both wisdom and inquisitiveness—she has an understanding of the overall process that will be facilitated, but works collaboratively with her clients to discover the specific dynamics that play out in their lives. This role is emphasized in the following types of verbal interactions and interventions used in the therapy.

SOCRATIC DIALOGUE

As with a number of other therapy models, CFT makes extensive use of Socratic dialogue to help clients explore their experience. Such interactions involve questions and reflective restatements designed to prompt clients to look deeply into the feelings, motives, and behaviors of themselves and others, as well as the causes and conditions that serve to create and maintain those experiences. There are myriad uses for Socratic dialogue, including increasing clients' awareness of their own thoughts and emotions, teaching the evolutionary model, facilitating mentalization, doing functional analysis of behavior, and facilitating shifts to a compassionate perspective—as we saw in the case example of Jenny in chapter 1. Here are a few common examples of Socratic dialogue that I find myself using a good bit in my own practice of CFT:

- Given what we know about your history, how does it make sense that you might feel/think/act in that way?

- (*After noticing nonverbal behavior signaling an emotional shift*): What just happened there? What feelings came up for you just then?

- If you were to… (*name behavior the client has been avoiding*), what would be the threat in that? What would you be afraid might happen if you did that?

- What might help you feel safe as you work to address this challenge at work?

- If someone you really cared about and wanted to help were struggling with… (*name a situation similar to what the client is facing*), what would this kind, wise, confident version of you want her to understand? How might you comfort or encourage her?

The idea behind Socratic dialogue is to facilitate the client's exploration of his experience (and that of others) in an *active* manner, so that realizations are being made from the client's side, rather than interpretations being provided by the therapist.

EXPERIENTIAL EXERCISES

Much of the latter half of the book will be spent presenting techniques employed by CFT therapists, many of which are centered around creating opportunities for experiential learning and the development of compassionate capacities in the client. Examples of such strategies include mindfulness practices, guided imagery work, perspective-taking exercises, chair work, and thought and behavioral experiments. We'll be exploring these in depth as we go on, but the role of therapist-as-facilitator is consistent throughout: setting the stage for the exercise by offering preparatory instruction, guiding the client through the experience, assisting in identifying and working with obstacles that may arise, and prompting client exploration of the experience afterward.

Considering mindfulness training, for example, the therapist begins by giving the client basic instructions on the practice, as well as specific instructions designed to circumvent common obstacles (we'll explore these in chapter 7). He then guides the client through the mindfulness practice, offering more extensive description and prompts initially, then phasing these out as the client becomes more familiar with the practice. Following the exercise, the therapist and client have a discussion in which they explore the client's experience of the exercise—what they observed and learned—as well as any obstacles that may have come up during the practice.

EXPLORING INTERPERSONAL DYNAMICS

As in other therapy models, it isn't unusual for CFT therapists to shift the discussion to focus on patterns of interaction playing out within the therapeutic relationship. Often, clients manifest repetitive relational patterns in therapy that mirror their outside relationships (Teyber & McClure, 2011). Rather than *reacting* to client resistance, capitulation, or passivity, we want to consider *what it means*. Shifting the discussion to *what is happening between us* in therapy can bring awareness to these dynamics, and set the stage for considering how best to work with problematic relational patterns of which the client may not previously have been aware. This can be done in a collaborative, non-shaming way: "I'm noticing that we seem to be falling into a pattern where I'm making lots of suggestions that don't seem to be helpful to you—I feel like I'm getting 'shot down' a lot. Could you share your experience so we can figure out how best to go forward?" or "I'm noticing seems to be happening in our relationship. Have you ever noticed patterns like this playing out in other relationships?"

WORKING COLLABORATIVELY WITH OBSTACLES

You'll note that in the mindfulness example given above, much attention was given to potential obstacles, both in preparation for the practice and in the discussion afterward. This is important, as obstacles and roadblocks will frequently arise in therapy—frequently enough that entire books have been written to help therapists work through them (e.g. Leahy, 2006; Harris, 2013)—so we need to be prepared to work with them. Sometimes obstacles involve vague understandings or misconceptions on the part of the client regarding what is to be done. Sometimes it's a motivational block. At other times, there are pragmatic factors in the client's life that get in the way (such as not remembering to practice). We can never fully anticipate what anyone's experience of a given practice is going to be, but we can be assured that it will often go far awry of what we may hope for when introducing a practice or homework exercise.

In CFT, we always want the therapeutic relationship to be a collaborative one, in which the client and therapist *work together* to discover ways to address challenges in the client's life and to facilitate compassionate growth. This is particularly true when it comes to working with obstacles. When challenges arise in therapy, it can be easy to fall into roles in which therapist and client both feel a bit threatened and become rigid—the therapist on one side, trying to get the client to do something, and the client on the other side, resisting. If allowed to play out, this dynamic can easily lead to ruptures in the therapeutic relationship.

In CFT, we consider things in terms of evolved emotion-regulation systems and also consider social mentalities—evolved motivational orientations that organize our interactions with others (Gilbert, 2014; 2010). In the language of CFT, if a client is operating out of the threat system (feeling threatened, anxious, or angry in relation to the therapist or therapy) and relating to the therapist via a defensive social mentality (in other words, her interactions with the therapist are organized around defending herself or her position), it can be easy to get stuck in therapy. We want the therapist and client to be on the same side, collaboratively working *together* to explore and address the obstacles that will inevitably come up in the therapy.

We start by assuming that there are valid reasons behind clients' reactions, emotions, and behaviors, and so when obstacles come up, we try to model compassionate reasoning. Instead of judging and labeling the client as resistant (which they very well may be, for very valid reasons), we seek to *understand* the resistance, using the same process of guided discovery that permeates the rest of the therapy—and engaging in some mentalization as we work to understand the experience from the client's side. *How does it make sense that this client is responding in this way? What would be helpful as we seek to address this obstacle?* This brings us to the next role of the therapist, that of a secure base for exploration.

Secure Base

As I've mentioned, a basic goal in CFT is learning to work with evolved emotions and motivational systems. As the evolved roots of emotional safeness lie primarily in our connections with others (particularly in nurturing relationships with caregivers), John Bowlby's attachment theory is core to the therapy (Gilbert, 2010). Bowlby viewed the *attachment behavioral system* as being designed by evolution to facilitate survival and reproductive success by aiding organisms in responding to perceived threats (Bowlby, 1982/1969; Wallin, 2007; Mikulincer & Shaver, 2007). Attachment theory informs many aspects of CFT, beginning with the nature of the therapeutic relationship itself.

In attachment theory, a *secure base* operates as an interpersonal context that fuels exploration (Wallin, 2007; Ainsworth, 1963). Such secure bases, in the form of secure attachment figures offering characteristics such as proximity, accessibility, and availability, provide individuals with a nurturing place to return to when things become overwhelming. Having such a secure base facilitates exploration of the novel, the unknown, and the threatening, because the individual knows that should he need assistance or comfort, it is available to him. A particularly important piece here is the individual's *felt sense* of security: the perception that the caregiver is emotionally responsive and will be there when needed (Bowlby, 1973; Sroufe & Waters, 1977; Wallin, 2007).

Attachment theory posits that over time, individuals develop attachment-based *internal working models*—internal representations of attachment relationships that impact how they will experience threats and respond to them in the future (Wallin, 2007). These can be played out in terms of attachment styles, which are relatively enduring but can vary across different relationships (Wallin, 2007; Mikulincer & Shaver, 2007). These attachment styles have implications not only for how individuals respond to threats, but also how they experience other people (as available and helpful or as unavailable) and themselves (as worthy of kindness and caregiving or as unworthy and flawed).

Many of our psychotherapy clients will present with insecure attachment histories. They may have learned that others are unavailable when needed, or that they are unpredictable, or that they are likely to respond to the client's communications of distress with escalation rather than comfort. Some clients will have been harmed or abused by those who should have cared for them, and have learned to associate connection and affiliation with threat rather than safeness.

Increasingly, we're learning the importance of the therapist functioning as a secure base for clients to explore and work with difficult experiences (Wallin, 2007; Knox, 2010). This function is particularly important in CFT. A primary goal in CFT is to assist clients in getting the safeness emotion-regulation system online and working for them—to help themselves access feelings of safeness, even in the face of threatening experiences and emotions. Human beings evolved to feel safe in the context of affiliation, such as that offered through warm, secure attachment connections (Gilbert, 2009a, 2010, 2014). In addition to promoting exploration, secure bases also facilitate confidence and self-development (Feeney & Thrush, 2010). Consistent with CFT's emphasis on assisting clients in developing compassionate characteristics, Mario Mikulincer, Philip Shaver, and their colleagues have conducted a series of studies linking the experience of attachment security to increases in compassion, empathy, and altruistic behavior (Mikulincer et al., 2001; Mikulincer & Shaver, 2005; Gillath, Shaver, & Mikulincer, 2005).

In serving as a secure base for clients, the CFT therapist seeks to embody certain qualities within the therapy session. We want the overall context of the therapy to be one of warmth, in which the client feels accepted, heard, supported, and encouraged as she contacts and explores difficult emotional material. Mikulincer & Shaver (2007) characterize the role of therapist as secure base in this way:

> *Therapists should provide safety, comfort, and unconditional positive regard, and help the client manage the distress associated with exploring and articulating painful memories, thoughts, and feelings. They should also affirm the client's ability to handle distress and problematic life situations, not interfering with exploration by offering inappropriate interpretations, and admiring and applauding the client's efforts and achievements in therapy. In other words, like a good parent, a good therapist [assures] the client that the therapist can be relied upon for safety and support, while the client becomes increasingly capable of dealing with distress autonomously. (p. 410–411)*

To create this overall context requires that the therapist be reliable, attentive, and empathic—able to understand the emotional perspective of the client (Bowlby, 1988).

From a CFT perspective, which deliberately targets the development of self-compassion as a treatment goal, the ability of the therapist to take on the role of a secure base and to foster attachment security in the patient is particularly important. Difficulties experiencing self-compassion have been linked with insecure attachment histories and styles (Pepping, Davis, O'Donovan, & Pal, 2014; Gilbert, McEwan, Catarino, Baiao, & Palmeira, 2013). Many of our clients may present with difficulties accepting compassion from others and directing it to themselves—difficulties that have been referred to as fears of compassion (Gilbert, McEwan, Matos, & Rivas, 2011). A growing body of literature documents the relationship between such fears of compassion and experiences of depression, anxiety, and stress (Gilbert et al., 2013), with research indicating that creating attachment security experiences for others can lead to increases in their self-compassion (Pepping et al., 2014). So in relation to the goal of increasing our clients' ability to engage courageously with difficult life experiences and cultivate compassion for themselves and others, the therapist's ability to serve as a secure base is important. We can take this even further with the next role served by the therapist in CFT: a model of the compassionate self.

Models of the Compassionate Self

CFT emphasizes helping clients develop compassionate qualities that will enable them to have happy, meaningful lives. As we explored in chapter 2, in CFT, compassion is operationalized in the form of attributes to be cultivated through specific practices, which will be presented in the latter chapters of this book (Gilbert, 2010). CFT also seeks to assist clients in developing other, related compassionate capacities, such as mindfulness and emotional courage, which we see as necessary for the skillful application of compassion. Overall, the goal is to assist clients in cultivating an adaptive, resilient, compassionate version of themselves, which serves as a framework for the integration of all of these capacities. In CFT, we call this the *compassionate self*, and when we're at our best, CFT therapists serve as a living embodiment and model of this compassionate self.

If that sounds like a tall order, I'm not trying to suggest that as therapists we have to be perfect, compassionate, enlightened beings. In fact, if we were to succeed in creating that impression, our clients probably wouldn't be able to relate to us very well at all. Psychologist Kristin Neff (2011, 2003) includes common humanity as a core component of self-compassion; we'd like our clients to experience us *both* as competent helpers and as real human beings who have sometimes struggled with some of the very things that trouble them. This common humanity is also reflected in our own ability to grasp our clients' experience; we can understand and connect with their suffering in part because we've experienced aspects of it in our own lives—sadness, fear, anger, uncertainty, insecurity, and struggle. So the point isn't to be perfect models of compassion. Rather, we want to *practice what we teach*—to model and cultivate in ourselves the very strengths that we're seeking to help our clients develop.

Such an approach has a number of potential advantages. First, it provides clients with a living example of the compassionate characteristics they're trying to develop in therapy, and what such characteristics *actually look like* in the context of working with suffering. We're not working toward a compassion that is vague and aspirational—we have to put it into practice in the real world, developing these strengths by applying them to working with real challenges and emotions. Second, because they're the recipients of our compassion, clients get to have the experience of receiving compassion within the context of a safe therapeutic environment, helping them gradually learn to feel safe in the context of a relationship with another person who genuinely cares about them. This can be both comforting and challenging for those clients with insecure attachment styles, who may have great difficulty feeling safe in connection with others.

Even for people who *are* generally able to feel safe in relationship to others, therapy work often involves overcoming tendencies to avoid difficult emotions and situations and learning to instead approach and work with them. In this way, compassion involves the development of *emotional courage*—the willingness to engage directly with difficult experiences. As therapists, we can both model this courage and kindly support our clients in developing it for themselves. The courage of compassion—the confident willingness to engage with and explore the hurts and the scary stuff—needs to be held within a relational context of warmth and genuineness. Warmth is a particularly important quality for us to model so that clients feel socially safe in exploring the things that scare them (Gilbert, 2010), and so that they can learn to relate warmly to *themselves* when they observe themselves struggling. Of course, the degree and manner in which this warmth is expressed will vary considerably based on individual client characteristics, attachment styles, and ability to tolerate connection with others.

As therapists, we're sensitive to the fact that we're asking our clients to explore very uncomfortable territory, *and* we keep moving forward, knowing that we're doing so for very good reasons. This process exemplifies the meaning of compassion itself—sensitivity to suffering combined with the willingness to *approach it* and do what is necessary to address it. In this way, compassion represents the union of strengths: kindness *and* perseverance; warmth *and* resolve. One thing I took away from my early experiences with dialectical behavior therapy (Linehan, 1993) were the dialectics surrounding the therapeutic relationship—the ability of the therapist to be *both* warm and confrontational; *both* a genuine, real human being and a knowledgeable authority of sorts; *both* reverent and playful. To that last piece, I've found that compassion works much better when it contains lightheartedness.

In conducting CFT in a wide variety of settings (including with angry men in prison—not exactly people we might think of as keen on compassion work), I have consistently received feedback from clients that tells me that the experience of *receiving* compassion from me and other therapists was an important part of the work, opening them up to having compassion for themselves. When we care about others and believe in them, after a while they can begin to care about and believe in themselves. When they know we won't judge and attack them, they can take more risks and be more honest with us—and with themselves. Finally, serving as models of compassion in this way creates a resonance and consistency in the therapy—the *process* of the therapy reinforces the *content*, and vice versa.

So I'd like to suggest that if we want to help our clients cultivate compassion in their lives, part of our preparation should involve working to purposefully cultivate these qualities in ourselves. While the empirical literature on therapist use of compassion meditation is in its infancy, there is research linking such meditation with increased empathic accuracy (Mascaro, Rilling, Negi, & Raison, 2013). I also think CFT therapists specifically will benefit from cultivating compassion because it gives us an inside view of how the practices work, as well as a sense of the obstacles and challenges that come up, and it enhances our ability to model compassionate presence with our clients.

So how do we actually do this? Probably the most important piece is to practice committedly engaging in the various compassion practices that we intend to utilize with our clients—many of which are featured in the remainder of this book. Doing this, we'll see how challenging it is to create space for the practices in our lives. We'll be faced with resistance that we'll have to learn to work with. And we'll see the benefits of cultivating compassion firsthand, giving us a deep understanding of just why the process is worth it. As guides for further exploring CFT practices from the inside out, I'd recommend *Mindful Compassion* (Gilbert & Choden, 2013) and *The Compassionate Mind* (Gilbert, 2009a). There are also other resources available that provide clear, direct instruction for the cultivation of compassion (Kolts & Chodron, 2013) and mindful self-compassion (Neff, 2011; Germer, 2009).

For those who'd like a head start for their compassion practice, here's a brief imagery practice that we can use to begin cultivating various compassionate qualities in our daily lives—consider it a preview of the Compassionate Self practice we'll learn about later. We'll get into the nuances of imagery practice in chapter 11, but for now, just keep in mind that we're trying to create a mental experience—it's not about constructing vivid visual images, so much as felt experiences in the mind.

CONNECTING WITH COMPASSIONATE QUALITIES

To begin, let's sit quietly, and allow our breathing to take on a slow, soothing rhythm. Let's spend thirty seconds to a minute breathing in this way, focusing our minds on the sensation of slowing...slowing down the body, slowing down the mind. When you're ready, bring to mind a compassionate quality you'd like to develop. Perhaps it's the kind motivation to be helpful. Perhaps it's the confidence and courage to stay and work with difficult situations, even when things get tough—the knowing that whatever arises, you can find a way to work with it. Perhaps it's the ability to tolerate distress. There are many other compassionate qualities you might choose to cultivate, like patience, kindness, warmth, wisdom, or perseverance.

Choose one of these qualities, and bring it to mind. Imagine what it would be like to be filled with this quality. As you prepare to go about the rest of your day, imagine how you might think, feel, and behave as you embody this compassionate quality. Bring to mind a specific task you might do. How would this quality impact how you understand and go about this activity? Imagine yourself in the activity—thinking, feeling, and acting from a compassionate place of kindness, confidence, wisdom, patience, or gratitude. Spend five to ten minutes, or as long as you like, in this way. As you finish the practice, try to keep this quality in mind as you go about your day, and see if you can bring it into the actual moments that present themselves in your life.

The above practice is similar to the intention-setting exercise we did earlier, except that we're anchoring our intention to a specific quality we want to cultivate. Later, in the Compassionate Self exercise, we'll broaden our scope to contain multiple compassionate qualities, but the goal is the same. We want to help ourselves and our clients activate and establish mental patterns associated with compassionate ways of feeling, thinking, and behaving. With a bit of practice, this exercise can be done in just a few moments. You might even consider doing it first thing in the morning, between waking and getting out of bed—what we in CFT circles call "compassion under the duvet" (Gilbert, 2009a).

Putting the Roles into Play

In this chapter, I've presented four roles embodied by the CFT therapist: teacher, facilitator, secure base, and model of the compassionate self. While it may sound like a lot, I'm betting that you already have many of the qualities involved in these roles. Many of them are common to most modern therapeutic approaches—things like genuineness, reliability, accessibility, empathy, warmth, and unconditional positive regard. The process of guided discovery in CFT makes extensive use of the skills provided in therapist training programs, including empathic understanding, Socratic dialogue, validation, and reflection of feelings. Taking on the roles of secure base and compassionate model aren't so much about learning a new way to be a therapist as they are about bringing a bit more intentionality and awareness to the things we already do. For example, basic therapeutic responses like noting a shift in client nonverbal behavior that signifies an affective shift ("Could you say something about what just happened there for you?") or reflecting back the client's feeling ("So it sounds like you're feeling really anxious about this") demonstrate attunement and connection, imply caring, model confident willingness to explore emotions, and warmly prompt exploration.

As we explore CFT together, you'll learn many things that will relate to the experiences your clients tell you about, and to the experiences of your own life. As we go I'll be offering examples and suggestions that will help us deepen our use of these roles and bring them to life in the therapy room. For now, perhaps consider what we've explored so far, and how you might bring what you've learned into your work with current clients, or your clinical training, or your daily life.

It's also worth noting that although I've discussed them separately, these roles overlap, deepen, and support one another. While we're teaching the CFT model—introducing many of the concepts we'll explore in the next chapter—we'll be doing so via a process of guided discovery. As we use Socratic dialogue to prompt clients to explore difficult experiences and to consider their challenging emotions through the lens of evolution, we'll do so warmly and compassionately—serving as a secure base while modeling the kind willingness to approach and work with the things that can make us most uncomfortable. I often find that the process of therapy is like a dance that unifies these roles: we move forward to confront and work with really difficult material; we step back to self-soothe and shift into a compassionate perspective; we move forward again to work compassionately with the scary or uncomfortable stuff...

Keeping in mind the therapeutic roles we've discussed, let's revisit the case of Jenny, who we met in chapter 1.

Therapist: Jenny, in our last session we spent some time discussing your anxiety around social situations, and it sounded like you connected these fears to some experiences in your childhood. Those experiences seemed important, and during that session we talked about revisiting them today. How would you like to proceed?

Jenny: (*Facial expression shifts noticeably; looks down.*)

Therapist: (*Leans slightly forward; speaks with a gentle, curious tone of voice.*) What just happened for you there, Jenny? What are you feeling right now?

Jenny: (*slightly tearful*) It's just that...when you said that, I could imagine being back in that room in sixth grade, with those girls glaring at me. Pointing at me and talking about me. It feels terrible.

Therapist: So the image of being back in that room, it brings up some powerful feelings in you right now. Could you talk about that?

Jenny: (*crying*) I guess so. I feel so sad. I just wanted them to like me. I just wanted to fit in.

Therapist: You just wanted to be liked and accepted, and instead you were rejected.

Jenny: (*still crying*) Yes. It was so hard.

Therapist: (*Remains silent; leans in, with a kind, attentive facial expression.*)

Jenny: (*After a minute or so, crying softens and breathing starts to stabilize.*)

Therapist: Jenny?

Jenny: Yes?

Therapist: I wanted to make an observation. Do you remember when we talked about those two parts of compassion—about being moved by suffering, and wanting to help?

Jenny: Yes.

Therapist: I wanted to point out that the sadness you felt just now...that's the sadness of compassion. When you brought to mind that sixth-grade version of yourself, sitting there, being ridiculed when all she wanted was to be accepted—sadness came up in you. You were moved by her suffering. You could see how terrible that was for her, and it made you sad. Does that make sense?

Jenny: Yes. It was terrible for her—for me. It makes me so sad to think about it, and scared that it could happen again.

Therapist: So you feel sad for that sixth-grade self, and it feels very threatening that you could be rejected like that again? That does sound scary. Does it make sense to you that remembering this would bring up such strong feelings?

Jenny: Yes, I guess it does. That experience was so awful. Of course it would bring up strong feelings in me.

Therapist: I'm wondering if we might be able to have compassion for both of those versions of you—the sixth-grade version of you sitting in that classroom, and the adult version of you sitting here, feeling sad about what your childhood self had to experience, and afraid that it could happen again. Could we try to understand both of those perspectives, and see if we could find a way to work with that fear and sadness?

Jenny: I think I'd like that.

In the brief example above, we see aspects of all the various roles described earlier. The therapist serves as a secure base by demonstrating availability and attunement with Jenny's experience, kindly supporting her as she comes face-to-face with a difficult memory and feels the emotions associated with it. Compassion is modeled throughout, in both verbal and nonverbal expressions of warmth and support, as well as in modeling emotional courage around exploring a difficult memory and related emotions. In doing this, Socratic questioning was repeatedly used to facilitate the process of exploring the memory, identifying the emotions, and introducing the shift to a compassionate perspective. Finally, an opportunity was used to teach an aspect of the CFT model—in this case, the definition of compassion—in a way that related it to the client's present emotional experience.

THERAPIST USE OF SELF-DISCLOSURE

In considering the roles we've discussed above, we should visit the topic of therapist self-disclosure. The appropriate use of self-disclosure can help clients understand the therapist as a real human being. It can also be experienced by clients as validating and depathologizing, emphasizing the common humanity emphasized by Neff (2003) as a core component of self-compassion. On the other hand, if used unskillfully, it can distract from the therapeutic work, shift the focus from the client to the therapist, muddy the boundaries of the therapeutic relationship, and even shift the client into the role of the caregiver. As I mentioned earlier, the CFT therapist is both a real, genuine human being *and* a knowledgeable guide. We need to be relatable, and at the same time perceived as knowledgeable enough, wise enough, and kind enough to serve as a secure attachment figure who can respond confidently and assertively to our clients' distress.

There are no hard-and-fast rules about when and how often one should use self-disclosure in CFT, and it's safe to say that CFT therapists (like other types of therapists) vary considerably from one another in this regard. I sometimes use self-disclosure in my own practice of CFT, but I do so fairly sparingly. In considering your own potential use of self-disclosure, I'd encourage you to apply the following guidelines. These can be useful in considering other potential therapy practices that you might be wondering about as well.

- Imagine that at any point, a colleague, supervisor, or trainee could walk into the therapy room, magically stop time—freezing the client in place—and ask, "What is it you are doing with this client, and how does it relate to your conceptualization of his case and the direction of therapy?" (Or less dramatically, imagine a supervisor reviewing a video of the session, and pausing and asking the same question.) Can you answer that question?

- Relatedly, consider your motivation for the disclosure. If it's based more in affect—in other words, you just *feel* like you want to tell the client these details about yourself— refer back to the point above before continuing. Our own affective responses aren't irrelevant or necessarily faulty, but a feeling of urgency around disclosure or another intervention could signal that this behavior is driven by our own threat or drive responses (we'll explore this more in chapter 5), rather than what will best serve the therapy process.

- Consider whether you would feel comfortable talking about this self-disclosure with your supervisor or in peer-supervision with your colleagues. If the answer is *Absolutely,* *because it relates to the therapy in this way...*that's a pretty good indicator. If the answer is *I'm not sure...*then I'd recommend consulting *before* using the self-disclosure. And if the answer is a feeling of discomfort accompanied by some variant of rationalization like *Well, they really wouldn't understand the context...*it may mean that you're working to convince yourself to do something in therapy that is rooted more in your own needs than in those of the client and the therapy.

- When in doubt, discuss things with a colleague beforehand. Colleagues can often give us valuable perspectives that dramatically expand our understanding and expose our own blind spots. The process of peer-supervision and asking for help or advice can also help us deepen our own compassionate qualities, like courage, distress tolerance, and humility.

SUMMARY

The first layer of compassion in a course of CFT is the therapeutic relationship. In this chapter, we explored the various roles embodied by the CFT therapist, and touched on how they can be integrated into the session. Cultivating these roles is a gradual process that develops over time. Let's lightly keep these roles in mind as we explore the foundational pieces of CFT therapy in the next few chapters. In the next chapter, we'll begin exploring the second layer of compassion in CFT: compassionate understanding.

CHAPTER 4

Compassionate Understanding: How Evolution Has Shaped Our Brains

As I've mentioned, shame and self-criticism underlie a wide range of mental health problems (Gilbert & Irons, 2005; Gilbert, 2014). A primary goal in CFT is to help clients shift the relationship they have with their internal experiences from a perspective of judgment and condemnation to one of understanding and compassion. A core theme in this work is to help clients recognize that many aspects of their experience are *not their fault*—things that they neither chose nor designed—while helping them *take responsibility* for working directly and actively to improve their lives. This shift to compassion begins with helping clients understand their emotions and motives in relation to how their brains and minds have evolved, and how evolution has presented human beings with some interesting problems. So in CFT, compassion begins with understanding the mind.

OLD BRAINS AND NEW BRAINS

In the 1990s, Paul Maclean introduced the concept of the *triune brain* (Maclean, 1990), which described the human brain in terms of three parts, reflecting different stages of brain evolution. The triune brain included a reptilian brain, which is responsible for basic bodily functions as well as aggressive and reproductive drives; a paleo-mammalian brain—the *limbic system*, having to do with memory, emotion, and learning; and the neo-mammalian brain (the cerebral cortex), which does the heavy lifting in terms of things like self-awareness, symbolic thought, problem solving, and other higher-order cognitive processes. While the reality of how the brain works isn't quite so straightforward (Cozolino, 2010), Maclean's work highlights some of the challenges presented by how evolution has shaped our brains, and gives us a nice way to explore these dynamics with our clients.

In CFT, we discuss this concept with clients using the language of "old brain" and "new brain" (Gilbert 2010). In therapy, it can sometimes be useful to use the term "emotional brain" synonymously with "old brain" when we're specifically talking about the dynamics of emotion. Because different parts of the brain evolved at different times in our evolutionary history and served different purposes for our ancestors, the ways our old brains, new brains, and bodies interact can be tricky and can create problems for us. Understanding this can be very freeing for our clients, as it helps clarify why their emotions can feel so out of control, and why it's not their fault.

Let's look at some ways to explore this idea with clients. When we're introducing it, we want to provide information, but not go on with lengthy monologues. Here's an example of how we might initially approach the concept with Josh:

Therapist: Josh, we've been discussing your anger, which you've struggled with for some time. In learning to work with emotions like these, it can be useful to explore where they come from, and how they work in our brains and minds. How about we chat about that for a bit?

Josh: All right.

Therapist: If we look through the lens of evolution, we see that the human brain is actually very tricky. It's kind of like we have an *old brain*, which takes care of all the stuff that kept our ancient ancestors alive—basic emotions and motivations that helped them protect themselves from threats and do the things needed for survival—and a *new brain*, responsible for things like problem solving, mental imagery, self-awareness, and deep thinking—about what sort of person we want to be, what it all means, that sort of thing. Does that make sense?

Josh: Yeah, I think so.

Therapist: Let's think about this in terms of a situation you've discussed. You mentioned that you sometimes become angry at work. Could you talk a bit about that?

Josh: It's mostly when my coworkers question me, or don't do something they said they were going to do. I get really pissed off then.

Therapist: So your coworkers question something you've asked them to do, and your old, emotional brain registers that as a threat, and here comes the anger. Does it come up pretty quickly?

Josh: Oh yeah. I get angry sometimes even before they ask a question. If they make a face, or look at me like they disagree with what I'm saying, I start getting angry. I just want to set them straight, like "Can't you ever just shut up and do what you're asked to do?"

Therapist: From an evolutionary perspective, our old, emotional brains are designed to help us identify and respond to threats—just like they did for our ancestors, who lived in a world with lots of real physical threats. You know—lions, tigers, bears, and the like. Anger is a threat emotion that prepares us to fight. It sounds like your emotional brain has learned that your coworkers questioning you or not doing what they've agreed to do are potential threats, and your brain responds like they're tigers out to get you.

Josh: (*With a look of consideration.*) I guess so. I mean, it is threatening.

Therapist: Let's explore that. Let's explore what's going on in your new brain while this is happening. When your coworkers are questioning you or fail to do what you've asked of them, what thoughts are going through your mind? What are you thinking?

Josh: (*Pauses, thinking.*) I'm thinking that they're challenging me—like they don't respect me or trust me. If they respected me, they'd just do what I ask, right? And then I'm thinking that things aren't going to get done, or aren't going to get done right, which will then come back to me. My boss is going to let me have it, even though I did everything I was supposed to do.

Therapist: (*Nods.*) Is there any mental imagery—like pictures or movies playing out in your mind—that goes along with those thoughts?

Josh: (*Thinks for a moment.*) Yes. It's like I can see it happening in my mind. I can picture them rolling their eyes, talking about me behind my back, and blowing me off. I can just see my boss coming to me, asking me what the problem is—blaming me for stuff not getting done. It's maddening, you know?

Therapist: (*Nods and speaks sympathetically.*) That does sound maddening. So in addition to that old-brain anger, the new brain is piling on a *lot* of other stuff—thoughts of being mocked and blown off, and images of the consequences—your boss coming down on you. There's a lot of stuff going on when that anger comes up.

Josh: Yeah, I guess there is.

The Old Brain: Powerful, But Not Very Wise

One thing you'll frequently hear CFT therapists say when exploring the idea of the old brain and the new brain with clients is that our "old, emotional brains are very powerful, but they aren't very clever or wise." Many of us may have experience explaining the basic cognitive behavioral model to our clients and using Socratic dialogue to explore how different patterns of thinking can lead to different types of emotion and behavior (and vice versa). In CFT, we want to understand and explore these dynamics in relation to the evolved brain.

Our old brains evolved to motivate our ancestors to do what was necessary to survive, and they did this via the evolution of basic emotion systems (fear, anger, desire, lust, and so on; Panksepp & Biven, 2012; Panksepp, 1998) and archetypal motives (caregiving, competitive, sexual), many of which are socially oriented (Gilbert, 2010; 2014). When triggered by an external or internal stimulus, working through the action of various neurotransmitter and hormonal systems, these emotions and motives can very powerfully orient and shape our attention, thinking and reasoning, mental imagery, and motivation (Panksepp & Biven, 2012; Gilbert, 2010). We'll discuss this process further in chapter 5, but the idea is that these old-brain emotions and motives can organize our minds and bodies in ways that make it easy for us to feel trapped inside challenging affective experiences. For example, when Josh is feeling anger related to his coworkers' behavior, he experiences a narrowing of attention onto the perceived threat (their questioning him, things not getting done, the idea of being humiliated and reprimanded), threat-related perseverations in the form of thoughts and imagery, and the motivation to set his coworkers straight. Of course, our old, emotional brains are also associated with patterns of bodily experience as well, patterns which play a large role in shaping how the emotion is *felt*.

While the old, emotional brain is powerful in how it can organize our minds, it's not very good at distinguishing thoughts and fantasies from actual stimuli coming in from the external world. Our emotions occur largely as a result of *implicit* (nonconscious) processing systems that are triggered by various inputs—information from the outside environment; from our own thoughts, memories, and imagery; and from our bodily experience (Gilbert, 2010). As a result, our emotional brains and underlying biological systems can respond powerfully to thoughts and imagery, almost as if they were real. This is why we engage in things like sexual fantasies—sexual *imagery* stimulates parts of the brain and endocrine system that produce sexual *feelings*, with corresponding activity in the body to produce sexual *responses*. Changing emotion is all about working with and changing implicit inputs to the emotional brain.

The good news is that we can choose to focus our thoughts and mental imagery in ways that help produce the sorts of affective experiences we want to have. We'll be exploring this dynamic a great deal in the second half of this book. The *challenging* news is that interactions between old brain, new brain, and body can create an emotional inertia, in which conditioned emotional activation in the limbic system triggers new-brain thoughts, imagery, and memories (as well as bodily responses) that then feed *back* to old-brain structures like the amygdala to fuel the very emotional response that created them. Of course, it can work the other way around, beginning with a memory, thought (*he doesn't respect me*), mental image, or bodily sensation that the old brain registers as a threat, leading to related emotional experiences, with the process continuing. This is fertile ground for exploration with clients, as they begin to understand how different emotions and motives are associated with specific patterns of attention, thinking, imagery, motivation, and bodily experience, and then learn skillful ways to work with these experiences and the emotions and motives that underlie them.

This is a simplified version of how things play out in the brain, but it's based in affective neuroscience research (e.g. Panksepp & Biven, 2012). Learning about these brain and body interactions can also have a number of positive effects for our clients, all of which fit with our focus on compassion:

- Shifting from judging and avoiding their challenging emotions to curiously examining and understanding how they play out in the mind.

- Recognizing that the way their emotions work isn't their fault, but occurs because of how our brains evolved and the ways different parts of our brains and bodies interface with one another.

- Giving clues as to how they can begin to compassionately work with their emotions—through creating new, helpful inputs to their old, emotional brains.

Let' consider how we might introduce this concept:

Therapist: Jenny, I'd like to chat a bit more about this old-brain/new-brain piece, because I think it might help us understand your anxiety a bit better. To start, I'd like to use an analogy. Do you have any pets?

Jenny: Yes, I love pets. I have a dog named Penelope.

Therapist: Penelope—what a wonderful name! We have a dog named Sadie. Do you have a fenced-in yard for Penelope?

Jenny: Yes, I've got a fenced backyard.

Therapist: We don't—the area behind our house is wooded, so we've decided to leave it open, to enjoy the view of the woods.

Jenny: Nice.

Therapist: It is nice, but it sometimes presents challenges. We let Sadie outside sometimes, and she'll hang out in our backyard. But because we don't have a fence, sometimes another dog will wander through—you know, sniff around, pee on a few rocks, that sort of thing.

Jenny: (*Nods.*)

Therapist: When another dog wanders in, Sadie can get pretty defensive.

Jenny: She's defending her territory.

Therapist: Exactly! So she'll sort of size up the other dog. If she thinks she can take it, she'll make a threat display—stand tall, with the hackles on the back of her neck standing up, growling a bit. On the other hand, if the dog looks big and scary, she might make a submissive gesture instead—maybe cowing down, as if to say, "No need to have any trouble here." (*Makes bowing-down gesture.*)

Jenny: (*Laughs.*) Yeah, I've seen Penelope do the same thing at the dog park.

Therapist: (*Smiles.*) So let's imagine that this happens to Penelope or Sadie. Things get a bit tense, but after a little while, the other dog gets bored and wanders off to pee on someone else's yard. Five minutes later, how is Penelope?

Jenny: She's fine. Right back to normal.

Therapist: Sadie, too. While she was initially upset because this dog invaded her territory, five minutes later she's coming to get scratched, begging for a treat. (*Moves head back and forth a bit, smiling.*)

Jenny: Exactly. (*Smiles.*)

Therapist: So now let's imagine that this same thing happens to you or me. We're at home, and a stranger walks into the house, wanders around looking at things, maybe grabs something out of the fridge, pees on the corner of the couch…

Jenny: (*Laughs.*)

Therapist: Sorry…took the dog analogy a bit too far! If this were to happen, we might respond like Sadie or Penelope. We'd likely feel somewhat threatened, and probably want to protect our territory. If the situation seemed manageable, we might get assertive—"Hey, this is my house. I'd like you to leave at once."

Jenny: Yeah. (*Nods.*)

Therapist: On the other hand, if the intruder seemed very dangerous—say, he was holding a gun, we might make a submissive display. (*Holds hands up in an open gesture.*) "It's okay. Take whatever you want…there's no need for anyone to get hurt…" We'd respond in ways that aren't terribly different from how Sadie or Penelope might.

Jenny: (*Continues to nod along.*)

Therapist: So here's the question. Let's imagine that after a while, the intruder gets bored and leaves. How would you or I be doing five minutes later? Five hours later? Five days later?

Jenny: (*good-naturedly*) I'd be freaking out!

Therapist: (*smiling*) I probably would, too. Why would we be freaking out? What would be going on in our minds? What thoughts or images might play out for us?

Jenny: I'd be thinking about what could have happened. That he could have really hurt me. I'd be worried that he might come back, thinking about what he might do the next time.

Therapist: What images might be coming up in your mind?

Jenny: I'd probably be picturing it happening again and again.

Therapist: And those thoughts and fantasies might fuel your fear, keeping you afraid?

Jenny: They sure would.

Therapist: Exactly! That's the difference between you or me and Penelope or Sadie. It has to do with the tricky way our old and new brains communicate with each other. The dogs have those old-brain threat reactions, but when the threat is gone, they'll tend to calm down fairly quickly. We, on the other hand…

Jenny: We keep it going.

Therapist: Our thoughts and mental images feed back to our emotional brains, and fuel the fear that caused them—like pouring gasoline on a fire. So our emotions can focus our attention and trigger thoughts and images in our minds— thoughts and images that can then come back and fuel the very emotions that triggered them. Does that make sense?

Jenny: (*nodding*) Like how those thoughts I have in the classroom about people laughing at me fuel my fear.

Therapist: Just like that. It's important to realize that this isn't our fault. You and I didn't *choose* to have brains that work in such tricky ways; it's just how they work— what we were born with. But if we're going to work with emotions like fear and anxiety, it can help to know how these brains work.

Jenny: Mmm-hmm.

Therapist: One last thing. Thinking scary thoughts can fuel feelings of being scared. One of the scariest thoughts we can have is, *There's something wrong with me.* (*Pauses.*)

Jenny: (*Pauses and looks down.*) I have that thought all the time.

Therapist: (*Pauses, then continues with a kind tone of voice.*) And how does it feel when that thought comes up?

Jenny: Terrible.

Therapist: (*Nodding.*) It *does* feel terrible. That's why in CFT we focus on developing compassion and kindness for ourselves and others—we want to find ways of thinking and acting that help us feel safe, rather than threatened.

Jenny: That would be really nice.

Therapist: Well, let's work on that, then.

The example above demonstrates how a CFT therapist might introduce old-brain/new-brain dynamics with a client. The use of the dog analogy is meant to reinforce the evolutionary model, initially demonstrating the evolved aspects of our emotional responses and behaviors that are similar to other mammals, and then exploring differences (the tricky old-brain/new-brain dynamics) that set us up for unique problems. You'll note that there was a good bit of therapist talking there, as the analogy was explained. While it's hard to convey in print, I've tried to give a sense of how the therapist would monitor the client's nonverbal behavior and use questions, pacing, body language, tone of voice, and attempts at humor to maintain engagement and create an interactive experience, even when the focus is on explanation. Whenever possible, we want to link such discussions to the client's experience early and often—even within the analogy (which is why the therapist asked Jenny about her own dog). We also see the therapist doing some mirroring of the client's affective experience—using humor when she is smiling and nodding along, and then reverently slowing things down when the discussion bridges to the Jenny's own experience of self-criticism and things get a bit heavy.

In doing this, we want to keep our focus on the *process* we're trying to explore with the client. Some clients might argue that the threat-driven thoughts that accompany fear of the intruder are completely valid, and could trigger behaviors (installing an alarm system, for example) that could help us avoid victimization in the future. They'd be right about this. We're not trying to convey that the ability of our thoughts and imagery to fuel and be fueled by our emotional brains is bad. It's neither good nor bad—it's just the way things work. The point is that this dynamic can be tricky for us, and can sometimes fuel threat responses that aren't terribly helpful. This sort of interchange can be useful in modeling compassionate reasoning—helping clients shift from *judging and labeling* (thoughts and emotions as either right or wrong, good or bad) to a perspective that instead is focused on *understanding* (thoughts and emotions as mental experiences, and the sometimes tricky dynamics between them). Finally, you'll note that as the vignette concludes, the therapist links the example back to a larger theme in the therapy—how Jenny's self-criticism functions to keep her threat response activated, and how compassion can help with this.

Emotional Inertia

As the above vignette demonstrates, we can explore how interactions among old-brain emotions, new-brain thoughts and imagery, and bodily sensations can work to maintain the energy of an emotion. For example, if a threat is registered in either the new or old brain (via a thought such as *She doesn't like me* or a previously conditioned threat trigger—like smelling the cologne that was worn by a rapist), it can trigger emotions of fear or anger, which themselves can give rise to thoughts and imagery associated with the emotion, as well as bodily sensations of arousal and tension (racing heart, shakiness, tensed jaw, tight shoulders, and so on). Once this cascade of experience occurs, each element of the system (new brain, old brain, bodily experience) can serve to trigger the others, fueling the ongoing emotional response. New-brain images and thoughts, bodily experiences, and the environments we are in (themselves shaped by emotion-driven behaviors) can all serve as ongoing inputs to the old, emotional brain—for good or ill.

This exploration can be useful to clients, as we can frame much of the work we do in therapy (and homework) as working with various inputs to the emotional brain. We work to develop compassionate ways of thinking and compassionate imagery to help ourselves feel safe rather than threatened, and to find helpful ways of working with situations rather than threat-based rumination. We work to develop ways of behaving that are effective in getting our needs met. And we work with the body to help ourselves find balance rather than panic.

In facilitating this discussion, I sometimes find it useful to draw it out on a piece of paper or whiteboard. I start by drawing a rudimentary brain. Then I'll mark a red area in the middle of the brain, about where the limbic area is, to represent the old, emotional brain. I'll then draw a box around the front fourth of the brain to represent the new-brain thinking centers. While discussing things, I'll draw arrows from the emotional brain to the new-brain "thinking box," and then back, to demonstrate the cyclical nature of how old and new brain can interact to fuel an ongoing emotional response. We can also draw similar arrows going down to and back from the body, to demonstrate how bodily responses can be a part of the cycle that maintains an emotion.

SOOTHING RHYTHM BREATHING

As I mentioned above, our emotions occur largely as a result of implicit processing systems which respond to a wide range of inputs—information coming in from the outside world through our senses, information coming down from the newer parts of the brain that produce thoughts and imagery, and information coming up from the body. Increasingly, we're discovering that working with that input from the body can play a powerful role in helping to balance emotions. So one of the very first interventions we introduce in CFT is specifically targeted at the body. In CFT, we call this *soothing rhythm breathing (SRB)*, and it involves purposefully slowing down the breath.

In SRB, we guide clients to slow down the pace of their breathing and focus their attention on the sensation of slowing. It's important to note that this is different from mindful breathing, which we'll introduce later, in chapter 7. With mindful breathing, we focus attention on the normal process of breathing as an anchor for the attention, and bring our attention back to the breath again and again. In SRB, the focus is on creating a sense of *slowing*—slowing down the body, and slowing down the mind. This slowing can help clients soften the intensity of threat emotions by activating the parasympathetic nervous system, and hence begin to shift away from the new-brain/old-brain/body inertia that drives these emotions. Let's consider how we might introduce SRB to a client:

SOOTHING RHYTHM BREATHING

Now, I'd like to introduce a practice called soothing rhythm breathing. *This practice involves slowing down our bodies and minds by working with the breath. Specifically, we're going to be slowing down the breath, and focusing our minds on the sensations of slowing.*

- *Let's start by sitting in an upright posture, with both feet flat on the floor, and perhaps folding the hands in the lap. The head is held in an upright, dignified but relaxed posture. As you gain experience with the practice, you'll be able to use it in all sorts of situations and body postures, but we'll start like this, with a nice, comfortable, upright posture.*

- *If you like, allow your eyes to close, and bring your attention to the sensation of your breath entering and leaving your body. Just notice this sensation of breathing. (Pause ten to twenty seconds.)*

- *Now we're going to slow down the breath. Allow your rate of breathing to slow, taking four to five seconds on the in-breath, pausing for a moment, and then taking four to five seconds on the out-breath. Breathing in deeply—1—2—3—4. (Pause for a moment.) Then slowly breathing out—1—2—3—4.*

- *Let's take a couple of minutes to breathe in this way. As we do, let's focus our attention on the sense of slowing—slowing down the body, slowing down the mind. If this rate of breathing is too slow, see if you can find a rate that is comfortable and soothing for you. The idea is to breathe in a way that is slowing and soothing.*

- (Wait two minutes, or however long you choose to do the practice. The timing should be based on making it a successful learning experience for the client—not an aversive one in which he loses himself in thoughts about how much he hates it! So if it's clear that the client is resistant, we can start with thirty seconds.)

- *When you're ready, allow your breath to return to its normal rate, and gently allow your eyes to open. (Wait until client's eyes are open.) Let's explore what that was like.*

Once the SRB exercise is over, we'll take a few minutes to explore the client's experience of the practice. As with all relaxation exercises, the effects of SRB increase with practice, so we shouldn't expect clients to have immediate dramatic effects. We can explain that slowing down our breathing in this way doesn't make threat emotions go away, but can *soften* them, and create some space for other things to happen (like mindful observation of our thoughts and emotions, and shifting into compassionate ways of thinking). I usually assign SRB as homework after the first session—often having clients practice it for thirty seconds at a time, two or three times per day. We'll need to problem-solve with clients around how they will remind themselves to do it, as the biggest obstacle is often forgetting to practice. Setting phone alarms can serve as a prompt for SRB practice, as can planning regular times to do it (for example, at specific times of day, or—if the person is a television watcher—during the first commercial of every program). SRB also provides us with a nice way to introduce the idea that therapy will involve regular home practice, and to shape homework participation—almost anyone can find thirty seconds to practice a couple of times per day. This gives us the opportunity the create a nice routine in which we explore, at the beginning of each session, how the home practice went. We can then give them positive reinforcement for practicing, work collaboratively with them to overcome obstacles that may have arisen, and then help to develop a new home practice plan as the session winds down.

Some clients may hate focusing on the breath or body, due to trauma conditioning or other factors. If this is the case, we don't want to turn the exercise into an exposure trial (which we may very well want to explore later)—the purpose here is to help them focus their attention in a *soothing* way. For these folks, we can choose one of the many excellent progressive muscle relaxation practices that have been developed, or even work with them to find something they could focus their attention on that would be soothing. (One group of Paul Gilbert's decided to hold tennis balls and focus on their texture.) The point is to come up with ways for clients to focus their attention in soothing ways that don't take extraordinary amounts of time or effort.

SUMMARY

In this chapter, we explored ways to help clients consider the manner in which their brains evolved and how this can create challenges for them. The goal is to begin facilitating a shift away from judging and attacking themselves (and others) for their emotions and reactions, replacing these habits with a curiosity-driven *understanding* of how and why their brains (and minds) work the way they do. In the next chapter, we'll deepen this discussion to explore three evolved emotion-regulation systems, and how evolution shaped these systems to organize our minds and bodies in very different ways.

CHAPTER 5

Compassionate Understanding: Three Types of Emotion

As we've discussed, in CFT, the groundwork for self-compassion is laid in helping clients understand their challenges in relation to the ways that our brains and minds work. In chapter 4, we explored how tricky dynamics between old brain, new brain, and body can serve to perpetuate emotional responses even when the external events that triggered them are long gone. In this chapter, we'll introduce a model of emotions that will allow us to quickly increase clients' understanding of why and how their emotions work the way they do, and how this makes sense in the context of evolution.

Modern research in affective neuroscience has identified a number of basic emotion systems that have evolved in humans and other animals (e.g. Panksepp & Biven, 2012; LeDoux, 1998). CFT has drawn upon this research to articulate a model of emotions that helps clients understand their feelings and related experiences as the result of human evolution. In this way, instead of seeing emotions such as fear, anxiety, or anger as *something that is wrong with me*, clients can instead see them as *part of what helped my ancestors survive.* By considering emotions and motives in terms of their survival value to our ancestors, clients can begin to see that how these experiences operate within us makes perfect sense. This process—helping clients consider their emotions, motives, and challenges through the lens of evolution—is sometimes referred to as *evolutionary functional analysis* (Gilbert, 2014).

THE THREE-CIRCLES MODEL OF EMOTION

In CFT, emotions are grouped into three emotion-regulation systems, related to their evolved functions, as shown in figure 4.1. First, we have emotions like fear, anger, and anxiety that function to help us identify and respond to threats (the threat-protection system, or "threat system" for short). Second, the drive-and-resource-acquisition system ("drive system") emotions motivate us to pursue goals and resources, and reward us for attaining them. Finally, the safeness-soothing-contentment system ("safeness system") emotions help us feel safe, peaceful, and calm when we're neither defending against threats nor pursuing goals. Let's briefly consider these systems individually.

Three Types of Emotion Regulation System

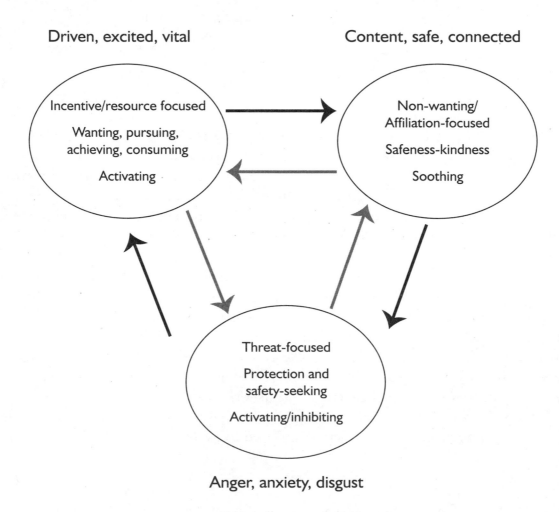

Figure 4.1: Three Types of Emotion-Regulation System. (From Gilbert, *The Compassionate Mind* [2009], reprinted with permission from Little, Brown Book Group.)

The Threat System

The threat system involves emotions that orient us toward perceived threats, assisting us in identifying and responding to things that may harm us. This system includes many emotions that our clients may struggle with, including anger, fear, anxiety, and disgust. The threat system picks up on threats very rapidly, and activates powerful bursts of feelings that alert us, orient us toward perceived threats, and motivate us to action—fight, flight, or freezing/submission (Gilbert, 2010).

Research has shown that we're biased toward processing threat-related information, with negative information capturing our attention and memory more powerfully than does positive information (Baumeister, Bratslavsky, Finkenaurer, & Vohs, 2001). Threat emotions organize us in powerful ways, narrowing our attention, thinking, mental imagery, and motivation onto the source of threat in "sticky" ways—we can struggle to disengage from these emotions, even when we want to. From an evolutionary perspective, it makes sense that these emotions would be equipped to push other, more positive experiences out of the way—our ancestors faced a harsh world filled with very real dangers. These ancestors were able to survive and pass their genes along to us partially because they possessed these threat emotions, resulting in our having brains designed to prioritize threat-processing through the action of structures such as the amygdala and hypothalamic–pituitary axis (LeDoux, 1998). These emotions were shaped by evolution to play out powerfully within us, and they operate on a "better safe than sorry" basis. Threat-based learning can occur very efficiently, with many of our clients experiencing significant distress stemming from a single threatening incident.

As we discussed in the previous chapter, new-brain abilities of fantasy, meaning-making, and rumination allow us to keep this system running even in the absence of any genuine external threat. Through new-brain activity that allows humans to form mental connections that go well beyond our original learning experiences, fear stemming from a powerful initial experience can come to impact many areas of our clients' lives. In this way, new advances in our understanding of learning, such as relational frame theory (Hayes, Barnes-Holmes, & Roche, 2001; Törneke, 2010), have harrowing implications for how experiences of threat can be magnified and multiplied in our minds. (We'll explore this more in chapter 6.) When it's balanced with the two other systems, the threat system helps alert us to potential threats and obstacles we need to deal with, to keep our lives moving in desired directions. However, it's easy for this system to take up more than its share of mental energy, so we need to help clients learn to find balance when they've spent lots of time living in states of threat.

The Drive System

In addition to defending themselves from threat, our ancestors also needed to acquire the things needed to survive and prosper—things like food, shelter, comfort, mates, and social position. This is the job of the drive-and-resource-acquisition system (or "drive system," for short), which is associated with feelings like excitement, lust, and ambition. Through the activity of chemicals like dopamine, this system alerts us to opportunities for pursuing goals and resources, helps focus and maintain our attention on pursuing them, and is associated with experiences of pleasure when goals are attained (Gilbert, 2009a; 2010). Like the threat system, this system can be very activating and motivating, and can powerfully focus our attention on what we are pursuing—which can be tricky when the blind pursuit of our goals can be harmful to others or ourselves. We can also develop powerful cravings for the intermittent rushes of pleasure that come when goals are attained—likely one reason things like videogames can be so addictive. However, when it's balanced with the two other systems, the drive system helps keep us activated in the pursuit of important life goals.

The Safeness System

In Western cultures at least, our clients will likely be familiar with emotional experiences associated with the previous two systems. Experiences of threat and drive are powerfully motivating, a fact used liberally by advertisers and political groups to activate people around their products and platforms. These emotions are important, but they can also be linked with problems when the systems are out of balance—mapping nicely on to the sources of suffering described in Buddhist psychology: attachment (going after what I want) and aversion (moving away from what I don't want).

Unlike these systems (which activate us), the safeness system is associated with feelings of being safe, calm, peaceful, and content. These emotions help balance us out when there are no threats to defend against and no goals that must be pursued. Safeness emotions are experienced positively, but are very different from the activating experiences of the drive system (Gilbert, 2009a; 2010).

As you may suspect after our discussion of the roles of the therapist in chapter 2, the safeness system is typically linked with experiences of affection, acceptance, kindness, and affiliation. Such interactions soothe us, and can help us feel safe and calm. Through the action of chemicals like oxytocin and the endorphins, these interactions can reduce stress, affect pain thresholds, impact immune and digestive functioning, and reduce threat activation in the amygdala (Gilbert, 2010; Depue & Morrone-Strupinsky, 2005). In contrast to a mind that is narrowly focused on threats or goals, when we feel safe, we can experience relaxed, reflective attention and we tend to be exploratory, prosocial, and altruistic (Gilbert, 2009a, 2010). Fueled by warm connections with others, the safeness system helps balance out the other two systems, helping us approach life in an open, kind, and reflective fashion.

The linkage of the safeness system to social connectedness presents therapists with both challenges and opportunities. Unfortunately, many of our clients will present with maladaptive attachment histories or interpersonal trauma, from which they will have learned to feel *unsafe* in connection to others. Closeness then becomes associated not with safeness, but with threat. This presents us with a primary challenge—what to do when our clients' experience has taught them to fear the very connections that should help them feel safe (evolutionarily speaking). As we'll see, the linkage between safeness and social connection makes the therapy room a perfect laboratory to do exactly this work. Done skillfully, therapy can be utilized to help clients "get the safeness system online" and help them face sources of threat in their lives, and in their minds.

ORGANIZING OUR EXPERIENCE

If you spend much time in CFT circles, you'll quite commonly hear therapists talk about how different emotions and motives "organize the mind." It can be very useful to introduce this concept to clients while we're helping them understand the three-circles model. The diagram in figure 4.2 illustrates what we mean by this.

Figure 4.2: How the Threat System Organizes the Mind. (From Kolts, *The Compassionate Mind Approach to Managing Your Anger* [2012], reprinted with permission from Little, Brown Book Group.)

The idea is that different emotions (such as anger, excitement, safeness) and related motives (such as aggressive, competitive, connection) are associated with distinctly different patterns of attention, felt emotion, thinking and reasoning, mental imagery, motivation, and behavior. This diagram can be used to guide Socratic dialogue with our clients to help them learn about how these emotions play out in them and to relate that organization to the evolutionary origins of the emotion. Let's consider a case example:

Therapist: Jenny, now that we've introduced the three circles, I'd like to talk a bit about how these emotions play out in us. In CFT, we talk about how different emotions can "organize the mind" in different ways, as I've demonstrated in this "spider diagram" here (*points at diagram*)—although that's kind of a silly name because it only has six legs.

Jenny: (*Nods.*)

Therapist: In addition to the feelings we get with different emotions, we also experience differences in how we pay attention, think about things, and imagine things in our minds when these emotions come up. (*Points at "attention," "thinking and reasoning," and "imagery and fantasy" circles on diagram, sequentially.*) They also affect what we want to do (*points at "motivation"*) and what we actually do (*points at "behavior"*). So with any emotion we feel, there's actually quite a lot going on—which is why it can be so easy to feel trapped in a feeling. Does that make sense?

Jenny: (*Nods.*) It's kind of like what we talked about last time—that different thoughts can fuel different feelings, which bring up more thoughts.

Therapist: (*Smiles.*) Exactly! Now we're going to explore how your threat system and safeness system organize your mind in very different ways. First, let's consider a time when you've felt very threatened. You've brought up a couple of situations like that—fears about going on a social outing with friends, and being afraid that you'd be called on in class. Want to focus on one of those situations?

Jenny: How about going out with friends?

Therapist: Sounds good. Could you briefly describe a situation that brings up feelings of threat in you?

Jenny: Sure—one happened just the other day. Some girls from my floor stopped by to ask me to go out with them this Friday night, like to eat and go to the bars, that sort of thing.

Therapist: Perfect. Now let's work our way around the spider diagram. What emotion should we put in the middle, here?

Jenny: Definitely fear or extreme anxiety.

Therapist: (*Writes "fear/anxiety" in the center of the circle.*) Okay, so let's start with this "felt emotion" circle. To start, it can be helpful to consider how emotions feel in the body.

Jenny: When they asked, my heart started pounding, and I had troubling concentrating. It's like the world was closing in on me. I just sort of nodded and said I'd let them know. After they left, I calmed down a bit, but I was really tense and scared. Even now, it's hard to think about it.

Therapist: Let's talk about that—what you think about it. What thoughts come up when you're feeling anxious about going out?

Jenny: Like I want to do it, but also that I really *don't* want to do it. I think that it would be fun, for any normal person, but that I would screw it up. I think of all the millions of things that could go wrong. I even have thoughts that they don't really want me along—that they're just inviting me so they can watch me squirm, or to have someone to make fun of.

Therapist: It sounds like those thoughts may have some pretty powerful images along with them. When you're feeling anxious, what are you imagining?

Jenny: That I'll do something stupid—wear the wrong thing, say the wrong thing, whatever—and they'll regret bringing me. That they'll talk about me later, making fun of me, or even decide they don't want me around and leave me at the bar. (*Appears anxious.*)

Therapist: That sounds terrifying. When you're in this space, what do you want or plan to do? What do you usually do?

Jenny: I just want to stop worrying about it, to stop feeling this way. So I usually back out…tell them that I remembered that I have a big exam the next week or something.

Therapist: So this whole thing (*gestures toward spider diagram*) is organized around how terrible this could turn out, motivating you to escape the situation—which is what you would normally do?

Jenny: (*Pauses a bit, with sad look on her face.*) Yes.

Therapist: We can also notice that even *remembering* this threatening event organizes things in specific ways right now—feeling anxious and tense, focused on the threat. It's almost like these experiences combine to create an anxious version of you—completely focused on the fear and anxiety. Does that sound right?

Jenny: It's absolutely right. I spend a lot of time feeling like that.

Therapist: So "Anxious Jenny" has been hanging around a lot lately.

Jenny: She sure has.

> *Therapist:* Let's thank Anxious Jenny for sharing her perspective with us, and see if we can get to know what "Safe Jenny" is like.
>
> *Jenny:* I'd like that. I don't know if there is a Safe Jenny, though.
>
> *Therapist:* Well, I'm here to help you find her.

In helping clients observe how they are organized very differently by varying emotions, it can sometimes be useful to refer to these as "different versions of the self," noting that our bodily experience, attention, reasoning, imagery, motivation, and behaviors can all be very different depending on the emotion or motive that we're experiencing. It can seem like we're different people when we're caught up in these different emotions. Using terms like "Anxious Jenny" can help clients recognize that as powerful as these experiences are, this is only one version of the self, and that we can develop other, adaptive aspects of the self (paving the way for the idea of the compassionate self). This language can also help set the stage for distinguishing "Anxious Jenny" from the current, experiencing self—the self that is observing and aware of the emotion (rather than caught up in it), which ACT therapists refer to as "self-as-context."

Now that Jenny has explored how her anxiety organizes things, let's consider how the therapist might continue to then introduce the safeness system. When making such transitions, it's good to do a little soothing rhythm breathing, to slow down the breath, get the parasympathetic nervous system going, and help us shift into a compassionate state of mind.

> *Therapist:* Jenny, now that we've explored how the threat system organizes the mind, I think it would be good to look at how the mind is organized very differently when we feel safe. We want to get to know what Safe Jenny feels like. How does that sound?
>
> *Jenny:* Sounds like it's worth a try.
>
> *Therapist:* Let's start by doing a minute or so of soothing rhythm breathing. Breathing in this way can help us balance things out after we've been working with threat emotions. Let's take a few moments to slow down the breath.
>
> *Jenny:* (*Closes her eyes; slows her breathing.*)
>
> *Therapist:* Slowing down the body…slowing down the mind. (*Waits one minute.*)
>
> *Therapist:* Opening your eyes, returning to the room. (*Waits a few moments until Jenny's eyes are open and she's orienting.*) How was that?
>
> *Jenny:* Better.
>
> *Therapist:* Good. It's good to learn that we can move into the perspective of an emotion like anxiety, and look closely at how it's organizing our minds, and then we can choose to shift back out of it. Soothing rhythm breathing can really help with

that. Don't worry if some of that anxiety sticks around—you've spent a long time learning to be anxious. Anxious Jenny has been going to the gym for quite some time.

Jenny: (*Smiles.*) She sure has!

Therapist: I'm here to help with that. Now let's explore how feelings of *safeness* organize the mind and body. Have you had times when you felt completely safe and at ease—maybe when spending time with someone you felt really comfortable with?

Jenny: (*Thinks for twenty seconds or so.*) Yes. I did have one friend in high school. Her name was Sophie. We had so much in common—she was even anxious, too. (*Brightens; speech takes on a comfortable pace.*) We used to do all sorts of things together. We'd spend hours talking on the phone, or sitting at a coffee shop talking. We'd go down to the beach sometimes, or just hang out wherever was convenient. I really miss those times.

Therapist: That sounds wonderful. Do you see Sophie anymore?

Jenny: Sometimes on holidays. We graduated, and she went to one college, and I went to another. We kept in touch really well for the first few months, and then gradually talked to each other less and less. Life gets busy, you know?

Therapist: It sure does. For now, I'd like to focus on a time you were with Sophie, and felt completely safe and comfortable. Can you recall a time like that?

Jenny: Yeah. There was this one time we picked up mochas at our favorite coffee shop and went down to the beach in the evening. We climbed up the lifeguard tower to watch the sunset. We just sat there, wrapped in blankets, talking for hours. It was wonderful.

Therapist: That does sound wonderful. As you remember that time, imagining being back there, how did you feel?

Jenny: Really relaxed, like I didn't have a care in the world—just enjoying the coffee and the sunset over the ocean, and talking.

Therapist: So it sounds like your attention was wide open—enjoying the coffee, the beautiful sunset, maybe the sights, sounds, and smells of the sea?

Jenny: Yes, it was so beautiful there. I love the ocean.

Therapist: I do, too. You mentioned that you and Sophie spent a lot of time talking. What did you talk about?

Jenny: We talked about all kinds of things: where we wanted to go to college, and what we wanted to major in. What sort of careers we wanted to have. Boys we liked. Movies and music. All kinds of things.

Therapist: Notice how it feels as you describe this. This is a perfect example of how the safeness system organizes the mind. I can just imagine you there, feeling completely comfortable. Attention open to notice all the wonderful sensations that surrounded you. Thinking open and flexible, able to think about the sort of lives you two would like to have, able to let your thoughts go wherever they took you…

Jenny: It was so nice.

Therapist: It *is* nice. Notice how the imagery—the pictures in your mind—work when you're feeling safe. Even now, bringing up that memory feels soothing, doesn't it?

Jenny: It feels great. I miss those times.

Therapist: I'd miss them, too. Then, I imagine your mental imagery was flexible and open like your thoughts—imagining what your future would be like, what you'd like to do…

Jenny: Yeah. The future seemed more interesting then, like I was excited about going to college, even though it was also a little scary.

Therapist: So feeling safe there with Sophie, you were able to even be somewhat excited about something that you also found a bit scary.

Jenny: Yeah. Now it's mostly just scary.

Therapist: (*soothingly*) Yeah. (*Pauses for a few moments.*) But would you say that in thinking about that time, you were able to connect with a little bit of what Safe Jenny was like?

Jenny: (*thoughtfully*) I was.

Therapist: So let's review what we've learned about how different emotions organize the mind. Notice that when we considered the threatening situation—friends asking you to go out—your attention, thinking, mental imagery, and motivation were all very narrow and focused on the perceived threat. All of that was focused very narrowly on fears of being embarrassed or humiliated.

Jenny: (*Nods consideringly.*) Mmm-hmm.

Therapist: And then when we brought up that memory with Sophie, all that changed. You remembered feeling safe, comfortable, and connected.

Jenny: (*Smiles thoughtfully; nods gently.*)

Therapist: Feeling safe, your attention opened wide to the things you appreciated about your surroundings, to your future, the things you wanted for your life…Your thoughts and mental imagery were flexible and open as well, as you imagined the sort of life you'd like to have. You chatted about all sorts of things. Your motivation was no longer captured by feeling like you needed to protect yourself, and you could imagine doing all sorts of things…even feeling excited about doing something that was also a little scary, like going to college. Notice how different your mind was organized from when you felt threatened? Notice what Safe Jenny was like?

Jenny: It was a lot more open and free. I wish I felt like that more often.

Therapist: How about we work on that?

Jenny: Sounds good.

In the vignettes above, the therapist guides Jenny through an exploration of how these different emotions organize her mind. This is done in two ways—exploring how her mind was organized within the situations she is recalling, and exploring the affective reactions she experiences in the present, due to bringing up these memories. While we're primarily focused on highlighting the former (exploring how attention, thinking, imagery, motivation, and so forth are organized during different affective states of threat and safeness), highlighting the way these memories shape current emotions helps pave the way for future imagery work, and for understanding memory as a powerful stimulus to the emotional brain.

The therapist prompts Jenny to bring up memories associated with threat and safeness, and guides her in exploring different ways these emotions organize her experience. Reflections of feeling and validating statements are peppered throughout, to deepen the affective experience and reinforce the connection between client and therapist. When Jenny begins to shift offtrack (for example, when she becomes wistful about missing "those times," expresses regret over the loss of relationship with Sophie, or comments that now things are "just scary"), the therapist compassionately validates her experience and then quickly brings her back to the focus of the exploration. The therapist also attempts to create safeness within the therapeutic relationship, making statements that communicate warmth, confidence, and support: "That's what I'm here to help you work on." "How about we work on that?" We revisit "Anxious Jenny," this time accompanied by "Safe Jenny," reflecting the idea that powerful emotions and motives can organize us as different versions of the self—versions that we can understand and value, and that we can selectively choose to strengthen. This sets the stage for compassionate-self work, as we work to develop and strengthen a perspective that is compassionate, kind, wise, and strong.

WHAT ABOUT SADNESS?

You may have noticed that in talking about the three emotion-regulation systems, we haven't really discussed sadness. Sadness is an interesting emotion that is challenging to categorize using the three systems, because it doesn't easily fit. While sadness can be seen as threat-related in that it often is linked with experiences of loss or disappointment, its physiological and psychological profile is very different from other threat emotions, which involve heightened arousal, tension, and a narrowing of thinking and attention. In contrast, sadness typically involves lower levels of arousal, and sometimes involves more open thinking and attention—for example, reminiscing and reflecting on life's meaning. Sadness also can serve to elicit caregiving responses from others, perhaps serving a safeness-eliciting function, and it usually involves a deactivation of drive pursuits.

While research is needed to further explore the ways that sadness organizes us, I think rather than trying to simplify things by forcing it into the threat circle, we're perhaps best served by considering sadness in terms of patterns of activation, and in relation to the contextual factors (such as loss) that trigger it. From this perspective, we can perhaps see normal sadness as a state involving low-to-moderate levels of perceived threat (loss but no active danger), low drive, and moderate safeness (we feel safe enough to really connect with the experience of loss and what it means to us). This can also help us in guiding treatment interventions for clients experiencing the deep experiences of sadness linked with major depression, which might involve much higher threat activation (as depression often involves significant anxiety—for example, with losses that threaten one's entire way of life) combined with very low drive and low-to-moderate safeness. In such a case, we'd want to help clients increase feelings of safeness to balance out the threat activation, but also get the drive system moving as well—as attested to by research showing the beneficial effects of behavior activation therapy with depression. For example, behavior activation around increasing positive social experiences might help to serve both of these purposes.

MOTIVES AND SOCIAL MENTALITIES

In addition to the emotions associated with the three circles, CFT also emphasizes that we can be powerfully organized around evolved motives. We can see motives as being the motivational and behavioral extensions of the three circle emotions—for example, motives to connect, pursue goals, attack, assert social dominance, defend oneself, mate, and play. These motives can manifest interpersonally in what Paul Gilbert has called *social mentalities* (Gilbert, 2009a; 2010; 2014). We can consider social mentalities to be organizing frameworks that structure our social interactions around certain motives. It can be quite useful to explore with clients how different social mentalities can organize their experience in entirely different ways. For example, we can use the spider diagram presented earlier to compare and contrast how defensive, competitive, caregiving, and sexual social mentalities are associated with very different patterns of paying attention, thinking, mental imagery, felt experience, motivation, and behavior. Such awareness (and the consideration of what sorts of social mentalities would be helpful) can be of great use in helping clients understand and work with relationship difficulties.

SUMMARY

In this chapter, we introduced the three-circles model of emotion. This model serves a number of purposes in CFT. It helps decrease shame in our clients' relationship with their emotions, as their understanding of these emotions shifts from *something that is wrong with me* to the realization that we *all* have these feelings because they helped our ancestors survive. Through this lens, they can see many of their unwanted emotions as their evolved brains' efforts to keep them safe when threats are perceived. Rather than condemn these efforts, a compassionate approach seeks to validate, soothe, and find more helpful ways of working with these experiences.

The model also helps pave the way for compassion as a way to work with suffering. We can help clients recognize self-attacking as serving to continually reactivate the threat system, and compassion as a way to get the safeness system working for them as they take responsibility for working with difficult feelings and life challenges. Finally, this model can serve as a sort of shortcut for developing mindful awareness of emotions. We might suggest to clients that when they are struggling, they could bring to mind the three circles and consider where they are in each—perhaps by quickly rating their threat, drive, and safeness on a 1-to-10 scale. As one of my graduate students (who was also a cheerleading coach) suggested, "When in doubt, circle out!" If our clients do this and observe that they are stuck in the threat system, it can be a prompt to slow down with some soothing rhythm breathing and then work with the emotion and situation using the compassionate strategies I'll be introducing later in the book.

CHAPTER 6

Compassionate Understanding: The Social Shaping of the Self

As we've discussed, compassion for self and others in CFT begins with the realization that many of our clients' challenges have to do with factors they neither choose nor design. We explored the first piece of this in the past two chapters—the recognition that we have tricky brains shaped by evolution to produce emotions that can be very difficult to manage. However, there is a second realization as well. From the moment of our birth, our evolved genetic potentials (genotypes) interact with and are shaped by another set of factors we don't get to choose or design—our early social environments.

As infants, we find ourselves entirely dependent upon caregivers who may or may not be equipped to nurture us and help us learn to manage these powerful emotions. We now know that different people are born with very different temperaments—more or less likely to experience emotions such as anxiety and irritability. These temperaments interact with our early social environments over time to shape the people that we will become.

A growing body of research shows that these early environments powerfully impact our developing brains, in particular those areas associated with emotion regulation and the processing of social information (Siegel, 2012; Cozolino, 2010). As we grow into childhood, adolescence, and early adulthood, we have growing influence over the contexts we inhabit, but are still shaped by social forces that can serve to model and reinforce habits that can cripple us later in life. Recognizing the ways in which we are shaped by social forces can support our clients' development of self-compassion, as they realize that the aspects of themselves they feel most ashamed of did not develop by accident, and are not caused by some inherent flaw they possess.

DIFFERENT VERSIONS OF THE SELF

If you attend very many CFT workshops, you're likely to hear a story like the following:

> *I was born into an educated, middle-class family with loving parents who were able to take care of me and provide me with the things I needed to survive and thrive—food, shelter, clothing, nurturing, and access to fun activities. They supported and encouraged my education, and taught me the skills I'd need to survive—how to study, manage my finances, and countless other things. But let's imagine that instead, I was born to a single, drug-addicted mother in an impoverished inner-city slum. Let's imagine that I often went hungry and alone, with no one to care for me when I needed help, abused by those who could have helped me. Let's imagine that I had to learn to steal to feed myself, fight to protect myself, and sell drugs or commit other crimes to earn the money needed to live. Would the current version of me—the university professor, psychologist, and author—even be possible? Would it be likely?*

We all have basic needs, and we learn to produce behaviors that allow our needs to be met within the contexts in which we find ourselves—contexts we often don't get to choose, but to which we have to adapt if we want to survive. The idea here is that we all represent only one version of what we could have become—a version that is defined by the unique pattern of interactions occurring between our life experiences and our genetic makeup. We, and all of our clients, were powerfully shaped by our early attachment relationships, as well as early and ongoing learning experiences. Considering these social forces can be a powerful step in helping our clients develop compassion for themselves and others. It can also help them take responsibility for working with their *current* social and physical environments, as they develop a growing awareness of how these environments can impact the course of their lives.

THE SOCIAL SHAPING OF THE SELF

In therapy, it can be useful to help clients explore the ways their current experience is related to the social contexts of their lives. Let's briefly touch on a few of these here, and how we might bring them into the therapy room. We have limited space, so I'll be moving through these topics fairly quickly, but there are *lots* of other resources available for those who wish to dig deeper.

Attachment History and Attachment Style

In the previous chapter, we explored how humans evolved to feel safe primarily in the context of connection with others who accept us and care about us (Gilbert, 2009a; 2010). John Bowlby and attachment researchers who followed him described how our early social environments can shape our most basic understandings of other people, and of ourselves in relation to others. In this way, early attachment histories give rise to relatively enduring attachment styles that shape how we will experience our relationships with others, and our ability to feel safe in the world.

Different authors have used different methods for categorizing and labeling attachment styles. For our purposes, I'm going to discuss attachment in terms of three processes that can impact emotion regulation: *attachment security*, *attachment anxiety*, and *attachment avoidance*. Attachment security tends to result from interactions with nurturing caregivers who are responsive to our needs. Secure individuals learn that help is available if they need it, and develop a repertoire of effective emotion-regulation strategies they can draw upon (Mikulincer & Shaver, 2007). From a CFT perspective, secure attachment relationships prime the safeness system, laying down and strengthening the neural networks that facilitate individuals' capacity for soothing themselves as they work effectively with threat-based emotions. Able to self-soothe, secure individuals can remain open to their emotions—acknowledging, feeling, and expressing them in adaptive ways (Mikulincer & Shaver, 2007). These individuals also learn to value themselves—their history of being cared for having taught them that they are *worthy* of caring and kindness.

Attachment anxiety tends to result from rearing environments that were unreliable and inconsistently responsive to the child's distress. Attachment anxiety is associated with desiring connection but being unable to trust that it will be there when needed, or fearing that it can disappear unpredictably. Hence, such individuals may find themselves unable to feel soothed even when social nurturing or connection is present. Clients with high levels of attachment anxiety may experience threat emotions in exaggerated, very intense ways—perhaps implicitly shaped by caregivers who provided nurturing only when the child displayed extreme levels of distress (Mikulincer & Shaver, 2007). Struggling to self-soothe or regulate their emotions, these individuals may seem to live in the threat system, ruminating on perceived threats, and hypersensitive to signs of social threat. They tend to be interested in others, but have difficulty managing relationships, and may be terrified of rejection.

In contrast, individuals high in attachment avoidance employ lots of strategies to inhibit, suppress, or avoid their emotional experiences. Often raised by unavailable or unresponsive caregivers, avoidant individuals can tend toward interpersonal distance and "going it alone," and may see support-seeking as risky, uncomfortable, or futile. Unable to soothe themselves through feelings of connection and support, these individuals turn instead to avoidance strategies—distancing, denying, and minimizing their emotions. These strategies can get in the way of effective coping, as clients avoid rather than engaging in problem solving, seeking support, or reappraising their situation in more helpful ways (Mikulincer & Shaver, 2007). Like anxious individuals, from the CFT perspective, avoidant folk are seen to have underdeveloped safeness systems to draw upon in soothing themselves and working with their emotions, instead relying upon threat-based avoidance strategies (called *safety strategies*), which often have crippling long-term consequences.

Our clients don't get to choose whether they feel safe in relationships with others, whether they feel confident in dealing with emotions, and whether they experience themselves as connected, vulnerable, or isolated. If these were choices, of course we'd all choose to feel safe, confident, and connected. We can't change the past, but we can help our clients begin to understand how they came to be this way, and that these experiences are *not their fault*:

Therapist: Jenny, in our last session we talked a bit about how we come to feel either threatened or safe, and how these experiences organize the mind—how we pay attention, experience emotions, think, and so on...

Jenny: Yes, I remember.

Therapist: Excellent. In CFT, we also consider how people *learn* to feel either safe or threatened—and a lot of times, this relates to our history of relationships with other people. We've talked about this before a bit—how you learned to feel unsafe in social situations after that terrible experience you had with the other girls in middle school.

Jenny: That's right. That was awful. It made me terrified of being around other people.

Therapist: It made it hard for you to risk trusting others, and scared of having relationships?

Jenny: It's almost impossible.

Therapist: When that happened—when you moved to the new school, and the other girls were so mean to you—did you talk with anyone about it?

Jenny: I tried to talk with my mother, but she didn't really help. I mean, she tried, but I don't think she understood. She told me that girls were just like that sometimes, and that I shouldn't make such a big deal out of it.

Therapist: So she wasn't really able to help you?

Jenny: Well, she wasn't doing too well herself. She and my father had just divorced, and their marriage had been bad for a while. It was really ugly. He had cheated on her, and she'd been doing a lot of drinking. It was bad enough that we moved after the divorce.

Therapist: So her life was enough of a mess that she had a hard time being there for you?

Jenny: Yes. I mean, she tried. She really did. It's like she could tell that she wasn't really doing a good job as a parent. She even said that sometimes, and she'd try to make up for it. She'd buy me stuff—expensive jeans, that sort of thing. But most of the time... (*Shakes her head and sighs.*)

Therapist: Most of the time?

Jenny: Most of the time she just didn't have it together. When Dad was there, she seemed unhappy, and after we moved, she just... (*Pauses.*) She was never mean to me. She just seemed caught up with her own stuff most of the time.

Therapist: How about your dad?

Jenny: He was kind of your absent father. He mostly seemed to be away a lot—working a lot, or whatever he was doing.

Therapist: Did you have much of a relationship with him when he was around? Do you remember doing things with him?

Jenny: I loved spending time with him, but he just wasn't there much. And after the divorce, he said he wanted to have a relationship with me, but he never really followed through. He'd call and schedule a time to pick me up for the weekend, but half the time he wouldn't show. After a while he just sort of stopped calling. I guess he was more interested in his new family. (*Looks down, a bit tearful.*)

Therapist: (*Waits in silence.*)

Jenny: (*Sighs.*) I guess I had some crappy parents, huh?

Therapist: It does sound like they had a lot of their own stuff going on, which got in the way of being there for you. Remember how we talked about the safeness system, and how we tend to feel safe through our connections with others who care about us? As we think about all of this, does it make sense that you might have a hard time feeling safe in relationships—have a hard time trusting that others will be there when you need them?

Jenny: It does make sense.

Therapist: Instead of learning that you could rely on others for help when you needed it, you learned that *sometimes* they'd be there, and…

Jenny: And a lot of the time they wouldn't.

Therapist: Jenny, given this learning, do you think it's your fault that you feel unsafe in relationships? Is it your fault that you have trouble trusting others to be there when you need them, or is that something your life has taught you? Is that your fault?

Jenny: No, it's not my fault.

Therapist: (*Pauses for a bit.*) Could you say that again?

Jenny: (*crying*) It's not my fault.

As the vignette above demonstrates, in CFT, the focus isn't upon categorizing people in terms of attachment style, but on helping our clients understand their emotions, motivations, and behaviors in nonshaming, compassionate ways. There are lots of ways clients can learn to feel unsafe, or develop habits that don't fit with the lives they'd like to have. Let's explore a few more.

Learning Theory and Behavior Therapy

Learning theory and behavior therapy have been successfully applied to the understanding and treatment of a wide variety of emotional and behavioral problems. CFT is quite compatible with these approaches, and optimally, a CFT therapist will have received training in basic behavioral principles and how they apply to understanding and treating psychological problems. Although behaviorists and behaviorism aren't always thought of as warm and compassionate, if we look closely, we see that behavioral understandings inherently undermine shame and self-attacking at their core. They help us, and our clients, clearly understand how their problems were *learned*, and how these challenges make complete sense when we consider the contexts in which they occur. Recognizing these challenges as learned rather than as *something that is inherently wrong with me* can help our clients have compassion for themselves (*It's not my fault that I have these struggles*), and can give us direction as we compassionately work to address them. There are many excellent resources on learning theory and behavior therapy, so I won't go into detail here, but I did want to briefly mention some methods of learning and ways we can bring such understandings into CFT.

OPERANT CONDITIONING AND FUNCTIONAL ANALYSIS OF BEHAVIOR

A functional analysis of behavior can be very useful as we help clients answer the question, *Why do I do this stuff?* Conducting a functional analysis involves figuring out the factors that control the occurrence of a given behavior—what factors set the stage for the behavior to occur, and what consequences follow it. This process is often communicated using the acronym A-B-C, which stands for *antecedent*, *behavior*, and *consequence*. When doing a functional analysis, we start by selecting a specific behavior. This could be something observable that the client does, or private behavior such as thinking (for example, self-attacking or rumination).

Once we've figured out the behavior we're interested in, we look for antecedents to the behavior—factors that precede it and signal its likely occurrence. Antecedents can be external factors (*stimuli*) that signal the presence of a punisher or reward, triggering the occurrence of related behaviors (called *discriminative stimuli*, because they allow us to detect or *discriminate* the presence of threats and rewards). Antecedents can also be internal experiences that aren't related to the availability of things the individual does or doesn't like, but instead involve motivational states that "set the stage" for certain behaviors to occur, impacting whether or not a behavior is likely to have pleasing or displeasing consequences. Hunger is a good example. We can see how this works: Regardless of the general availability of food, eating is much more rewarding to us when we are hungry. In this way, antecedents can either let us know that a reward is available (serving a discriminative function) or motivate us to go looking for one (serving a motivational function) (Törneke, 2010). Key is the understanding that antecedents orient us to the potential that desirable or undesirable consequences will follow our behavior, setting the stage for these behaviors to occur.

Once we've specified the behavior we're interested in and the antecedents that precede it, we can explore the consequences that follow the behavior and impact its likelihood of occurring in the future. Some consequences are reinforcing, increasing the likelihood that a behavior will be repeated. This can be either because the consequence is something the individual prefers, such as receiving a good grade after studying for an exam (positive reinforcement), or because it involves the termination or removal of an experience that the individual dislikes—like medication getting rid of a headache (negative reinforcement).

Other consequences, called punishers, decrease the likelihood of behaviors being repeated. This can occur because the consequence of the behavior is aversive and nonpreferred (called *punishment* or *positive punishment*—where positive refers to the *addition* of the undesirable consequence), such as being laughed at after attempting to answer a question. Punishment can also occur when consequences involve the termination or removal of something the individual prefers, as in having friends pull away and distance themselves from you after you tell an offensive joke. This is sometimes referred to as *negative punishment*—where negative refers to the *removal* of the preferred state or situation—or *response cost* (as in, the behavior or response has a *cost*).

Conducting a functional analysis with our clients can assist them in understanding how the behaviors they engage in—of which they may feel very ashamed and self-critical—actually *make sense* when we consider them in context. The prison inmate's aggression makes a whole lot more sense when we see that he has always lived in dangerous environments, and that being aggressive meant that others would leave him alone rather than target him for victimization.

Chris: After I almost killed that guy, the others left me alone. I guess they decided it wasn't worth it—and that was fine by me. They knew I could go off at any time. They knew that if you fucked with me, you would get hurt, and hurt bad.

Therapist: It sounds like you learned to be violent in the effort to feel safe—that if you were tough enough, people would leave you alone—and it worked. If we think of it like this, does it make sense that you would learn to be violent, to keep up that image?

Chris: It sure does. But that's not who I want to be. That's not the dad I want my son to have.

Therapist: So that violent version of you served his purpose, but we don't want to leave him in charge. How about we work to develop another version of you that fits with the sort of dad you want to be?

Chris: Sounds good.

Likewise, when we recognize that our client's cutting has provided her with temporary relief from terrible emotional pain, we can compassionately understand why she may be reluctant to give this strategy up. Both of these clients may experience intense shame and self-criticism as they observe themselves struggling to stop performing behaviors that create great problems for them and don't fit with who they want to be, but which serve (or served) a very real purpose in their lives. This shame and self-criticism can paradoxically keep them stuck in the threat system and potentially prevent them from taking responsibility for changing the behavior, as they work to avoid shame-related discomfort by blaming others, rationalizing their behavior, or simply shifting their attention elsewhere. We see these themes occurring again and again, in clients who struggle with the very behaviors that their lives shaped in them—behaviors they developed in the effort to meet their needs and keep themselves safe. Helping clients understand how these behaviors *make sense* given their histories can help shift the focus away from self-attacking and toward compassionately finding more helpful strategies for pursuing these very admirable goals—*keeping themselves safe* and *working with their suffering.*

In the language of CFT, we find that many of our clients seem to live in the threat system—with their lives and behaviors centered on efforts to reduce or avoid uncomfortable experiences. This is what behaviorists sometimes refer to as behavior being "under aversive control" (Skinner, 1953), and which Buddhists refer to when they talk about aversion. In CFT, we help clients learn to not just reduce experiences of threat and discomfort, but to cultivate and strengthen a compassionate version of the self that is oriented toward helping themselves feel safe (undermining the aversive control), exploring what will be helpful in addressing their challenges (versus merely trying to avoid or escape unwanted emotions related to those challenges), and moving *toward* the way they want their lives to be (versus away from how they don't want it to be). In this way, we see that CFT has much in common with approaches like ACT—which heavily emphasizes values work—and DBT, in emphasizing the development of adaptive skills like distress tolerance and emotion-regulation skills.

RESPONDENT CONDITIONING

In addition to learning connections between antecedents, behavior, and consequences, our brains are also highly efficient at learning connections between different stimuli. Certain stimuli—events, experiences, things in our environment, even ideas or mental imagery—have the natural capacity to produce certain responses in us. We can consider this process for each of the three emotion-regulation systems we discussed in the previous chapter (threat, drive, and safeness).

For example, being in a life-threatening situation such as a car accident can naturally produce fear. Sexual stimulation can naturally lead to sexual arousal. Warm conversations with dear friends over dinner can lead to feelings of comfort and safeness. Let's imagine three different people, one in each of these situations—a terrifying car wreck, a heated bout of passionate lovemaking, and a warm dinner with a dear one. Since each of these situations naturally produces a response, we call them unconditioned (unlearned) stimuli, and the responses that result from them (fear, sexual arousal, safeness), by virtue of arising naturally in response to the stimuli, are called unconditioned (unlearned) responses.

Let's imagine that in each of these situations, the same song is playing on the radio in the background. Our brains are very efficient at linking things together, so for each of these people, this song can become associated with the situation (car wreck, sex, warm interactions with dear friends).

In the future, these individuals could come to have very different *learned* reactions to this song, through its connection with the situations. The individual in the car wreck hears the song and experiences a rush of fear. The lover hears it and feels a rising of sexual feelings. The friend hears it and feels a warm arising of safeness and peace. The *form* (what it is) of this stimulus—the song—is the same for each of these individuals, but its *function* (its effect—what it *does*) is entirely different, due to its previous pairing with these different situations. In each case, the individual has learned to have an emotional response to the song, which now functions as a conditioned (learned) stimulus in its ability to provoke conditioned (learned) responses—fear, sexual arousal, or safeness. This learning process is an example of respondent conditioning (also known as classical conditioning).

It's worth mentioning that evolution has shaped us so that not all learning is created equal—some types of learning, sometimes called *prepared learning*, had much more survival value for our ancestors, and so we adapted such mental connections much more quickly and efficiently. In the case of powerful threat emotions like fear or disgust, for example, we can learn such connections in a single trial—so even after only one car accident, the survivor may experience extreme fear when he next hears that song. In the case of the sexual situation, it may take a few such spicy encounters before the song acquires the ability to trigger sexual feelings on its own (particularly if the song is also heard at other times). We might need an entire summer of barbecues with good friends at the lake before the song strongly brings up feelings of safeness. In particular, our brains are biased toward processing threat—which is why it can be easy for clients to learn to feel threatened in response to a variety of situations and triggers, and more difficult for them to learn to feel safe, particularly when their early environments didn't often provide them with experiences of safeness.

Many clients will report overwhelming emotions in response to what seem to be relatively minor situations, or even occurring "out of the blue," in which powerful feelings of fear, anger, or sadness arise in them with no warning or explanation. These experiences can be terrifying, potentially leading clients to *fear their own emotions* as powerful, unpredictable forces capable of striking at any time, with the clients feeling "crazy," vulnerable, and helpless in the face of these feelings. We can imagine how such experiences might lead clients to find their own emotions threatening, and strive to avoid them. Such experiences can also prompt self-criticism in our clients, as they observe *there's no reason for me to feel this way...there must be something wrong with me*. The logical new brain often can't see or understand what the old, emotional brain is responding to, so it blames the victim.

Here again, we can help our clients explore how they *learned* these emotional responses, and how, given these learning experiences, their emotional responses and related motives (for example, desires to escape or avoid situations that trigger the emotions) *make complete sense*. There's nothing wrong with them—they simply have tricky brains that are working very hard to keep them safe, by identifying every possible signal they've previously learned to connect with danger—even when these signals (like our song) aren't at all dangerous. Often, our clients won't even be aware that they've heard the song at all—the feelings just seem to come up on their own. Understanding that these emotions are *echoes*—occurring because of previous learning—can help them to make sense of these experiences, and to understand how very powerful emotions can arise even when the situation seems perfectly safe to our logical new brains.

RELATIONAL FRAME THEORY

Historically, even radical behaviorists have occasionally had to admit that their theories had certain limitations—most notably in explaining the nuances of verbal behavior (Törneke, 2010). However, the last few decades have been exciting ones for behaviorists, as these limitations have been addressed with the development of relational frame theory, or RFT (Hayes, Barnes-Holmes, & Roche, 2001; Törneke, 2010). RFT can be complicated, and we don't have space to explain it well here (and I'm not qualified to do so). However, this theory is important enough for understanding threat system dynamics that I'll attempt a brief explanation to suit our current purposes.

All of the previously described forms of learning—learned connections between behaviors and consequences and between different stimuli presented at the same time—are observed in animals as well as humans. However, our ability for symbolic thought allows us to form much more complex networks of learned relationships, even between things that have never been linked together in our actual experience. For example, if I teach you that A is like B, and B is like C, you will *derive a new relationship between A and C*—concluding that A is like C, and that C is like A. This may seem simple, but its implications are significant—once derived, you can then project this relationship into the future and consider what that means for you (if, for example, you identify with something about A, B, or C). You can also form loads of other derived relationships, if, for example, you've previously learned that B is like Q, which is like P, which is like R. You can then derive relationships linking A and C with Q, P, and R, multiplying across a network of mental connections like a spiderweb—tug one point, and the whole web shifts. These are things that other animals, lacking our fancy new brains, just can't do. It's hard to get the real significance of these relationships by using an example that features printed letters, so let's consider how this learning might play out in one of our clients.

The implications of our ability to mentally derive different relationships can be harrowing for understanding how we process threat. Suppose Lauren considers herself to be feminine, and that she has harbored a dream of becoming a successful scientist. She is quite intelligent and is attending school in pursuit of this dream. Let's imagine that through her exposure to various media and culture—say, movies, cable news channels, conversations, that sort of thing—she learns to connect femininity with weakness, helplessness, or incompetence at science. Perhaps punctuated by a particularly powerful learning experience in which she overhears a male authority figure making a nasty gender-based slur about women in the sciences, we can imagine Lauren deriving a connection between herself (via her own experience of identifying as feminine) and helplessness or scientific incompetence.

Given her goal of becoming a scientist, how would Lauren feel? How might she feel about her goals and her ability to attain them? We can also imagine how the various aspects of her life that are linked with femininity—the way she dresses, habitual behaviors, the things she likes—can be tainted by these derived relationships—their effects (in RFT lingo, their *stimulus functions*) transformed so that instead of being things she enjoys that help her feel comfortable, these reflections of her femininity are now triggers for feeling helpless and weak, and thinking that she'll never be a competent scientist. Even Lauren's *preferences* are now signs of weakness.

Let's imagine that Lauren wants to be a scientist so badly that she begins to *reject* these aspects of herself, in the effort to become less feminine and have a chance at pursuing her goal. She exchanges her dresses for pants, changes her hairstyle and her color palette. And then, one day, she's watching a cable news program in which the hosts are viciously attacking a female politician for appearing *masculine*—ridiculing her appearance, labeling her assertiveness as "bitchy," and deriding her sexuality. We can imagine another set of relationships being derived in Lauren's mind, in which everything about her that seems in any way masculine is now tainted with negative implications—her behavior, her clothes, even her ambitions to enter a stereotypically male field. How is Lauren ever to feel comfortable with her gender identity? How can she feel comfortable and confident in pursuing her goals? This brilliant young woman's completely realistic aspirations can be crushed, all due to culturally based lies being multiplied through a complex network of derived relationships in her mind.

This is tricky business indeed, and what I've described is really just the tip of the iceberg when it comes to RFT and the nuances of verbal behavior in humans. I'm not suggesting that we give our clients lessons in relational frame theory. But we can help them recognize that our brains are very good at linking and translating things in our minds so that given a powerful learning experience, perceptions of threat can be magnified and multiplied almost exponentially across time, situations, experiences, and thought. *This is not our fault.* It is a result of the evolution of our brains, and it's a capacity that has allowed us to do amazing things as a species, as we use these abilities to solve complex problems. Again, the key is to help clients recognize that these experiences and feelings they struggle so greatly with are *learned*, that they *make sense* in the context of their lives and the way their evolved brains work, and that we can help them work with these struggles in empowering, compassionate ways.

SOCIAL LEARNING

We can learn not only through direct experience, but through our observations of others. We can learn to fear by watching others experience punishment (for example, being ridiculed when they speak up). We can learn behavior through seeing it modeled by others (for example, how our parents behave when they are experiencing emotions, or how to play a song on the guitar by watching a YouTube video). Often without our awareness, our minds are constantly storing information about what the world is like, what we are like, our relationships with others and what they mean, and what we should do as we go through life. Helping clients discover how their lives are shaped by these learning experiences can pave the way for compassion to arise—compassion for themselves *and* others.

In session, this exploration isn't done by mechanistically running through someone's learning history, using lots of technical jargon like some of the terms I introduced above. Rather, it happens organically, through discussions around topics like *what things were like growing up*, or *what it was like around the time of the trauma*. As our clients are acquainting us with their history—as we're constructing an understanding of *how things came to be this way*—we can compassionately explore (again, using techniques like Socratic dialogue) how they learned to fear certain things, or to react in certain ways. In this way, we can help them form a compassionate understanding of how it *makes sense* that they would be this way. Let's consider how we might bring some of this into the therapy room:

Therapist: Jenny, we've been exploring some of the situations that bring up anxiety in you, and what you've learned from them. Does it make sense that after your experience of being ridiculed by your middle-school peers, you would learn to be afraid of forming relationships with classmates or of speaking up in class?

Jenny: It does, but… (*Pauses and makes a considering facial expression.*)

Therapist: Looks like you're not quite sure there…

Jenny: It's just that, yeah, what happened to me in junior high does help me understand why I would have problems making friends. But I get really scared of lots of other situations, too. I'm terrified of dating, and I really need to get a job, but I can't go on interviews.

Therapist: So there are other situations that don't seem to really make sense—situations that cause lots of fear in you, but don't seem to be related to your past experiences.

Jenny: Yes—it's maddening. (*Shakes her head a bit side-to-side.*)

Therapist: (*Nods.*) I can see how it would be. Let's see if we can make some sense of it.

Jenny: That would be nice.

Therapist: Jenny, do you remember when we talked about how our brains can be very tricky, and can lead us to struggle with things in ways that animals like Penelope or Sadie don't have to worry about? The new-brain/old-brain stuff we chatted about?

Jenny: Yeah.

Therapist: Well, one of the things our brains are very good at is linking things together—forming connections between different experiences, thoughts, and feelings. Our brains evolved to do this—to help us quickly make sense of the world, so we could understand how things work, without having to experience everything firsthand.

Jenny: Mmm-hmm.

Therapist: Well, this can work against us, too. If we experience humiliation in *one situation*—say, being the new kid at a school and being ridiculed in class, or in the hall—our brains can figure out that being the center of attention in *any situation* is dangerous. We can form this connection between being the center of attention and being rejected and humiliated. Remember, our threat systems work very hard to help us identify threats and protect ourselves—*better safe than sorry.*

Jenny: (*Nods.*)

Therapist: When we have a really terrible experience, we can project that learning into the future, imagining that it will always be this way. We can also project that learning onto lots of different situations—like dating relationships and job interviews. So one really powerful learning experience in the sixth grade can result in our threat systems being activated by lots of different situations, for a long time to come. This is particularly true if we haven't learned how to help ourselves feel safe. We can develop a version of ourselves that is really scared of all sorts of different situations, and that thinks that avoiding them is the only way to stay safe. Does that make sense?

Jenny: It sure does. That's exactly what it feels like for me—I'm terrified of all these situations, even ones I've never been in. I thought I was going crazy!

Therapist: It can feel like that, can't it? But which sounds more likely—that you're just crazy for no good reason, or that your threat system is using what you've learned to work *really* hard to protect you, to make sure you're never hurt like that again? (*Smiles.*)

Jenny: (*Smiles.*) Okay, okay. I think I get it. That makes a lot more sense. (*Pauses and looks down a bit.*)

Therapist: (*Remains silent.*)

Jenny: It still sucks, though.

Therapist: (*Waits a moment, then speaks warmly.*) It sure does. That's why we're going to send your safeness system to the gym, and develop a version of you that is confident, wise, kind, and compassionate—to help that vulnerable part of you feel safe.

Jenny: I'd like that.

WORKING WITH FEARS OF COMPASSION

In this chapter, we've explored various forms of learning that can be problematic for our clients. As we've discussed, a primary goal of CFT is to help clients learn to access feelings of safeness—initially through the therapeutic relationship, and in going forward, through learning to direct compassion to themselves, to receive it from others, and to form and maintain nurturing relationships. Connection is important, as we evolved primarily to feel safe through affiliation with others—others who accept us, who like us, and who can support us when we need it.

Unfortunately, some clients will have learned to associate interpersonal connection with threat rather than safeness. Through trauma, abuse, difficult attachment history, or other experiences, our clients may have learned that to care about others or to allow themselves to be cared about is dangerous. They may actively resist kindness and compassion, even feeling as if they don't deserve it. This presents us with a fundamental question: *If the connections that are supposed to help us feel safe (evolutionarily speaking) instead become associated with threat, how do we ever feel safe?* Some of our clients will present with exactly this conundrum. Even if they consciously want to build connections and feel safe, powerful implicit learning experiences lead them to feel really threatened as soon as they start to really connect. You've probably had experiences like this with clients; just as the therapeutic relationship is getting closer and it seems like the client should be feeling safer, they actually become destabilized and uncomfortable.

I like to talk about this using a metaphor. A store near my home in Spokane, Washington, sells bags of nice big frozen prawns at a very reasonable price. They're great if you're having a last-minute get-together—just pick up a bag, thaw them out, whip together some horseradish and catsup to make cocktail sauce, and you've got a nice hors d'oeuvre. But you've got to plan ahead, as the thawing instructions are very specific: *Thaw in the refrigerator overnight. Do not force-thaw under running water.* It turns out that if we attempt to force-thaw the frozen shrimp by placing them under running water, it will often create a boundary disturbance—the shrimp will absorb way too much water, and become mushy and gross.

I think humans are a lot like these prawns. We can't be force-thawed. When we're frozen—when we've learned to feel unsafe in connection with others and to avoid such connection—attempts at forcing us to thaw too quickly can lead to peril. Many of us have had clients that we tried to force-thaw, moving too quickly to places the client wasn't yet ready to go. In such situations, it's easy to have relationship ruptures that create obstacles in the therapy, or even to have clients drop out of treatment.

I think the best way for us humans to "thaw" is to place ourselves in an environment that contains the necessary conditions—the causes and conditions that make thawing *possible*—and then to give it some time. With clients like this, there's no one thing we can say that will lead their emotional brains to conclude, *Oh, I can go ahead and feel safe, now.* Our clients may be frustrated by this, too (and may benefit from hearing the metaphor), as they may consciously know that they'd benefit from feeling safe in relationships, and may desperately want to do so. They're not *choosing* to panic at the first sign of closeness. They may not even recognize what is happening. They've learned that *closeness is dangerous,* and their old, emotional brains are trying to protect them. *It's not their fault.*

This is why I think the layered approach we're taking is so important. We can think of the consistent, warm-but-not-overwhelming, compassionate presence of the therapist as an external factor that facilitates "thawing." These feelings can be thawed from the inside as well, softened as clients begin to understand how and why they feel unsafe in relationships, that this isn't their fault, and commit to helping themselves work with this. Mindful awareness can help clients identify when they begin to feel unsafe in connection with others, and to pause and observe rather than habitually pull back. Finally, the compassion practices we'll explore later can help clients begin to actively cultivate feelings of warmth and connection, and to kindly coach and reassure themselves as they courageously participate in relationships they would have previously avoided. But we need to have patience and help clients have patience with themselves, recognizing that this thawing is something that happens over time. It can't be forced.

SUMMARY

In CFT, one of the foundational layers underlying self-compassion is composed of *understanding*. As we've seen in the past few chapters, clients are helped to understand where their emotions and motives come from, how they organize the mind and body in powerful ways, and how people are often shaped by social forces that they neither choose nor design. As we see in the clinical example above, helping clients understand how their challenges were learned can help shift their understanding of these challenges from *something that is wrong with me* to *my brain working to protect me in situations that it wasn't designed to deal with*. It can also help undermine fears of their own emotions, as they come to understand these experiences not as random, uncontrollable jolts of pain from out of nowhere, but as understandable reactions that *make sense* given their previous life experience. In the next chapter, we'll continue the work of helping our clients develop a more helpful relationship with their thoughts, emotions, and behavior—exploring *mindfulness* as a method to help clients relate to these experiences with compassionate awareness.

CHAPTER 7

Compassionate Awareness: Cultivating Mindfulness

In the layered approach we're taking to understanding the process of CFT, we began by first considering the therapeutic relationship, in which compassion is modeled by the therapist, who serves as a secure base for clients to begin feeling safe so they can approach difficult emotions and experiences. We then spent chapters 4 through 6 developing the next layer—helping clients develop a compassionate *understanding* of their emotions in relation to evolution and the developmental factors that shaped them. This understanding is in the service of helping clients relate compassionately and nonjudgmentally to their difficulties—many of which they didn't choose or design, but must cope with nonetheless. In this chapter, we'll consider the next layer of our approach to CFT: mindful awareness. It's important to recognize that all three of these layers will be present from the beginnings of therapy, with the relationship developing from the point of initial contact, and the therapist weaving in the understanding and mindful awareness pieces even during the first few sessions.

Over the past few decades, mindfulness has become one of the most used and studied practices in contemporary psychotherapy. It has provided the basis for mindfulness-based cognitive therapy (Segal, Williams, & Teasdale, 2001), and has long been featured in other "third wave" cognitive behavioral approaches, including DBT (Linehan, 1993), ACT (Hayes, Strosahl, & Wilson, 1999), and others. A body of evidence supports the use of mindfulness-based interventions for a host of problems, particularly depression and anxiety (Hofmann, Sawyer, Witt, & Oh, 2010). There are many existing resources for learning about mindfulness and using it in therapy, so I won't be attempting an exhaustive introduction to mindfulness here. Rather, I'll briefly discuss the concept of mindfulness and how it fits into CFT, introduce a couple of mindfulness practices commonly used in CFT, and touch on some tips for effectively engaging clients in mindfulness practices.

MINDFULNESS

Mindfulness involves a particular sort of awareness. Probably the most common definition of mindfulness comes from Jon Kabat-Zinn (1994): *paying attention in the present moment, on purpose, nonjudgmentally.* Mindfulness means intentionally directing our present-moment awareness in a way that allows us to see what is before us, both in our external environment and in our minds, exactly as it is. With mindful attention, we refrain from judging, criticizing, clinging to, or rejecting our experience. Rather, we allow ourselves to notice, accept, and curiously explore the contents of our experience—whether that experience comes to us from the outside world through our senses, or is the product of our own internal experience, as in thoughts, feelings, motivations, and bodily sensations. With mindful awareness, we allow ourselves to curiously observe all of these experiences—noticing them for exactly what they are, neither clinging to them nor pushing them away.

Mindful awareness can be a very useful ability for clients, particularly those who are haunted by powerful shaming and self-critical thoughts. The problem is not that they *have* these thoughts—to a greater or lesser extent, pretty much all of us do from time to time. The problem is that they ruminate on these thoughts, rehearse them, and *believe them.* Clients will also sometimes present with powerful emotions that seem to take them by storm, powerfully organizing their bodily experience, attention, thinking, motivation, and behavior in ways we've discussed in previous chapters. Such clients can find themselves feeling trapped in the immediacy of such emotional experiences. The experiences can trigger unwanted feelings and problematic behaviors in the present moment, but can also lead clients to fear thoughts and emotions themselves—potentially leading to the development of unhelpful patterns of experiential avoidance as they try to manage these scary and seemingly uncontrollable mental experiences.

Practicing mindfulness can help address these challenges, and help prepare our clients (and ourselves) for compassion. Mindfulness involves numerous potential benefits that are relevant to CFT. Mindfulness training can give clients increased awareness of and control over their attention, helping them learn to direct their attention in helpful ways. It can help them learn to notice movement in the mind, to more quickly become aware when unhelpful thoughts and feelings arise. When these thoughts and emotions are noticed, the observing quality of mindful awareness can help keep clients from becoming stuck and fused with these experiences—instead relating to them as temporary events playing out in the mind and body. In this way, clients can come to understand thoughts and emotions as mental and bodily experiences rather than *who I am.*

Relatedly, the accepting, nonjudgmental quality of mindful awareness can help clients refrain from reacting to or elaborating upon these experiences in unhelpful ways (such as ruminating, or criticizing themselves for feeling anger or thinking certain thoughts that don't fit with the person they want to be). The ability to mindfully observe one's difficult thoughts and emotions without either fusing with them or avoiding them by redirecting the attention can also help our clients develop distress tolerance, which is of vital importance for compassion. If we're going to overcome avoidance and *work* with suffering, we have to be able to approach it and stay in contact with it while doing so. Mindfulness gives our clients a way to do that.

Preparing Clients to Work with Attention

As mindfulness is first and foremost a way of working with the attention, it can be useful to orient clients to this—to help them *get to know* their attention a bit before introducing formal mindfulness practices. This can be done quickly and easily with an experiential exercise in which we prompt clients to direct their attention to different targets—internal, external, broad, narrow, present, past, concrete, conceptual—so that they can see firsthand how their attention works. Let's consider an example of how this might be done:

Therapist: Josh, as we discussed in our last session, today we'll be introducing a practice called mindfulness. Mindfulness involves paying attention in a particular way that helps us to become more aware of our experiences and helps us keep from getting caught up in unhelpful thoughts and emotions. How does that sound?

Josh: Sounds like it's worth a try.

Therapist: Great. Before we dive into mindfulness, though, I think it might be useful to get to know what we mean by *attention*. We can think of attention as the "spotlight of the mind." That spotlight can be pointed at lots of different things, directing our awareness in different ways. Are you up for a little exercise?

Josh: All right.

Therapist: Fantastic. I'm going to simply say a series of words—and when you hear the word, try to direct your attention where the word indicates. So if I say, "Left elbow," you'll bring your attention to your left elbow. Got it?

Jenny: (*Nods.*)

Therapist: Okay, here goes: Right ear. (*Waits two or three seconds.*) Left foot. (*Waits two or three seconds.*) Your tongue. (*Waits two or three seconds.*) The feeling of your breath. (*Waits two or three seconds.*) The buzzing of the lights. (*Waits two or three seconds.*) Your favorite color. (*Waits two or three seconds.*) Tater tots! (*Waits two or three seconds.*) Justice. (*Waits two or three seconds.*) World peace. (*Waits two or three seconds.*) South America. (*Waits two or three seconds.*) What you'd like to have for dinner. (*Waits two or three seconds.*) And allowing your face to form a smile, the sensation of smiling.

Josh: (Smiles slightly.)

Therapist: What did you notice? Were you able to move your attention where I indicated?

Josh: Yeah. It was kind of interesting.

Therapist: Excellent. Did you notice how effortlessly you could move your attention around? When you moved your attention from one thing to another, did it happen quickly or slowly?

Josh: Quickly. Like, immediately.

Therapist: So you were able to very quickly shift your awareness from one thing to another. You may have also noticed how you were able to move the focus of your attention from external to internal bodily sensations, to ideas and memories, to the past and the future. You could also narrow it down to something like your elbow, and widen it onto broad ideas like *justice*.

Josh: (Nods.)

Therapist: What do you think? Pretty cool, eh?

Josh: (Smiles and offers a slight, good-natured eye-roll.) Pretty cool. (Pauses.) Actually, it *was* kind of cool. I never thought of that before.

Therapist: So that was just an example of how we can direct the spotlight of our attention in different ways. Let's continue to explore that by learning our first mindfulness exercise.

MINDFUL CHECKING-IN

The first formal mindfulness exercise I usually introduce in CFT is called Mindful Checking-In (Kolts, 2012). Mindful Checking-In involves bringing our attention sequentially to bodily experiences, felt emotions, and thinking, in fairly rapid succession. This exercise isn't meant to be an extended meditation, although clients can certainly spend as much time as they like. Rather, the practice has a few specific purposes:

- To help clients *develop the habit* of bringing their attention to their bodily experiences, emotions, and thoughts—to get used to noticing these experiences.

- To help clients begin to relate these experiences as they are—physical sensations, feelings, and words or images in the mind—without judging them.

- To help clients get used to practicing mindfulness exercises (and home-practice generally) in their daily life outside the session—starting small with something they can hopefully do with little difficulty.

Let's take a look at how this exercise can be introduced in a therapy session:

Therapist: The first mindfulness exercise we'll do is called Mindful Checking-In. Just like before, I'll prompt you to bring your attention to certain experiences. This time, we're going to direct attention to body experiences, emotions, and thoughts. Sound good?

Josh: Sure.

Therapist: In mindfulness, we want to be aware of these different experiences, bringing our attention to them. This is different from *thinking about* our experiences. So if your foot is cold, mindful awareness would involve noticing that it is cold, and maybe curiously paying attention to what those sensations of coldness feel like—as if you were going to describe them, or explain what the experience was like to someone who didn't have feet. That's different from thinking about having cold feet, which might involves words in our minds like *Crap, my feet are cold again. I should have worn my warm winter socks. Darn it!* Get the difference?

Josh: (*Chuckles a bit.*) I think so.

Therapist: So if you notice yourself thinking instead of observing—and you probably *will*—no worries. When you notice that, just try to bring your attention back to the experience. We'll talk more about the thinking bit and how to handle that later. I'm also going to turn on my digital recorder here so that we can record the exercise in an mp3 that we can load onto your phone before we finish today, so that you can listen to it if you'd like, when practicing at home. Sound good?

Josh: Sounds good. I can just record it on my phone right now.

Therapist: Great. (*Waits a few moments while Josh sets up his phone to record.*) First, sit up in an upright, alert posture, with your head up. We don't want to slump. Allow your breath to take on a comfortable rhythm, and if you feel comfortable doing so, allowing your eyes to close. If you prefer, feel free to keep your eyes open and lower your gaze onto the floor about six to eight feet in front of you, allowing your gaze to soften—to unfocus a bit. If you need to shift about a bit as we go, or clear your throat, or anything like that, to remain comfortable—don't worry about it; just do it.

Josh: (*Straightens his posture and closes his eyes.*)

Therapist: Let's start by bringing our awareness to the temperature in the room. Try to notice sensations of warmth or coolness… (*Waits fifteen to twenty seconds*)…

- Now bringing your attention to external bodily sensations…the feeling of your feet on the floor…legs, buttocks, and back on the chair…the sensation of your hands resting in your lap. (*Wait fifteen to twenty seconds.*)

- Now noticing information coming in through your other senses…sounds coming in through your ears…my voice, the rush of the heating system, the buzz of the lights… patterns of light on your eyelids… (*Wait fifteen to twenty seconds.*)

- Now following these sensations into the body, noticing any internal bodily sensations. Bringing awareness to sensations like hunger or fullness, tension or relaxation, comfort or soreness. Just noticing these sensations, just as they are. (*Wait five to ten seconds.*) If any of these sensations call out for your attention, let it go to them, settling on the sensation and noticing what it is like… (*Wait fifteen to twenty seconds.*)

- Now bringing awareness to the sensation of the breath. Noticing how quickly or slowly the breath enters and leaves your body. Noticing the heart rate… (*Wait fifteen to twenty seconds.*)

- Following these sensations of arousal or relaxation, shifting your awareness to any emotions you may be feeling. Interest? Boredom? Anticipation? Curiosity? Just noticing these feelings as events in the mind. (*Wait thirty seconds.*)

- Now that we've brought the attention to our feelings, allowing it to shift to another mental experience…thoughts. Notice any thoughts—any words or images—arising in your mind. Thoughts like, *Is he going to talk in that slow voice the whole time?* Just noticing any thoughts that might be coming through your mind, watching them arise and pass. (*Wait thirty seconds.*)

- And if you like, you might bring your attention to the relationship between your thoughts and emotions…perhaps noticing that when you have certain types of thoughts, certain types of feelings tend to arise as well. Perhaps noticing that when you're feeling certain emotions, certain thoughts tend to arise. (*Pause for thirty seconds.*)

- And when you're ready, allowing the breath to take a comfortable rhythm, gently opening the eyes, and returning the attention to the room…

The first time, this practice will take five to ten minutes to go through, but we want to let clients know that it can actually happen much more quickly. This practice isn't designed to be a long meditation—although it can certainly serve as one if the client wants to spend more time on any of these aspects of his experience. Rather, it is designed to be an efficient way for the client to learn to *establish the habit of checking in* with his body, emotions, and thoughts. The purpose is to establish the ability (and the tendency) to efficiently *notice* his bodily experience and what he is feeling and thinking; mindfully noticing and accepting these experiences exactly as they are—sensations, thoughts, and feelings. With a little practice, this check-in can be done in thirty seconds to a minute, as the client efficiently brings his attention to his body, feelings, and thoughts in fairly rapid succession. Learned in this way, the client won't need thirty minutes on a meditation cushion to mindfully connect with his experiences—he'll be able to do it during a television commercial, or stopped in traffic, or in the line at the supermarket.

When we're giving these instructions, we want to use a generally calm, slightly slowed tone of voice—but remember, we're not trying to put the client to sleep. I find that some natural variation in vocal tone and speed of speech can help keep clients engaged in the exercise. While the practice is fairly straightforward, it's also good to record the exercise so that the client can use it (or listen to it for a reminder of how to do the practice) at home. I have this exercise and a few others available on my website so that clients can access them that way as well. These days, many clients will have phone apps that can record the exercises during the session.

There are some variations of the exercise that clients may find useful. Once they've gotten the basic practice, we can suggest that they check in with their three circles. They can either try to notice which of the three circles (threat, drive, safeness) is most dominant in their bodies, emotions, and thoughts, or perhaps rate each of the three circles on a 1-to-10 or 1-to-100 scale. Again, the idea is to get clients in the habit of *noticing* how threatened, motivated, or safe they are feeling.

We can also suggest that they pause to do this whenever they notice the arising of (or after noticing they are caught up in) a particular emotion or string of thoughts. We can model this in session (for example, "It looks like something is happening for you right now. What's happening with those three circles? How is that playing out in terms of your bodily experience? What feelings are showing up? What thoughts are running through your mind?"). In this way, we're introducing clients to a nonshaming way of talking about and relating to emotional experiences that may previously have been experienced as unpredictable and overwhelming.

We can use these observations as a platform for helping clients explore and become familiar with how thoughts and emotions play out in their bodies and minds. This can help take the sting out of such experiences as we look closely and curiously at them not as something to fear, but as *valid aspects of their experience that we seek to understand.* We're helping clients learn to approach these basic human experiences in a curious, manageable, and helpful way—which is a core part of compassion.

MINDFUL BREATHING

While the Mindful Check-In gives us an easy way to introduce mindfulness to clients that doesn't require extensive practice time, there is much to be gained from longer, more meditative mindfulness practices as well. First, there's a growing body of scientific literature that supports the ability of such practices to quite literally grow the parts of our brains that are involved with things like emotion regulation and interpersonal relationships. Second, more extended mindfulness sessions are likely to be more helpful in assisting clients in developing attentional control, the ability to notice movement in the mind, and the capacity to tolerate distress.

Teaching Mindful Breathing

In essence, mindful breathing is a fairly straightforward practice: we're training the client to settle her attention on the sensation of the breath, and to bring it back to the breath whenever she notices the attention has strayed. *Notice and return*—that's the practice. While different mindfulness teachers will give the instructions in slightly different ways, there are some basic components that tend to be present:

- Sitting in an upright, comfortable posture.

- Eyes closed, or gaze lowered to a spot six to eight feet in front with an unfocused, or "softened," gaze, or a gaze focused on the tip of the nose.

- Breathing at a natural, comfortable rate.

- The attention settled on the breath, wherever it can be found most easily. This can include the tip of the nose, where it enters and leaves the body, the rise and fall of the abdomen, the path of the breath through the body, or any place the client finds it comfortable to anchor the attention.

- When the client notices her attention has wandered—distracted by thoughts, emotions, or sensations—she gently brings it back to the breath. Some teachers prompt the practitioner to label the distraction: *thinking, listening,* and so on.

- It's good to set an external timer to remind the meditator that the session is completed. There are numerous meditation timer applications with soothing gong tones that work well for this purpose.

Let's look at an example of how this exercise can be introduced in a session:

Therapist: Jenny, I'm glad you found time to do the Mindful Check-Ins we introduced last session this week. How did you like them?

Jenny: In the beginning, it was hard to remember to do it. So I started setting the timer on my phone. That really helped.

Therapist: Good thinking. What did you notice about the practices?

Jenny: One thing I noticed was that it made it easier to get things done.

Therapist: (*leaning in a bit, with an interested look*) Tell me more about that.

Jenny: Well, a lot of the time when I start to do something, I'll have lots of thoughts like, *Why should I do this? There's no point to it.* Or I'll go through all the different ways that it could go wrong. This week, a few times, I was able to notice those thoughts, but keep going anyway.

Therapist: So "Anxious Jenny" still had a lot to say, but you were able to let her have her say and keep going anyway. That's great.

Jenny: Yeah. I do find myself wondering when someone besides Anxious Jenny will have something to say.

Therapist: No worries—we're going to work on developing "Compassionate Jenny" as well—a version of you that is compassionate, kind, strong, wise, and confident.

Jenny: I'd really like that.

Therapist: Actually, it sounds to me like Compassionate Jenny is already showing up. That's the version of you that kept you going even after Anxious Jenny shared her reluctance.

Jenny: Hmmm. (*Looks a bit thoughtful.*)

Therapist: We're going to be sending Compassionate Jenny to the gym, and one way to begin doing that is by introducing that second mindfulness practice we mentioned last session—mindful breathing. How does that sound?

Jenny: Sounds good.

Therapist: Mindful breathing *is* quite literally sending Compassionate Jenny to the gym— there are scientific studies showing that practicing mindful breathing over time can actually grow the parts of the brain that help us with managing our emotions and relationships with others. To start, let's sit up in a comfortable, upright position, head held up but not too high. (*Models position.*)

Jenny: Like this?

Therapist: Just like that. This exercise will take a bit longer than the check-in, so again, if you feel the need to shift, clear your throat, swallow, or anything like that— don't worry about it, just go ahead and do it. You may also find it useful to have your mouth slightly open, with the tongue touching the roof of the mouth just behind the teeth.

Jenny: (*Shifts a bit.*)

Therapist: Now, allowing your eyes to close…

Jenny:	(*Closes eyes.*)

Therapist: Breathing in and out through the nose, allowing your breath to take on a comfortable rhythm—just breathing naturally, not attempting to slow down or speed up anything. Settling the attention on the breath, wherever you feel it most easily. That could be the tip of the nose where the breath enters and leaves the body, the rise and fall of the abdomen, or following the breath in and out of the body. (*Waits thirty seconds.*)

As you breathe, you'll sometimes find your attention moving away from the breath as you become distracted by thoughts, sounds, or other things. This isn't a bad thing. It actually helps us learn to notice movement in our minds. When this happens, whether you've been distracted for a moment or for quite a long time, just notice the distraction and gently bring your attention back to the breath, over and over, again and again. This is the practice—settle the attention on the breath, notice the distraction, gently come back to the breath. Notice, and return.

Jenny: (*Sits quietly, breathing.*)

Therapist: (*Waits thirty seconds.*) Notice the distraction, return to the breath.

Therapist: (*Waits one minute.*) Notice and return.

Therapist: (*Waits one minute, thirty seconds.*) And when you're ready, gently opening the eyes, bringing your attention to the room.

Jenny: (*Slowly opens her eyes over the course of thirty seconds or so.*) Mmmm.

Therapist: So that was three minutes or so after I stopped giving instructions. What did you notice?

Jenny: It felt like a really long time. It was relaxing, but also a little frustrating. Overall, I liked it.

Therapist: So it felt like longer than three minutes?

Jenny: A lot longer. I never just sit quietly like that.

Therapist: It can feel like a lot longer, particularly when our minds are used to being so busy all the time. It can take a while for them to get used to sitting quietly, watching the breath. You mentioned a little frustration—did you find yourself getting distracted?

Jenny: That's when I'd get frustrated. It seemed like I'd be focused on the breath for just a second and then I'd start thinking, over and over again.

Therapist: (*Smiles and chuckles a bit.*) Yep—that's just what it's like! The same thing happened for me when I was learning. Sometimes it *still* does.

Jenny: Really?

Therapist: Oh yeah! Sometimes I'll have really sneaky thoughts—I'm sitting there like, *This is a great meditation session. I'm completely focused on my breath. No thoughts at all. I'm getting really good at this.* I'm thinking the whole time!

Jenny: (*Smiles and laughs gently.*)

Therapist: It's easy to get frustrated if our drive system sets up sticking to the breath as a goal. When we get distracted, we think we're failing at our goal. The key is to remember that one purpose of the practice is learning to *notice movement in the mind.* And these distracting thoughts give us the perfect opportunity to do this. If we never got distracted, we'd never learn to notice what it feels like when thoughts take us away. So it's not a problem—does that make sense?

Jenny: That helps.

Therapist: Want to try it again—say, for five minutes this time?

Jenny: Sounds good.

Therapist: Excellent. I'll set my timer then, and let's move into an upright posture, close our eyes, and bring the attention to the breath…

The above example demonstrates one way of presenting mindful breathing to clients. Again, assuming that mindful breathing will be assigned as homework, it's good to record the exercise or to provide the client with links to online mp3 recordings of the practices. Notice that in the vignette above, the therapist introduces the practice by giving brief instructions on how to hold the body and speaking briefly to various obstacles that might come up (instructing Jenny to shift if she needs to, for example).

It's also important to follow up after the practice, to see how the client experienced it, and to explore, validate, and address any obstacles that may have come up. Notice also that the therapist refers to his own practice, and shares his own challenges with the client, using a bit of humor along the way. Doing so underscores the importance of the practice (it's important enough that the therapist practices as well), validates the difficulty, and reduces the likelihood of related self-criticism (the "expert" therapist sometimes struggles with the same things), and models how to handle such obstacles with good humor (working to soften the implicit frustration response with a bit of levity). Also note how the therapist utilizes the language of CFT, referring to "Anxious Jenny," "Compassionate Jenny," and the drive system—helping shape her mastery of the CFT concepts she's been learning.

One last comment: I strongly, strongly advise, if you're going to be using mindful breathing (or any other mindfulness practice) in therapy, that you will have practiced using the technique yourself (and optimally will have an ongoing practice). It will give you an experience of the practice to draw upon when explaining it to the client. It will help you observe the obstacles from the inside out, and what it takes to work with them. Finally, mindful awareness itself produces many practical benefits that can potentially improve one's capacity to be an effective CFT therapist. At a practical level, think about it—mindfulness and compassion aren't just therapy "techniques." They are complex capacities and skills that we're helping clients develop. Would you choose to learn to play an instrument or a sport from someone who had never played it? While the best practitioners don't always make the best teachers (and vice versa), teachers should have some mastery of the skills they are instructing.

OTHER MINDFULNESS PRACTICES

There are numerous other mindfulness practices our clients might find helpful as they work to bring this purposeful, present-focused, accepting, nonjudgmental awareness into their lives. Almost any activity or experience can be chosen as a focus of mindfulness. The idea is that we select where we're going to focus our attention, bringing our awareness to this experience and then nonjudgmentally noticing and exploring it. Whenever distractions arise, we notice them, and bring the attention back to our chosen focus. Typically we'll want to start with sensory experiences like the breath, physical sensations in the body, or sensory input coming in from outside the body. However, we can also use mental images or even ideas as the focus of concentration, or we can rest in open awareness, not anchoring the attention to any specific focus, and simply noticing whatever arises in our experience without clinging to or pushing away any of it. Here are a few commonly used mindfulness exercises:

- Mindfulness of the Body—bringing nonjudgmental awareness to bodily sensations

- Mindful Eating—eating slowly and noticing all sensory aspects of the food or the eating

- Mindful Walking—walking slowly, bringing mindful awareness to all the sensations that come with walking

- Mindful Showering—showering while mindfully focusing on the feeling of water hitting the skin

- Mindful Task Completion—doing tasks like dishwashing or cleaning and mindfully noticing all the sensory experiences one has while completing the activity.

- Mindful Exercise—mindfully focusing the attention on physical activity (such as yoga)

The idea is to come up with a variety of activities in which clients can apply mindful awareness. We work collaboratively with them to come up with activities that *they* are interested in, to keep motivation for the practice high.

Over time, this sort of mind training can help clients learn to settle the mind, gradually quieting the endless torrent of thoughts as they get better and better at bringing their attention to the present moment. This can pave the way for lots of good things. As clients learn to endure the initial discomfort of sitting quietly with a busy mind, they learn to tolerate distress and persevere when things are difficult, and are reinforced as their efforts begin to pay off. These practices also set the stage for the development of compassionate wisdom. For centuries, Buddhist practitioners have used exercises like the mindful-breathing practice described above to prepare the mind for more involved analytical meditations—learning to stabilize the mind so that they could deeply contemplate things like compassion and the nature of reality. Once our clients have gotten comfortable with the more focused practices, they may wish to take some meditation time to explore the questions that compassionate reasoning will often bring up: *What sort of person do I want to be? What do I want my life to be about? How do I want to contribute to the lives of others, and to the world?*

WORKING WITH OBSTACLES IN MINDFULNESS TRAINING

When presenting clients with practices we'd like them to follow through with, it's important to troubleshoot around obstacles that might arise. There are some common obstacles that can get in the way when we're teaching mindfulness—particularly mindful breathing. The extent to which we can plan for and address these obstacles on the front end can increase the likelihood that clients will be able to establish an ongoing mindfulness practice.

Forgetting

Perhaps the most common obstacle is simply not remembering to practice. I'd recommend naming this as a likely obstacle when planning the homework to begin with, and working collaboratively with clients to plan good times to do it (for example, when they will be alert, not sleepy), and ways to prompt themselves (such as setting an alarm): "One common challenge that can come up when learning mindfulness is simply forgetting to do the practice. What do you think might help you remember?"

Avoidance and Low Motivation

In my experience, if I try to have clients start out by doing thirty minutes of mindfulness practice per day, they often won't be able do it, and may well not *want* to do it. That's a long time for someone with no experience of sitting quietly and watching the breath. We need to remember two things: First, consider how hard it can be to create twenty to thirty minutes of free space in *your life* to do something new—even when it's something you're motivated to do and know will be very good for you. Not so easy? It's the same for many of our clients. Additionally, many of our clients (like us) live in overstimulating environments filled with constantly shifting media, electronic gadgetry, text-message conversations, and so on, that may have tuned their neurological systems to expect high levels of ongoing stimulation. When you've adapted to function in the face of an ongoing cacophony of flashing screens, beeping phones, and rapid-fire interactions, the relatively quiet, inactive state of mindfulness meditation can initially feel disorienting, agitating, or downright uncomfortable.

So what to do? First, we can *acknowledge* these potential obstacles, so that if and when they arise, our clients understand them as common, completely understandable occurrences and not as *something that's wrong with me*. Second, we want to start small. While it depends on the individual client, I've often begun with two to five minutes per day of mindful breathing for the first week—then increasing by five- or ten-minute increments, paced according to how the client is feeling and how it's working. We want to start with a level of practice that can be sustained, and which gives clients a feeling of success when they're able to complete it. If we start with the bar too high, an initial failure to follow through can kill the client's motivation. However, if this happens at any point, we can problem-solve around obstacles with the client—in nonshaming, nonblaming ways which validate that there will often be obstacles that get in our way. Part of working compassionately with life challenges is learning to work compassionately with obstacles: "It can initially be really hard to keep up a mindfulness practice, and there are lots of obstacles that can get in the way. What got in the way of you being able to follow through with our plan? Let's see if we can figure out something that will help make it easier."

Feeling Like a Failure

If I had a dollar for everyone who has decided to take up mindful breathing and then has given it up soon after, feeling like they "just can't do it," I suspect I'd have enough money to fund my research assistants until I retire. The instruction to "settle your attention on the breath, and gently bring it back when you notice that it has wandered" seems like a simple one. It *is* simple. It's just not *easy*. Well-meaning practitioners will often start out very excited to have this tranquil meditation experience, only to give up in frustration as they observe that their minds are bounding about in every which way, with almost no time in which their attention is actually focused on the breath. Even if our fancy new brains *know* that our attention will wander and that this isn't a failure, our old-brain emotional centers will often register frustration as we find ourselves distracted by thoughts again and again.

To soften this tendency, we can let clients know ahead of time that they will become distracted, and that this isn't a bad thing. It's really *not* a bad thing. As I mentioned above, one goal of mindfulness is to learn greater control over the attention—and over time, practitioners will be able to keep their attention on the breath for longer and longer periods of time. However, we can emphasize that another goal of mindfulness meditation is learning to notice movement in the mind. When thoughts, emotions, and sensations take us away from the breath, we have the chance to *notice* this movement—an opportunity that wouldn't be there if our attention never strayed. So these distractions actually give us valuable opportunities to learn to notice the arising of thoughts and emotions, to notice when we've disappeared into them, and to bring our attention back to the breath when this happens.

One last piece: Clients will sometimes struggle with having thoughts that come up during meditation that they don't want to let go. This happens for me a lot, as I'll often do my mindfulness meditation in the morning before settling down to write. Thoughts come up that I'll want to include in my writing. As you might imagine, attempting to hold these thoughts in mind while simultaneously returning to the breath is problematic for the practice. But it's no problem—I keep a pad of paper and pen in close proximity to my meditation cushion so that I can jot down any thoughts I want to make sure not to lose. This practice can be useful for clients as well.

SUMMARY

Like relational safeness and understanding the unchosen factors that shape how we develop, mindful awareness is an important part of the foundation that underlies the development of compassion in CFT. Mindfulness practices help clients learn to observe their emotions and experiences in accepting, nonjudgmental ways; to notice movement in their minds, and to use their attention to work with and tolerate difficult emotions. These capacities set the stage for what will be our focus for much of the rest of the book: the purposeful cultivation of compassionate strengths.

CHAPTER 8

Committing to Compassion: Working with Self-Criticism

Hopefully by now, much of the foundation for self-compassion will have been laid, with self-blame softening as clients recognize that many of their struggles were caused and shaped by unchosen factors, and as they get a taste of what it's like to curiously observe their thoughts and emotions without judging them. From this point forward, we focus our attention solidly on helping clients cultivate compassion for themselves and for others, and applying that compassion in working with their difficulties.

For many clients, the idea of self-compassion can be very foreign—they may be able to connect with compassion for others, but have little ability or willingness to direct it toward themselves. Their internal self-critic may be a constant companion, and may have become the primary way they attempt to motivate themselves in life. Such clients can have great reluctance around disempowering their self-critic and directing compassion toward themselves. Some may fear that if this harsh but familiar voice is silenced, they will lose the ability to motivate themselves at all—perhaps bringing about the life outcomes they most dread. They may also feel that they *deserve* this shame and self-criticism, seeing self-compassion as indulgent or inappropriate.

In the face of such resistance, we may be tempted to *convince* our clients of the merits of self-compassion by telling them how it is better than self-criticism. While trying to sell clients on the virtues of self-compassion might be helpful, in my experience, this can sometimes paradoxically set them up to defend the self-critic. Instead, we can facilitate exploration on the part of clients, using Socratic dialogue and thought exercises to help them recognize compassion as a powerful way to motivate themselves—in a way that doesn't have the negative side effects of shame and self-criticism. Rather than argue whether or not they *deserve* criticism or compassion, we want to assist them in exploring what would be *helpful* as they work with their suffering, tackle the difficult aspects of their lives, and pursue their goals, dreams, and values.

SOCRATIC DIALOGUE

When we have clients who are reluctant to let go of self-criticism, it can be useful to explore their thinking around the function served by the criticism. We can use a rather standard "CFT move" in doing this, which involves asking the client a variant of "What would be the risk if you did _____? What are you afraid might happen if you did this?" Let's consider how we might use this strategy with someone having an extensive history of self-critical thinking:

Therapist: Jenny, we've been working on developing compassion. A big part of this is learning to relate warmly to ourselves when we observe ourselves struggling. This can be a big shift if we're used to criticizing and attacking ourselves. Some of us say harsh, critical things to ourselves that we'd never imagine saying to others.

Jenny: I'm like that. For years, I've constantly run myself down. It's so ridiculous. Everyone else can manage to do the things they need to without freaking out all of the time. What's wrong with me?

Therapist: So your internal self-critic speaks up loudly and often, running you down when you're having a hard time? Has it always been like this?

Jenny: For a long time, it has. It's like it's always there. Since I was a kid, anyway.

Therapist: So your self-critic feels very familiar—she's been around for a very long time. We're going to work with self-critical thoughts in the way that we've worked with the anxious ones—by noticing and paying a little less attention to that self-critical voice, and developing an encouraging, self-compassionate voice. How does that sound?

Jenny: (*Looks a bit skeptical.*) I don't know about that.

Therapist: (*gently smiling*) You don't know about that?

Jenny: It just doesn't seem realistic, you know.

Therapist: It sounds like there's some reluctance there—let's explore that. Let's imagine that you *were* able to stop listening to the voice of that internal self-critic, or that she were just to give up and go away. Would you be reluctant to give that self-criticism up?

Jenny: (*Pauses, thinking.*) I think I might. I think it would be hard to give it up.

Therapist: What would be the risk if you did give it up? What would you be worried might happen?

Jenny: Sometimes I think it's like, if I run myself down first, I'm making it so other people can't hurt me. If I say those things to me first, when they say it, it won't hurt as much.

Therapist: Whereas if you allowed yourself to relax and feel safe and comfortable with yourself…

Jenny: Then they could hurt me. Like when I was in school. I moved there, looking forward to meeting people, and they just came at me from out of the blue. Now, if someone were to say terrible things about me, it would be like, *Of course. What else you got? I already know that.*

Therapist: That makes a lot of sense to me. It hurt so much when that happened. You want to make sure you don't get blindsided again.

Jenny: Yeah.

Therapist: Are there any other reasons you might be reluctant to stop listening to the voice of that internal self-critic? Any other things you fear might happen if you were to stop running yourself down?

Jenny: I'm afraid I wouldn't do anything. It's really hard, but I manage to go to class and do the stuff I have to do, because I don't want to be even *more* pathetic. I guess I'm afraid that if I didn't have that self-critic, I'd just hide out in my room and not do anything. It's like this group project I told you about in my communications class. When the teacher first split us into groups, I thought about just sneaking out of the room—like I was going to the bathroom—and then not come back.

Therapist: And your internal self-critic kept that from happening?

Jenny: Yeah. I just thought, *Jenny, stop being so stupid. You're going to look like an idiot if you do this. Don't be a loser.* So I stayed. I hated it, but I stayed.

Therapist: So you use self-criticism as a way to motivate yourself, and you're afraid you wouldn't do anything if that critical voice were quieted?

Jenny: Yeah. I'm afraid I'd just hole up in my room, and eventually flunk out of school and have to move back in with my parents, which would be *awful.*

Therapist: It seems like we've learned some important things here, Jenny. It sounds like you feel your self-critic serves two important functions: to protect you from being blindsided by attacks from other people, and to keep you going, doing the things you need to do. Does that sound right?

Jenny: It does.

Therapist: So it sounds to me that if we're going to find a way for you to turn down the volume on the self-critic, then we need to find other, more helpful ways for you to feel safe and motivate yourself. Would you be interested in exploring whether your compassionate self could do those jobs at least as well as the self-critic?

Jenny: I'd be up for trying.

In the above vignette, the therapist uses Socratic dialogue to explore Jenny's resistance around giving up self-criticism, and in particular, identifying the *functions* she ascribes to self-criticism that might lead her to be reluctant to give it up. It is often the case that clients will feel their self-critic serves important functions in their lives—functions that will need to be met in other, more adaptive ways if clients are to commit themselves to developing more compassionate ways of relating to themselves. You might consider the ways you use self-criticism in your own life, and what you might be afraid of losing if you were to give it up. Let's explore a thought exercise that can help us try to build motivation around developing new, compassionate ways of relating to the self.

Two Teachers Vignette

While many of us may use self-criticism as an attempt to motivate, protect, or "keep ourselves in line," clinging to the self-critic for these purposes is based on a logical fallacy—that self-attacking is the *only* way to motivate ourselves, or perhaps the *best* way. Even if self-shaming and self-attacking do seem to serve some useful purposes, they do so at a great cost, keeping us stuck in the threat system (with narrowed attention and thinking, focused on threats) and diminishing our happiness. We want to help clients discover ways to encourage, motivate, support, and protect themselves that don't have these drawbacks. As we've seen, one way to do this is through the development of self-compassion—the ability to be sensitive, validating, and encouraging in the face of one's suffering and struggle. In the beginning, we may need to help clients develop motivation to make this shift from self-criticism to self-compassion. One of my favorite methods for doing this is the "Two Teachers" vignette, an experiential exercise commonly used by CFT therapists (Gilbert, 2009a):

Therapist: Josh, we've been talking about how you see your self-critic as working to protect and motivate you, and I've suggested that we might be able to find other ways to do those things. Related to that, I'd like to do a brief imaginal exercise and then ask you some questions. Would that be all right?

Josh: I guess.

Therapist: I want you to imagine a child that you care very much about—maybe it's your child, maybe someone else's—but you care very deeply about him. This child is learning a very difficult task, maybe learning to do algebra for the first time, learning a musical instrument, or to play a challenging sport. Have you ever done any of that stuff?

Josh: I play guitar.

Therapist: Then you know that when you first begin playing, it's really hard—and you have to practice quite a lot before you get to sounding very good.

Josh: You've got that right.

Therapist: So I want you to imagine that in learning this task, the child could have one of two teachers. First, let's imagine that he has a harsh, critical teacher, who tries to motivate him by running him down. Imagine how this teacher might interact with him: "No! ... No! ... Wrong again! ... Can't you get anything right? ... Not like that, like this! ... No! ... No! ... What's wrong with you? Are you stupid? ... No!"

Josh: Sounds familiar. My dad used to talk to me like that all the time.

Therapist: It's no secret where you learned to criticize yourself, is it?

Josh: (*Nods pensively.*)

Therapist: Now, let's imagine a second teacher this child could have. This teacher is compassionate, really wanting to help the child learn. He understands that this is a really difficult task, and that anyone would struggle with it, especially in the beginning. This teacher is wise, knowing that what he really needs to do is find ways to encourage this child to keep going—knowing that the key to mastering this task is for the child to keep working at it, and that he's more likely to do that if he enjoys the experience. Let's imagine how this teacher might approach this child: "There you go... There you go... Nice! ... Keep going... Not quite like that, like this... Yes, that's right... You're doing really well—this is tough but you're doing a great job keeping at it... There you go!"

Josh: (*Relaxes a bit; breathing softens.*)

Therapist: So now, a few questions. First, which of those teachers would you want this child you care so much about to have? Which would you hire to teach him guitar, the first or second?

Josh:	The second.
Therapist:	Me, too. Let's look a bit deeper, though. Even if you didn't particularly care about this child, which teacher do you think would do a better job at teaching him to do this difficult task?
Josh:	The second.
Therapist:	(*Nods.*) One last question. When you observe *yourself* struggling, which teacher does the voice in your head sound like?
Josh:	(*Pauses; looks down.*) You got me there. It's the first. Every damn time.
Therapist:	(*Pauses; leans in a bit in silence.*)
Josh:	I think I get it.
Therapist:	(*warmly*) Yeah. (*Pauses.*) So we've got some big tasks to tackle together. Which of those teachers do you think we should hire to help us? It sounds like that critical teacher has had his chance. Would you be willing to give that compassionate teacher a try, to see if he might be able to help us out?
Josh:	(*Nods consideringly.*) Yeah. That'd probably be worth a try.

Exercises like the one above allow us to introduce the idea and impact of compassion in a way that is *experiential*—operating at both the explicit (thinking about the benefits of compassion) and implicit (*feeling* the differential effects of criticism and compassion) levels. If it stays only at the thinking level, we may find little shift in the client, as these self-critical habits may be very deeply ingrained. We want the client to *feel the difference,* to connect with the realization that compassion is a more powerful way to get his needs met and pursue his goals. In the vignette above, the therapist works to accomplish this not just by describing the two teachers as critical or compassionate, but by acting out what they would say from these perspectives (which also provides some modeling— giving the client a glimpse into what compassion might look like in this situation). We see in the vignette that Josh reacted nonverbally to these depictions. We also need to allow plenty of time for the client to process what is happening within him, leaving plenty of space after the vignette to get to the questions that prompt self-reflection, so that the client has time to connect with certain realizations. You'll note that the therapist also matched the gender of both teacher and child to that of the client—setting up the realization that the client *plays both of these roles* in relation to himself.

Some clients will respond in very different ways from how Josh did—sometimes digging into the self-criticism, saying things like, "Well, that would work better for the child, but not for me," or "I had the harsh teacher growing up, and *I* learned to play." Again, we don't want to come straight at this resistance, setting ourselves up as a threat cue and positioning the client to defend his self-critic. Rather, we can explore with Socratic dialogue: "So for you, it feels like the criticism *worked,* and you're really reluctant to give up that strategy?" or "It sounds like you're reluctant to relate compassionately to yourself because you feel that you don't *deserve* to be treated kindly and compassionately?" We can explore these ideas with the client and see if he might be willing to try an experiment to see if compassion might work as an alternative to self-criticism.

Like any practice or technique, this practice requires attention to nuance, and won't work equally well for everyone. Combat veterans whose training involved lots of people who sounded just like that critical teacher may reply: "I'd want my kid to have the first teacher. That first teacher kept me alive." Using Socratic dialogue, we could help such clients explore the differences between the combat environment—an environment filled with physical threats—and civilian life, considering different strategies in terms of how they fit with the demands and concerns present in these different contexts.

SUMMARY

In this chapter, we considered how we might help clients apply compassion in working with self-criticism. Identifying the self-criticism, exploring reluctance to give it up, and prompting clients to consider compassion as an alternative can be important steps in helping them really commit to developing compassion for themselves. With clients who have well-entrenched shame and self-critical habits, working with these tendencies requires patience and steadfastness, as they gradually become better at mindfully noticing the arising of shame and self-criticism, acknowledging these tendencies, compassionately noting how it makes sense that they would experience them, and purposefully shifting into a more compassionate perspective. In the next chapter, we'll explore what such a perspective looks like.

CHAPTER 9

Cultivating the Compassionate Self

Compassion work first and foremost involves facilitating a shift in perspective, or *social mentality*, so that our clients can approach their difficulties with flexible attention and reasoning, feelings of safeness, and the courageous motivation to approach and work helpfully with suffering. We want to help clients shift from a threat-based perspective focused on avoiding or getting rid of feelings of threat or discomfort, and into an orientation centered on developing strengths to help them compassionately engage and work with whatever arises—in their lives, or in their minds. In CFT, we call this perspective the *compassionate self.*

THE COMPASSIONATE SELF

In CFT, we're less interested in teaching clients compassion techniques, and more focused on helping them cultivate compassionate *lifestyles*—ways of being in the world defined by open, courageous hearts, flexible minds, and a repertoire of effective behaviors to draw upon. The *compassionate self* provides us with an organizing framework for the compassionate strengths we'll help our clients develop—a compassionate version of the self that we'll continually be working to deepen and strengthen (Gilbert, 2009a; 2010). In this way, CFT isn't about getting rid of unwanted experiences. It's about cultivating this compassionate self that is wise, kind, confident, courageous, and committed to working with whatever life presents.

A Method-Acting Approach

After reading those inspiring bits above, you may find yourself thinking, *Well, this is all well and good, but it seems awfully pie-in-the-sky. My clients have lots of* real *problems. Their experience of life isn't anything like that. Actually, my life doesn't seem much like that, either.*

As you might imagine, this is very a common experience. For clients whose lives are dominated by one experience of threat after another, the idea of the compassionate self can seem impossibly distant—so far from their lived experience as to seem ridiculous. This idea, that *I am nothing like that,* can be a primary obstacle, so we need to find a way to work with it.

We work with this in CFT by taking a method-acting approach to the development of the compassionate self (Gilbert, 2010). Actors quite often have to portray characters that are entirely different from how they experience themselves, with traits and characteristics that are nothing like their own. How do they manage this? They do it by *imagining what it would be like* to be this character: *If I were this person, with these characteristics, how would I feel? What would I think? What would I be motivated to do?* Just as different emotions and motives organize our attention, felt emotion, thinking and imagery, motivation, and behavior in very different ways, we can prompt clients to consider how their minds would be organized if they possessed a deep wealth of compassionate qualities: compassionate motivation, wisdom, confidence, commitment, and emotional courage. Rather than getting caught up in debating whether or not they *have* these strengths, we assist them in *imagining what it would be like if they did* possess them. Using imagery, we can assist clients in exploring how they would feel, understand, and interpret situations; how they would relate to their own emotions and various "emotional selves"; and what sorts of things they would be motivated to do from this compassionate perspective. In this way, we can help them develop these compassionate ways of reasoning, feeling, and behaving without getting caught up in thinking, *I am nothing like this.*

The Compassionate Self Practice

Now that we've introduced the Compassionate Self practice, let's explore how we might teach it to clients. We begin by orienting clients to the method-acting approach, and then prompt them to imagine what it would be like to have various compassionate qualities. While we can vary the attributes featured in the exercise depending upon the needs of the client, we'll often anchor the exercise to qualities of compassionate motivation (committed desire to be kind and helpful), wisdom and understanding, and emotional courage and confidence. In general, we want to begin with soothing rhythm breathing, then move to bodily experiences of warmth and strength, and then lead the client through a process of imagining what it would be like to have various compassionate mental qualities:

Therapist: Jenny, now that we've committed ourselves to inviting that second teacher on board, I'd like to introduce the Compassionate Self practice. In this exercise, I'll ask you to imagine what it would be like to have various compassionate qualities—like a committed desire to help yourself and others, a deep wisdom to understand and work with difficulties, and the confidence and courage to face difficult situations and work with them. Before we begin, do you have any questions?

Jenny: (looking skeptical) That sounds like a stretch. It doesn't sound like me at all.

Therapist: That's the beauty of the exercise. We're going to approach this exercise like we're actors playing a movie role that may be completely different from how we think of ourselves. Instead of thinking about whether or not we're actually like this, we're going to *imagine what it would be like if we did have these qualities*—what it would feel like, what we would understand, how we would think…that sort of thing. Would you be willing to try that?

Jenny: Okay. I'll give it a try.

Therapist: So we'll start in a familiar way. Let's assume a comfortable, upright position, and take about thirty seconds to slow down our breathing. (*Waits thirty seconds to one minute.*)

Jenny: (*Straightens, closes her eyes, and slows her breathing.*)

Therapist: Now, allowing the breath to return to a normal, comfortable rate. (*Waits three to five seconds.*) Now I'm going to ask you to imagine what it would be like to have different qualities. As I describe the qualities, try to imagine what it would be like if you had them—what you would feel, think, and experience if you were a deeply compassionate person who had already succeeded in developing these qualities. If you struggle at imagining this, you might bring to mind someone you think has these qualities, and imagine how it might feel to be like that person. Give me a gentle nod when you're ready to continue.

Jenny: (*Nods.*)

Therapist: First, imagine that your body feels calm, peaceful, and safe—filled with warmth and strength. Allow a gentle smile to cross your face. (*Waits thirty seconds*)…

- Imagine that along with this warmth and strength, you are filled with a kind, committed motivation to help those who are suffering—yourself and others. Imagine that this kind wish to help fills you and builds within you, filling you with strength and purpose. Feel this deep wish to *help*. (*Waits thirty seconds to one minute.*)

- Imagine that along with this committed motivation, you are filled with wisdom. Imagine that you are able to think flexibly, and to see things from different perspectives. Aware that difficult situations and emotions come and go, you are able to keep from being

117

captured by these experiences, and can draw upon your life experience in working with them. Knowing that difficult experiences are just a part of life, you are able to keep from judging them or yourself, and can look deeply—to understand where these feelings and experiences come from, how they make sense, and what would be helpful in working with them. Imagine being filled with this wisdom. (*Waits thirty seconds to one minute.*)

- Imagine that with this kind motivation and wisdom, there arises a deeply felt sense of confidence. Feel this confidence filling you with courage. You're filled with the willingness to engage with difficult feelings and situations. It's a feeling of *knowing* that *whatever arises, I can work with this, too.* Feel this confidence and courage building within you, filling you with strength. (*Waits thirty seconds to one minute.*)

Jenny: (*Sits quietly, with her eyes closed.*)

Therapist: Imagining being filled with these qualities—kind, committed motivation to help; deep wisdom; confidence; and emotional courage. Notice what it feels like as these qualities build within you. (*Waits thirty seconds to one minute.*)

- Focus on the feelings in your body—calm, peaceful, and strong. Imagine how you would feel, and look, as this kind, wise, confident, compassionate being. (*Waits twenty seconds.*)

- Imagine how you would experience the world as this deeply compassionate being—what you would understand. (*Waits a few seconds.*) What sort of feelings would you feel? (*Waits a few seconds.*) What sorts of thoughts would you think? (*Waits a few seconds.*) What would you be motivated to do? What would you do? (*Waits one to two minutes.*)

Jenny: (*Sits quietly, with her eyes closed.*)

Therapist: And when you're ready, allowing your eyes to open, and returning to the room. See if you can carry a sense of wisdom, kindness, and confidence with you as we continue. Feel free to stretch a bit if you like.

Jenny: (*Slowly opens her eyes and stretches a bit.*) Mmmm. I liked that.

Therapist: (*smiling gently*) What did you like about it?

Jenny: It was really peaceful, and it was nice to think about being like that. Just really comfortable.

Therapist: What was it like to imagine feeling like a deeply compassionate person—kind, wise, and confident?

Jenny: It was hard at first, like I couldn't really feel it. But I kept telling myself to just imagine what it would be like. Toward the end, I could sort of feel it. It felt different, at least.

Therapist: That's an important observation. It can be hard to feel it in the beginning—so sometimes all we can do is to imagine what it might be like if we *could* feel it. If we focus on how we would see things from this compassionate perspective, it can help—imagining the sorts of things we would think or understand if we had these characteristics.

Jenny: It seemed to get easier as we went along.

Jenny's observation that it was initially hard to *feel* like the compassionate self is a common one. For many of our clients, this compassionate perspective is so different from their experience of daily life that it may take a while before the feelings show up. The key is to keep shifting into that compassionate perspective. It may help some clients to recall a time in which they really *were* compassionate, in which they were motivated to help someone else, did so, and felt good about it. It can also be difficult to imagine having these characteristics in a vacuum—it can feel vague to imagine being compassionate, kind, wise, or courageous without having a situation to reference. For this reason, it's good to move fairly quickly from imagining having these compassionate characteristics to imagining how we might *use* them. Let's consider a couple of ways we might do this.

Extending Compassion to the Vulnerable Self

One way we can help clients strengthen their sense of the compassionate self while also learning to apply compassion to *themselves* involves having them bring to mind a situation in which they were struggling, and prompting them to extend compassion to that struggling version of themselves from the perspective of the current, compassionate self. In guiding such an exercise, the therapist prompts the client to empathize with, sympathize with, and honor this previous, struggling version of the self—while imagining that she is extending compassion, encouragement, and understanding to that suffering self. Let's explore what this might look like:

Therapist: Jenny, now that we've gotten familiar with the compassionate self, I'd like to try one more exercise. These compassionate qualities can feel a bit vague if we just imagining *having* them—to make it feel real, it can help to imagine applying them in a particular situation. This is an exercise we can use to bring compassion to a situation you've been struggling with. How does that sound?

Jenny: Sounds good.

Therapist: Excellent. Hopefully, the exercise will also help you develop some compassion for yourself when you're struggling with the fear and anxiety we've been talking about. First, I'd like you to bring to mind a situation you've struggled with recently—perhaps one in which you were really anxious, afraid, or self-critical. Could you take a minute to bring up a situation like that and then tell me a bit about it?

Jenny: (*Sits quietly for a few moments.*) As I was telling you last week, one of my teachers announced that we'd be doing a group project in my communications course. She split us up into groups and told us to meet to work on the project outside of class. I was just sitting there, terrified. We exchanged phone numbers and we're supposed to be meeting sometime this week. I'm dreading it—it makes me feel sick to think about. I don't know if I can do it.

Therapist: What's the project like?

Jenny: We're supposed to do a group paper, and then give a presentation to the class. It's on effective communication with diverse groups—worth like one-third of the points for the class. It's an interesting topic, but I hate group projects.

Therapist: Does it make sense that this project would trigger your anxiety?

Jenny: Yep. It's all the stuff I'm scared of, wrapped up into one convenient bundle. I'm dreading our first meeting. We're supposed to split up duties and figure out who's responsible for what... It's hard for me to speak up, so I know they're going to think I'm a slacker.

Therapist: This sounds like a perfect situation for this exercise. Want to give it a shot?

Jenny: Might as well.

Therapist: Okay. Let's start by assuming a comfortable, upright position, closing the eyes, and doing thirty seconds or so of soothing rhythm breathing. (*Waits thirty seconds to one minute.*)

Jenny: (*Closes her eyes and slows her breathing.*)

Therapist: Now, feeling sensations of calm, warmth, and strength filling your body, let's bring to mind those qualities of the compassionate self. Allowing a kind smile to cross your lips, imagining what your body would feel like as this deeply compassionate person. (*Waits fifteen to thirty seconds*)...

• Imagine being filled with a deeply felt sense of kindness—a kind, committed desire to help yourself and all those who are suffering. Feel this kind commitment growing in you. (*Waits thirty seconds.*)

- Imagine that with this kind motivation, you are filled with a deep wisdom and understanding—able to think flexibly, see things from multiple perspectives, and figure out what to do. (*Waits thirty seconds.*)

- Imagine that alongside this wisdom, you experience a powerful feeling of confidence and courage—a deeply felt sense that *whatever happens, I can work with this, too.* It's a sense of *knowing*—knowing that you can help. (*Waits thirty seconds.*)

Jenny: (*Sits quietly.*)

Therapist: Now bring to mind that situation back in the classroom. You've been split up into groups. See that vulnerable, anxious version of you sitting there with this group of people, sharing her phone number. From this kind, wise, compassionate perspective, imagine looking in on that anxious version of you in that situation. See how she is feeling. Can you see how hard it is for her?

Jenny: I can. She's terrified. She doesn't know if she's going to be able to do it.

Therapist: From this kind, wise, confident perspective, see if it's possible for you to be touched by her suffering, to have compassion for this anxious version of you who only wants to get a good grade in the course. A long time ago, some classmates treated her terribly, and she learned to be really scared in situations like this. Can you understand why she would be so scared? Does it make sense that she would be terrified?

Jenny: It does. It does make sense that she'd feel this way. She's so scared that she's going to be embarrassed, or humiliated.

Therapist: It's not her fault, is it?

Jenny: No. It's not.

Therapist: Seeing how hard it is for her, is it possible for you to feel some warmth and compassion for her? To wish that you could somehow help her? How do you feel for her?

Jenny: I feel bad for her, and I do wish that I could help her. It's so hard for her.

Therapist: That feeling you're having—being moved by her struggle—that's compassion. Feel this compassionate wish to help her. See how courageous she's being, this anxious version of you, staying there even though she's terrified. (*Waits a few seconds.*)

Jenny: (*Sits quietly with eyes closed.*)

> *Therapist:* Imagine that this strong, compassionate version of you could be there with her. Imagine you're there with her, and only she can see or hear you. Consider how you would be there for this struggling version of yourself—how you might help her to feel safe, how you might encourage her. You know her better than anyone else, and you know what she would need. How would you help her?

> *Jenny:* I don't think I'd say anything to her. I'd just sit there with her, maybe holding her hand. Just trying to help her feel safe. To let her know she's okay, and that I'm here for her.

> *Therapist:* Imagine yourself sitting there with her, sending her kindness, understanding, and support. You understand what she's going through—you get how hard it is for her, and how hard she's working just to be there. She's so strong, facing these fears, but she doesn't yet understand that. Allow yourself to feel good about being able to support her in this moment, and imagine her being filled with the kindness, support, and encouragement you're sending out to her. Are you able to imagine that?

> *Jenny:* (*Sits quietly with her eyes closed, slightly tearful but voice clear.*) I am.

> *Therapist:* (*Waits a bit.*) Imagine her being able to receive this understanding and support from you. How might she feel?

> *Jenny:* (*Pauses.*) Better. Still scared, but better. Supported. She's got someone on her side.

> *Therapist:* From this compassionate perspective, what would you want her to understand?

> *Jenny:* That she's going to be okay. And that I'm there to help her.

> *Therapist:* (*Pauses, smiling.*) That's beautiful, Jenny. Let's take a few moments more, imagining being there with that anxious version of you, extending compassion and support to her.

When clients are able to connect with it, the experience of imagining oneself extending compassion to a struggling version of the self can be a powerful one. We want to help make the experience a vivid one, having them imagine what they are feeling, doing, and experiencing in this scenario with as much detail as possible. Clients with deeply entrenched shame and self-criticism may initially struggle with such exercises. We can help them, gently suggesting ways they might support their struggling selves. For such clients, it may be more useful to have them begin by imagining a situation in which someone else—someone they care about—is struggling, and imagining extending compassion to that person. Once their self-criticism has been softened a bit through compassionate thinking exercises or other practices, we can have them return to extending compassion to themselves either through this practice or through compassionate chair work, which we'll introduce a bit later.

Some clients may find it nearly impossible to imagine having these qualities. Such clients may, however, be able to bring to mind someone they think *does* possess these traits, and imagine what it would be like to feel, think, and act from that person's perspective. The key is for them to begin developing the ability to shift into a perspective that is organized by the experience of compassion rather than threat.

The Compassionate Self in Action

Once the Compassionate Self practice has been introduced, we want to strengthen this compassionate perspective by having clients shift into it as often and in as many different situations as possible. We can do this in session, both by beginning subsequent sessions with a brief Compassionate Self exercise and by pausing to shift into this perspective at different points in the session, particularly when it's clear the client is caught up in the threat system. It's important to note that in doing this, we aren't shaping avoidance—we shift our attention away from the threatening material or situation so that we can slow things down, shift into the perspective of the compassionate self, and then *come back* to work with the problematic situation or emotion. We're shaping a process in which clients learn to mindfully notice when they've been captured by experiences of threat and use this awareness as a cue to work with their emotions, balance things out a bit, and come back to work with things from a compassionate perspective. The coming back is crucial—otherwise, we're just helping the client establish patterns of experiential avoidance, which isn't at all helpful.

We can also collaborate with clients to develop a plan for practicing outside of the session. It's important that this practice is initially done when conditions are favorable (not when the client is completely overwhelmed by threatening emotions or situations). We can even work with clients to plan specific times when they can shift into the perspective of their compassionate selves—considering how they would feel, think, pay attention, and be motivated to behave from this perspective. Before walking into a meeting at work or beginning a project, before picking up the kids from school, as we're getting up in the morning or before going to bed at night—the key is to identify times to practice shifting into the perspective of the compassionate self. With practice, this shift in perspective can be accomplished fairly quickly, perhaps by simply bringing to mind words like *kind, wise, courageous, compassionate*. We can then have clients apply this new perspective increasingly to challenging situations in their lives—imagining how they might think, feel, pay attention, and be motivated to act from this compassionate perspective.

In planning such home practice, we want to approach it as we would any outside-of-session practice: by considering potential obstacles and hedging our bets for success. It can be key to work collaboratively with clients to plan how to keep motivation high (starting small, initially planning for situations in which there's a high likelihood of feeling successful) and to build in reminders so they don't forget to practice. We can use behavioral techniques such as activity scheduling (Persons, Davidson, & Tomkins, 2000) to increase the likelihood that they'll be able to follow through with the plan.

Additionally, we want to communicate that it can initially be difficult to shift into this perspective, and that they may find themselves resisting doing so for various reasons, including just not feeling like it. We want to emphasize that the point is simply to make the effort—to try to imagine how you might feel, think, pay attention, and behave in this situation from the perspective of this kind, wise, courageous, compassionate self. We can even make "not wanting to do the home practice" the situation that is targeted: "How would your kind, wise, confident, compassionate self understand your resistance to do this practice? What would she encourage you to do?" Home practice can be aided by the Threat Emotion Monitoring form—a basic cognitive behavioral monitoring form that includes prompts to consider the situation and one's responses from the perspective of the compassionate self. (This form is included in the appendix at the end of this book, and is also available online at http://www.newharbinger.com/33094.)

Compassionate Letter-Writing

Particularly with clients who struggle with social anxiety or difficulty concentrating, in-session practice applying the compassionate self can be challenging. They may find themselves feeling self-conscious or "on the spot," with threat arousal getting in the way of being able to connect with (or verbalize) this compassionate perspective. Compassionate letter-writing can help clients learn to extend compassion to themselves in a context that allows them to avoid the potential performance demands of an in-session exercise. It also provides as much time as they like to think about and craft a compassionate message to their vulnerable selves (Gilbert 2009a; 2010).

Additionally, this exercise produces a product—the compassionate letter—that can be read again and again in those moments when the client needs compassionate support, encouragement, and coaching. Such a letter can be composed in session, but I find that having clients complete the letter at home often leads to a more powerful letter, as they can spend several days considering what to write, can take as much time as they need in writing it, and can even develop multiple letters to support themselves in different situations. Below, I've included a sample set of instructions to send home with clients who will be composing a compassionate letter. (The instructions are also available for download at http://www.newharbinger.com/33094.)

INSTRUCTIONS FOR COMPASSIONATE LETTER-WRITING

This exercise is designed to help us develop the compassionate self. We want to build and strengthen mental patterns that will help us find the courage to work with difficult experiences, to accept ourselves, and to build a sense of peace within ourselves that we can share with others. Learning to think and behave compassionately can sometimes be helped by writing a letter to ourselves. In this exercise, you're going to write about difficulties, but from the perspective of your compassionate self. You can write a general letter to yourself, or you can tailor the letter to support yourself around a particularly challenging situation.

- First, get out a pen and paper. You might even pick out a special journal or notebook.

- Spend a few moments doing soothing rhythm breathing. Allow yourself to slow down and settle into your experience.

- Now try to shift into the perspective of your compassionate self. Connect with your compassionate self, imagining yourself at your best—your calmest, your wisest, your most caring, your most confident and courageous. Feel yourself filled with feelings of kindness, strength, and confidence. Imagine yourself as this compassionate person who is wise, understanding, and committed to helping. Imagine your manner, your tone of voice, and how you feel as this compassionate being.

- When we are in a compassionate frame of mind, even slightly, we try to use our personal life experiences wisely. We know that life can be hard. We can look deeply into the perspectives of ourselves and other people involved in difficult situations, and try to understand how it makes sense that they might feel and act this way. We offer strength and support, and try to be warm, nonjudgmental, and noncondemning. Take a few breaths and feel that wise, understanding, confident, compassionate part of you arise—this is the part of you that will write the letter.

- If thoughts of self-doubt, like *Am I doing it right?* or *I'm not really feeling it* arise, note these thoughts as normal comments our minds make, and observe what you are experiencing as you write the best that you can. There is no right or wrong…you're just practicing, working with your compassionate self. As you write, try to create as much emotional warmth and understanding as you can.

- As you write your letter, try to allow yourself to understand and accept your distress. For example, you might start with, *I am sad, and I feel distress. My distress is understandable because…*

- Note the reasons—realize that your distress makes sense. Then continue… *I would like myself to know that…*

- The idea is to communicate understanding, caring, and warmth while helping ourselves work on the things we need to address.

When you have written your first few compassionate letters, go through them with an open mind and see whether they actually capture compassion for you. If they do, see if you can spot the following qualities in your letter:

- It expresses concern, genuine caring, and encouragement.

- It is sensitive to your distress and needs.

- It helps you face your feelings and become more tolerant of them.

- It helps you become more understanding of your feelings, difficulties, and dilemmas.

- It is nonjudgmental and noncondemning, helping you to feel safe and accepted.

- A genuine sense of warmth, understanding, and caring fills the letter.

- It helps you think about behavior you may need to adopt in order to get better.

- It reminds you why you are making efforts to improve.

Let's consider an example of a compassionate letter:

Dear Josh,

This has been a rough week and it makes sense that you're having a hard time. You've been trying hard to work with your anger. It's easy to feel upset with yourself when you don't meet your standards. Remember that you didn't choose to have a threat system that makes this anger, and it's not your fault that you get angry. There's nothing wrong with you—it's just your old brain trying to protect you. You learned to be angry by watching your father, and when you were bullied in school. That isn't your fault, either. But you're taking responsibility for becoming a better man, and that takes a lot of courage.

I know this feels terrible and sometimes you want to give up, but you're doing better and I know you can do it. Although you're scared others will attack you like your dad and those kids at school did, things are really different now. He's gone, and Maria loves you and has stayed with you even when things were really bad. Chloe and Aiden look up to you and you care a lot about being a good father to them. You're making progress. You just need to keep going. This compassion stuff is helping you realize that being strong and being angry are two different things. You have what it takes to be a good man. You can do this. It will be hard, but you can do this.

If you're reading this, it's probably because you're having a really tough day. Maybe you did or said something that you're beating yourself up for. Remember that these times will pass. You just have to keep going. Think of all the times when things seemed bad, but you made it through. Maybe go to the gym and let off some steam. You know exercise helps. Hang out with Nathan. Slow down your breath. Mostly, remember why you're doing this. Remember your family, how much they love you, and how much you want to be there for them. You're safe, and there's nothing wrong with you.

Sincerely,

Josh

We can have clients bring their compassionate letters to session and, if they feel comfortable, read them out loud. It can be a powerful experience for clients to hear themselves speaking compassionately to their struggles in this way.

Some clients may find themselves stumped, unable to generate such a letter. If the issue is one of motivation, better to not push the issue and instead use Socratic dialogue to explore the resistance—again, we don't want to set our clients up to *resist* extending compassion to themselves because we're pushing it on them. On the other hand, sometimes it will be the case that clients simply don't *know how* to address themselves in this compassionate way. In such cases, we can do a Compassionate Self exercise in session as described in the examples above, and then (with both therapist and client operating from the perspective of their compassionate selves), collaborate to write the compassionate letter—with the therapist offering support, Socratic questions, and suggestions about how the client might relate to his struggles (and the struggling version of himself) in compassionate, supportive ways.

SUMMARY

In CFT, Compassionate Self work isn't just a technique. It can serve as a framework for integrating all of the other aspects of the therapy, and as a perspective from which our clients can learn to courageously approach and work with their struggles and suffering. Once this perspective has been established, it can be used as a reference point for problem solving ("What would your compassionate self think or do in this situation?"), for sympathy and empathy ("How would your compassionate self feel when she sees you struggling like this?" "What would your compassionate self understand about why you are feeling and behaving this way?"), and for motivating therapeutic work. Quite frequently, in developing a plan for home practice, I'll ask clients, "What would your compassionate self want to make sure you do over the next week?"

As we'll see in coming chapters, establishing the perspective of the compassionate self also sets the stage for important work occurring within the therapy session, such as compassionate chair work and the Multiple Selves exercise. Ultimately, a primary goal of CFT is the strengthening of this compassionate version of the self and the neural architecture that underlies it, so that these compassionate ways of being and relating to self and others become woven into the fabric of our clients' day-to-day lives.

CHAPTER 10

Compassionate Thinking and Reasoning

In its approach to thought work, CFT incorporates components of both mindfulness and more traditional cognitive therapies. Consistent with mindfulness-based approaches, CFT assists clients in developing an awareness and nonjudgmental acceptance of their unhelpful and challenging thoughts as mental events, refraining from clinging to these thoughts, arguing with them, or attempting to push them out of awareness. However, recognizing the power of thoughts both as implicit inputs to the emotional brain and as organizers of motivation and behavior, CFT shares ground with many cognitive therapy models in emphasizing the purposeful cultivation of helpful thinking patterns. Thought work in CFT is defined by an emphasis on compassionate thinking—thinking that is focused on understanding, bringing balance to the emotions, encouraging the self in facing difficult situations, and helping to develop compassionate strengths. As we saw in the letter-writing exercise in the previous chapter, compassionate thinking is warm, validating, flexible, and focused on facilitating helpful action.

Thought work in CFT is not seen as an isolated set of practices. Rather, it is a natural part of the continued development and elaboration of the compassionate self. *How would this kind, wise, confident, compassionate version of you think about this situation? How would you understand this experience from that deeply compassionate perspective? What would be helpful in working with this situation?* It's not just about generating compassionate thoughts—it's about learning to shift more fully into this compassionate perspective.

As we explore compassionate thinking with clients, we can remind them that different emotions and social mentalities organize our mental and bodily experience in very different ways, producing very different, interrelated patterns of attention, thinking, imagery, felt experience, motivation, and behavior—with compassion organizing the mind in ways that are particularly useful in confronting and working with suffering.

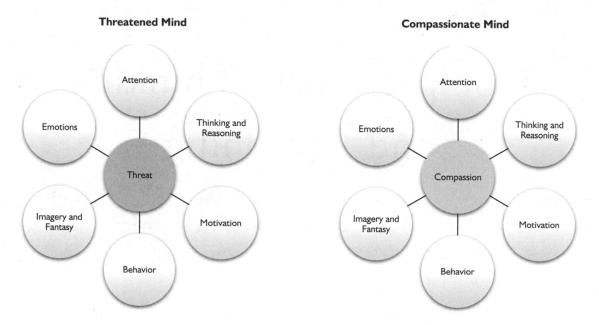

Figure 9.2: How threat and compassion organize our experience. (From Gilbert, *The Compassionate Mind* [2009], reprinted with permission from Little, Brown Book Group.)

Before doing compassionate thought work, it can be useful to have clients engage in a brief Compassionate Self exercise, to have them shift into the perspective of the compassionate self before going forward. In this way, we're linking the thought work to the overall story arc of therapy—the cultivation and reinforcement of this adaptive, compassionate version of the self.

WORKING WITH THREAT-FOCUSED THOUGHTS

Much of our clients' psychological suffering can be triggered and maintained through patterns of thinking, and it's well established that negative thought patterns regarding oneself, the world, and other people can play a central role in psychological distress (Beck, 1976). We've already introduced mindfulness, which plays an important role in compassionate thought work. Mindfulness practices help clients keep from becoming fused with such thoughts, as they become more adept at noticing the arising of unhelpful thoughts, refraining from judging them, and learning to redirect their attention rather than getting caught up in rumination.

As we've seen in some of the clinical vignettes, when clients have well-entrenched patterns of unhelpful thoughts, the CFT therapist will sometimes help them recognize these thoughts as products of how different threat emotions and learned patterns of responding organize the mind. This can be done using language like "the anxious self," "Depressed *(client name)*," or "the self-critic." "So,

Anxious Jenny is very good at listing off all of the ways this situation could go horribly wrong?" Or, "It sounds like your self-critic has a lot to say today."

Using such language helps clients step back from these thoughts or critical messages and relate to them in a nonblaming way. It also helps anchor these experiences to themes of compassionate understanding that are woven through the therapy—understanding these thoughts as natural products of how powerful threat emotions organize the mind as they attempt to protect us, or as habits that were learned via social shaping. We don't hate the anxious or angry self—we want to reassure and help her. Understanding such thoughts in this way can help take the sting out of them, and provides a structure for working with them compassionately. Let's consider what this might look like:

Therapist: Jenny, you've been able to keep up with your mindfulness exercises and have been practicing really consistently. Have you noticed anything new as you've been doing that?

Jenny: It took a few weeks to remember to do it consistently, but I'm doing better. I feel like I'm getting a lot better at noticing all the thoughts that come up throughout the day—especially the ones that get in the way of me doing things.

Therapist: That sounds great. Could you tell me more about what you've noticed?

Jenny: Well, I've noticed that before I do anything, I spend a lot of time thinking about all the things that could go wrong, particularly when it involves doing stuff with other people. I'm all the time having thoughts like, *This is going to be terrible,* or *I can't do this,* or *They aren't going to like me,* or *I'll look like an idiot.* That sort of thing.

Therapist: So it sounds like Anxious Jenny has a lot to say.

Jenny: (*Smiles.*) She sure does! Anxious Jenny is working very hard.

Therapist: She's working very hard to try and protect you, isn't she? She's been burned before, and she's working very hard to make sure you don't get hurt like that again. Can we understand her perspective? Given your experience, does it make sense that she might be really vigilant?

Jenny: (*Pauses thoughtfully.*) It does. It does make sense.

Therapist: The tricky bit is that Anxious Jenny has a perspective that is very limited—she sees only the danger, and sometimes sees danger when it really isn't there. Does that sound right to you?

Jenny: It does. I get worked up about all sorts of things. I get anxious about stuff I *know* isn't a big deal. Stuff that doesn't even matter. And I worry about it anyway.

Therapist: Have you seen those life-size cardboard cutouts of movie characters?

Jenny: Yeah. A girl down the hall from me has some of those in her room.

Therapist: From the front, they can look pretty real—they're life-sized, and have lots of detail. From a distance, you might even think it's a real person.

Jenny: Yeah. She's got Justin Bieber!

Therapist: Justin Bieber? (*Smiles.*)

Jenny: For real. She's got Justin Bieber. I know, right?

Therapist: (*Chuckles.*) That's actually a good lead-in to what I was getting at. If we think about Anxious Jenny—this version of you that is completely organized around fear and anxiety—it's like she's looking at a really scary cardboard cutout right from the front, so it looks like a real threat. So there's this cutout of someone laughing at you, or a teacher who's going to criticize you...or Justin Bieber. And this threat is right there, and from the front it looks really real. So she sees this, and gets really scared, and we can understand why.

Jenny: (*Nods.*)

Therapist: But imagine that Compassionate Jenny shows up, and she sees how scared Anxious Jenny is getting. Compassionate Jenny is kind, and wise, and courageous—courageous enough to walk around the room and look closely, seeing the situation from all angles. What would Compassionate Jenny see? What would she understand?

Jenny: She'd see that it wasn't real. She'd see that this scary person isn't really there, that it isn't really dangerous. It's just cardboard.

Therapist: Would she understand why Anxious Jenny was so worked up? That from her side, given her experience, it looks really scary?

Jenny: Yeah, she would.

Therapist: Anxious Jenny is there, reeling off all these scary thoughts: *Can't you see it's terrible? They're going to attack us! We can't handle this!* What does Compassionate Jenny think of this?

Jenny: Compassionate Jenny wouldn't think too much about it. She knows that Anxious Jenny is just freaking out because she's scared.

Therapist: That's it! *That's* the wisdom of compassion! So this compassionate version of you can see the thoughts, and can understand where they come from, but can keep from buying into them. If Compassionate Jenny wanted to help Anxious

Jenny feel safe, what might she do? If this kind, compassionate, wise version of you were there, what would she say—what would she want Anxious Jenny to understand? How would you reassure her? Would you tell her to stop being so stupid? (*Smiles.*)

Jenny: (*Smiles.*) No. (*Pauses.*) I'd tell her that it's okay, that these scary people aren't real, that they only look that way because of where she's standing. I might give her a hug and then take her by the hand and lead her to the side of the room, so that she could see they're only cardboard.

Therapist: That's beautiful, Jenny. How do you think Anxious Jenny would feel if you were to do that?

Jenny: I think it would help.

Therapist: It occurs to me that you also wrote down a lot of really encouraging, compassionate thoughts in the compassionate letter we reviewed last session. Have you reread that at all this week?

Jenny: I have, and it really helped. I really liked writing the letter, and reading it helped me calm down when those anxious thoughts were really getting ramped up. I read it before my small group met to work on the project in my communications class that I told you about, and it went pretty well. I even spoke up once or twice.

Therapist: Jenny, that's fantastic! Nice work. I'm proud of you.

Jenny: I'm proud of me, too.

In the vignette above, we see several aspects of compassionate thought work at play. First, we see a notable absence of *Let's replace that bad thought with this good one*. The therapist begins by anchoring the work in Jenny's ongoing mindfulness practice, and discussing the thoughts from a mindful perspective—looking at them from the perspective of a curious, nonjudgmental observer. The therapist then introduces the language of "Anxious Jenny," contextualizing the worrisome thoughts as products of how anxiety organizes the mind—setting up this anxious version of the self not as an enemy to be criticized or hated, but as a sympathetic figure who is trying to help, but whose limited perspective (characterized via the cardboard cutout metaphor) often prevents her efforts from being truly helpful. The therapist then prompts Jenny to shift into the perspective of the compassionate self, preparing her to connect with more reassuring, helpful ways of thinking that aren't focused on disputing or arguing with the anxious thoughts, but on soothing the anxious part of her, and broadening her perspective.

The architecture in place, this discussion could then progress to working with thoughts around a specific challenging situation, in which Jenny (from the perspective of her compassionate self) could be prompted to offer encouragement, understanding, guidance, and problem solving around how to meet and work with the situation. In the vignette, this took the form of bridging from the current discussion to the compassionate letter we introduced in the previous chapter, which Jenny had used to help herself work with a situation she'd been dreading. As the vignette closes, we see how this success was able to fuel positive self-to-self relating in Jenny, as she spontaneously relates to herself with warmth ("I'm proud of me, too") rather than criticism.

We don't have to use the "emotional self" language if we're not comfortable with it. Instead, we can simply label such thoughts as products of the threat emotions that prompt them: "Sounds like you were having lots of anxious thoughts." After clients are fairly well acquainted with the Compassionate Self exercise, we can prompt them to shift into this perspective: "What would your wise, kind, confident, compassionate self think about this situation? What might she advise us to do?" Again, the idea isn't to dispute threat-driven or self-critical thoughts. It's to acknowledge them and facilitate a shift to a gradually deepening compassionate perspective. Let's explore this a bit further.

COMPASSIONATE THINKING AND REASONING

A primary attribute of the compassionate self is the capacity to think and reason in compassionate ways, and to develop these ways of thinking as habitual patterns of mind. Compassionate ways of thinking and reasoning are anchored in two fundamental objectives: *understanding* suffering, and *helping* to address, alleviate, or prevent it. As we help clients understand what compassionate thinking looks like, it can be useful to contrast compassionate ways of thinking with threat-based ways of thinking:

Threat-Based Thinking	Compassionate Thinking
Narrowly focused on the threat	Broad, considers many factors in understanding the situation
Focused on judging and labeling	Focused on understanding
Inflexible and ruminative	Flexible, problem-solves
Activates the threat system	Activates the safeness system; helps us to feel comfortable and at peace
Directs hostility, fear, or disgust toward others and ourselves	Directs kindness toward others and ourselves
Judgmental and critical	Noncritical, empathic, and encouraging
Focused on avoiding, dominating, or punishing	Focused on helping ourselves and others, finding solutions that benefit everyone and harm no one

In exploring this contrast with clients, it's important not to set things up in a *threat-based thinking is bad, compassionate thinking is good* sort of way. Familiar with the three circles, clients can understand why the threat system organizes thinking in such narrow, constraining ways—it's designed to work that way in the face of immediate physical threats. However, they can come to recognize that in the absence of such threats, there are likely more helpful (or as ACT therapists might say, more *workable*) ways to understand and approach things. In contrast to threat-based thinking, compassionate thinking often takes the form of asking questions (Gilbert, 2009a):

- *How does it make sense that I (or he or she) would feel (or think or behave) in this way?*

- *What is triggering my threat system here? What feelings are coming up in me?*

- *How would I understand this situation from the perspective of my kind, wise, confident, compassionate self?*

- *What might help me feel safe so that I can work with this situation more skillfully?*

- *What might be helpful as I tackle this challenge? What resources might help me work with this situation?*

- *How might he or she be making sense of this situation?*

- *What would my compassionate self think (or feel or say or do) in this situation? What would he or she encourage me to do?*

Mentalizing

In helping clients emphasize compassionate understanding in their thinking, it can sometimes be helpful to introduce the concept of *mentalizing* (Fonagy & Luyten, 2009; Liotti & Gilbert, 2011). Mentalizing involves examining actions and emotions by considering what is going on in the mind of the person who is behaving or feeling that way. What are the desires, feelings, needs, beliefs, and motivations reflected in these behaviors? Such consideration puts even frustrating or extreme behaviors into a context that opens the door for compassion—such as the recognition that the patient who self-harms does so in a desperate attempt to reduce emotional pain.

Linking Thought Work to Compassionate Understanding

As we're helping clients develop compassionate patterns of thinking and behaving, it can be useful to relate what we're doing to how things work in the brain—linking the thought work back to the compassionate understanding we've been working to develop. We can prompt clients to consider that everything they do, say, think, or feel is reflected in the activation of corresponding patterns of cells in the brain, and that as these patterns are activated again and again over time, the pattern is strengthened and becomes easier to activate. As neuroscientists say, "Cells that fire together, wire together."

Over time, these connected patterns of cells become so well primed that they can be activated easily—often without the client's awareness—which is why longstanding habits like self-critical thinking can be so hard to break. The brain patterns underlying them have been strengthened over thousands and thousands of trials. This realization can assist the cultivation of self-compassion in two ways: First, it can help clients ease up on self-blame around their failures, as they understand that changing longstanding habits is *difficult*, not because they are weak or lack willpower, but because of how their brains work. It also helps clarify the way to change—establishing and strengthening *new* patterns in the brain by repeatedly shifting into the perspective of the compassionate self and practicing compassionate thinking, attention, and behavior consistently over time. Let's take a look at how this might play out in a therapy session, using a "path in the woods" metaphor:

Therapist: So we've chatted a bit about compassionate thinking and how it organizes us in different ways than anxious, threat-based thinking.

Jenny: (*Frowns and looks down.*)

Therapist: Jenny, it looks like something just happened there for you. Could you tell me a bit about how you're feeling right now?

Jenny: I'm just frustrated. We've been talking about this, but these anxious, critical thoughts just keep coming. I try to think more positively but it's like the anxious thoughts are always there, every time I want to do anything. It's really discouraging.

Therapist: (*Leans in; remains silent.*)

Jenny: It's like the thoughts are automatic. They just come up, and I get stuck in them.

Therapist: It makes sense to me that it would feel discouraging—some psychologists even call such thoughts *automatic thoughts.* I'd bet those anxious thoughts kind of *are* automatic, at this point. Like, *in your brain,* automatic. Would it be all right if we talked for a bit about why they're like that?

Jenny: (*considering*) Sure.

Therapist: Imagine that there are woods behind my house, and every day for ten years, I walked in these woods—walking a way that seemed to make sense, the same way every time. Over time, what would happen in the woods, on the ground where I was walking?

Jenny: You'd wear in a path.

Therapist: I sure would. And when it rains, where would the water run?

Jenny: Down the path.

Therapist: Exactly. Why would it do that? Would the water *choose* to run down the path?

Jenny: No, it just would. It's easier for it to run down the path than anywhere else. Like a path of least resistance.

Therapist: Exactly. So what if I suggested our brains are like this forest? Every time we think or behave in a certain way, we're walking a path—activating a pattern of cells in the brain—and the more we think or behave that way, the more "worn in" the pattern becomes. The pattern becomes strengthened over time, making it so that it lights up more and more easily. Eventually, it can light up almost automatically—you think about a social situation, and that self-critical pattern just lights right up, like a path of least resistance in your brain. So it seems like the self-critical thoughts just show up automatically. It's not our fault. It's just how our brains work.

Jenny: (*after a thoughtful pause*) That makes sense. It sucks, though.

Therapist: (*Smiles.*) It certainly can suck! But it also gives us a clue about how to create change in our lives. Let's say I was getting tired of that path—perhaps because every time it rained, the rain ran down the path into my backyard, flooding it. How would I change this, assuming I didn't want to give up going for walks?

Jenny: You'd need to stop walking on the path. You'd need to find some other way to walk.

Therapist: Exactly. I'd need to figure out a path that worked better, and walk that way instead. I'd probably forget sometimes, and walk the old path out of habit. So my job would be to try and notice when that happens, and then change over to the new path that goes where I want it to go. Can you see how this applies to those self-critical and anxious thoughts?

Jenny: I think so. They're the really worn-in path.

Therapist: Yeah. That path is really easy to walk—automatic, almost—because it's been worn in for years. The compassionate thinking path takes more effort.

Jenny: It sure does.

Therapist: But if I work really hard to notice where I'm walking, and remember to try and walk the new path most of the time, it becomes easier. Over time, the forest starts to look different, doesn't it? Eventually, the old path erodes, and the new one slowly wears in. But the forest doesn't change overnight just because I decide I don't like the old path, does it? It takes consistent effort over time.

Jenny: That makes sense.

Therapist: Over time, if I make effort to consistently walk a new way, the new path *will* wear in—it's just how it works. So if I find myself accidentally walking the old path out of habit, what's the best thing to do? I mean, besides getting really mad at myself? (*Smiles and speaks warmly.*) You know I'm joking, right?

Jenny: (*Smiles.*) I get it. No, you'd want to just stop, and go over to the new path.

Therapist: Exactly. This is the reason for the approach we're taking with these anxious and critical thoughts. We want to increase mindfulness so that you notice when they come up—when you are walking the old path out of habit…

Jenny: (*Nods.*)

Therapist: …so you can shift over and walk that new path, over and over, to strengthen brain patterns associated with compassionate ways of thinking. So that compassion becomes the path of least resistance. We're not arguing with the anxious or critical thoughts. We're just noticing that old pattern, letting go of it, and shifting over to strengthen the new one. What do you think about that?

Jenny: Sounds good. It makes sense, anyway.

Therapist: Let's think about a situation in which those old, anxious patterns show up. This group project you have in your communications class is ongoing, correct?

Jenny: (*Cringes a bit.*) Yeah…we're meeting twice per week for the next two weeks.

Therapists: Sounds like although you did well at the last meeting, you're still not really looking forward to it. Do those anxious thought patterns come up before the meetings?

Jenny: (*still cringing a bit*) Yeah. I still get really anxious about it.

Therapist: What are some thoughts that come up?

Jenny: That it's going to be awful. That I'll look stupid. Just running through all the different ways it could go wrong in my head.

Therapist: So that's the old path. Let's work on what the new path would look like. Let's imagine that we've mindfully noticed those thoughts and let them go. Now, let's shift into the kind, wise, confident perspective of your compassionate self. We'll start with thirty seconds or so of soothing rhythm breathing…slowing down the body…slowing down the mind.

Jenny: (*Shifts in her seat a bit, closes her eyes, and slows her breathing.*)

Therapist: (*Waits thirty seconds to one minute.*) Now imagining being filled with kindness, wisdom, and courage as you shift into the perspective of the compassionate self. This is the part of you that wrote that compassionate letter—the part that sees how hard it is for you to do things like that group activity, and wants to encourage you and help you feel safe. Give me a little nod when you feel like you've been able to connect a bit with that compassionate perspective.

Jenny: (*Waits a few moments; nods.*)

Therapist: What would this compassionate version of you think, as you prepare to go to the group meeting? How would you extend kindness and encouragement to the part of you that's so anxious? As this compassionate self, what would you say?

Jenny: I'd say that this is really hard, but I've done this before, and I can do it again.

Therapist: What are some other things you'd say from this compassionate perspective?

Jenny: That I'm not alone. There are other people in the group who seem to like me, people I like being around. I'd tell myself that I'm stronger than I think. I'd remind myself that when I spoke up last week, nothing terrible happened. That I can do this.

Therapist: How does it feel to hear yourself saying these things?

Jenny: It feels good. Kind of fake, but good.

Therapist: Does it make sense that the new path would take a while before it felt as easy and natural as the old one?

Jenny: It does. I need to remind myself of that.

Therapist: How would your compassionate self remind you of that, when the compassionate thoughts feel a little fake?

Jenny: She'd say that it's because it's a whole new way of thinking. Of course it wouldn't feel as natural as the old path.

Therapist: Exactly! It sounds like your compassionate self is figuring some things out.

Jenny: (*Smiles.*) She's trying.

At first, clients can become demoralized when the voices of the critical or threat-based selves seem so much more powerful than the new, compassionate ways of thinking. The idea is to provide clients with a context for understanding why this is so. This can even provide the basis for compassionate sympathy ("It's *really difficult* for me that these anxious thoughts come up so automatically"). Given such a context, clients can see the power of shifting into a compassionate perspective again and again—both for developing compassionate ways of thinking in the present moment, and for strengthening the underlying neural architecture that can make these ways of thinking more likely to arise in the future.

SUMMARY

In this chapter, we've explored ways to help clients apply compassion to their thinking and reasoning. The idea is to *cultivate* compassionate ways of thinking so that over time, such compassionate thoughts will spontaneously arise more and more often. We'll continue to explore how clients can relate compassionately to their struggles in the next chapter, which focuses on compassionate imagery.

CHAPTER 11

Using Compassionate Imagery

In order for compassion to become real for our patients, it needs to be felt at an experiential level. Increasingly, we're discovering that imagery is an effective method for facilitating experiential work with clients (Hackmann, Bennett-Levy, & Holmes, 2011). In the Compassionate Self exercise, we used imagery to help clients shift perspectives and practice compassionate ways of working with difficult situations. In this chapter, we'll explore ways to use imagery to help clients manage distress and balance their emotions.

AN ORIENTATION TO IMAGERY

Since CFT makes frequent use of imagery, let's consider how to effectively introduce clients to imaginal work. Often, when clients hear "imagine" or "imagery," they think it means, "creating vivid pictures in the mind." This idea can be an obstacle; while some clients will be able to effortlessly create such vivid mental pictures, many others will struggle to do so. The key to overcoming this block is to help clients realize that imaginal work isn't about making vivid pictures—it's about creating *mental experiences* (Gilbert, 2010). Let's explore a method for introducing this practice to clients, developed by Paul Gilbert:

Therapist: Jenny, as I mentioned in our last session, today we'll introduce some imagery exercises to help you bring up feelings of safeness to balance your emotions when your threat system is really going. I thought it would be useful to talk a bit about how to use imagery before we get started. How does that sound?

Jenny: Sounds good.

Therapist: Besides the Compassionate Self exercises we've been doing, have you ever used mental imagery? Perhaps closed your eyes and tried to imagine something?

Jenny: Last year I took a yoga class, and sometimes the teacher would have us imagine things—like being somewhere like a beach, or being a tree, with life flowing into us from the ground beneath us. That sort of thing.

Therapist: Cool—how did you like it?

Jenny: I liked it, but sometimes it worked better than others. I should take another yoga class, because it was really relaxing.

Therapist: Sounds like a good idea—yoga is fantastic, and it fits really well with what we're doing. It's good that you've had some experience with imagery. Sometimes people struggle with imagery work because they think it involves creating really vivid pictures in their minds. Some people can do that, but other people really struggle with it.

Jenny: I think I know what you mean. I'm not really good at that.

Therapist: (*Smiles.*) Me neither—I'm not good at "seeing things" in my mind. But here's the thing: what we're after isn't about creating vivid mental pictures, but creating mental *experiences*. Could we do a brief exercise to demonstrate what I mean?

Jenny: (*nodding interestedly*) Sure.

Therapist: Great. Let's start by shifting into that comfortable, upright position we've been using for our exercises…feet flat on the floor, back straight, eyes closed. Let's do thirty seconds or so of soothing rhythm breathing, slowing down the breath, and focusing on the sense of slowing. Slowing down the body, slowing down the mind.

Jenny: (*Closes her eyes and breathes slowly.*)

Therapist: (*Waits thirty seconds.*) I'm going to briefly prompt you to bring a few different situations to mind. As I do, just allow yourself to imagine the situation I'm describing.

Jenny: (*Nods.*)

Therapist: First, bring to mind how you got here this morning—imagining the route you took when you were driving, riding, or walking here. (*Waits thirty seconds.*)
Now, bring to mind your favorite dessert. (*Waits thirty seconds.*)
Now, bring to mind the last vacation you took, or if one doesn't come to mind, a vacation you'd like to take. (*Waits thirty seconds.*)
When you're ready, gently allow your eyes to open.

Jenny: (*Waits a moment, then slowly opens her eyes, shifts, and smiles a bit.*) Mmmm.

Therapist: Were you able to get a mental sense of all the things I mentioned?

Jenny: I was. It was nice. I didn't want to stop.

Therapist: Nice! It sounds like you were able to get a mental experience of those things—the route you took, the dessert, the vacation—and like some emotions came up as well?

Jenny: Yeah. It felt nice to imagine myself walking along the beach like I did last summer.

Therapist: Excellent! That's mental imagery. It's about bringing an experience to mind, so we've got a good sense of it. Sounds like you've already noticed one of the benefits of imagery—that our old, emotional brains respond to imagery by producing different emotions, like that pleasant feeling you got from imagining yourself back on the beach.

Exercises like this can give clients a sense of what imaginal work is like, and can give them confidence that they *can do it*. We want to create a mental context in which the client is able to focus on the imagery exercises, minimizing distractions caused by self-evaluative thoughts of whether or not they are doing it correctly.

CREATING A SAFE PLACE

One goal of CFT is to help clients learn to work with the three circles to balance their emotions, particularly when they notice themselves shifting into threat mode when a more balanced approach would be helpful, or when they observe they've been fueling feelings of threat through rumination or threatening imagery. Imagery can be a powerful tool for getting the safeness system online, and one way to do this involves *safe place imagery*. (Sometimes it's referred to as "soothing space" imagery for clients who don't like the term "safe place.")

In this practice, clients imagine themselves in a setting that creates feelings of safeness, calm, peacefulness, and belonging. Many therapists will have used imagery in this way. As in other such practices, we have clients focus on the various sensory details of this soothing place. In CFT, we add a dimension to the typical safe place practice by introducing an affiliative component to the imagery. This is done via specific instructions such as, "If there are other beings in this place, imagine that they welcome you, value you, and are happy to see you. In fact, imagine that this place itself values your presence—as if you complete it, and it is happy that you are here." Let's consider how this practice might be introduced and facilitated in a therapy session:

Therapist: Jenny, now that we've explored what we mean by imagery, I'd like to introduce a specific practice designed to help get your safeness system working for you—to help you connect with feelings of calm and peacefulness when you notice your threat system is really going. How does that sound?

Jenny: Why not?

Therapist: Great. In a way, you've got a head start on this one. A few moments ago, you said you enjoyed imagining yourself back on that beach from your vacation—so much that you didn't want to stop. What did you like about that?

Jenny: I love the beach. I love everything about it—the smell, the feeling of sand under my feet, watching and listening to the waves, the sun. I like to walk on the beach for hours. It's so peaceful.

Therapist: That does sound wonderful.

Jenny: It is. It's my favorite thing to do.

Therapist: That's a perfect segue into our next exercise. This is called the "Safe Place exercise." We're going to imagine being in a place that helps you feel safe, comfortable, peaceful, and soothed. The idea is to create a mental experience of this place and the feelings that go along with being there. Sometimes it takes time to figure out what sort of place to use—but it sounds like you may already have a good place in mind. Do you think the beach would work for this exercise?

Jenny: The beach would be perfect.

Therapist: Great. So let's go ahead and get started. We'll begin with some soothing rhythm breathing, to slow down our bodies and minds. Then I'll prompt you to imagine the beach. I'll ask you to describe what it's like on the beach—like it's really happening—so we can create a deep mental experience. Then I'll be quiet and leave you to the imagery for about five minutes. If your mind begins to wander or you get distracted by thoughts, that's no problem—just manage it like we do with mindful breathing, by noticing you've become distracted and gently bringing yourself back to the beach. Ready to go?

Jenny: Let's do it.

Therapist: Sitting in an upright, comfortable position, the eyes gently closing.

Jenny: (Shifts a bit, closes her eyes, and slows her breathing.)

Therapist: Allowing the breath to take on a slow, comfortable rhythm. Focusing on the sense of slowing. (Waits five seconds.) Slowing down the body, slowing down the mind. (Waits thirty seconds to one minute.)

Jenny: (*Breathes slowly.*)

Therapist: Now, imagining yourself on that beautiful beach. Opening yourself to the soothing experiences there. When you've got the image, describe what you're doing and experiencing. Imagine yourself, there on the beach, with all the sounds, smells, and images you love.

Jenny: (*Pauses for five to ten seconds.*) I'm walking down the beach, and I can feel the sand squishing underneath my feet. I like the way it feels on my toes.

Therapist: That's perfect, Jenny. What else are you noticing? What does it feel like?

Jenny: It's warm and peaceful. The sun is shining on my face, and the wind is gently blowing through my hair. I can hear the waves and the sound of the seagulls. (*Pauses for a few seconds.*) I can smell the ocean.

Therapist: Allow yourself to be filled with feelings of safeness, peacefulness, and joy at being in this wonderful place. Maybe allow a gentle smile to cross your face, as you enjoy being here.

Jenny: (*Smiles.*) Mmmm.

Therapist: Imagine that the seagulls you hear are happy that you are here with them. Likewise, if there are any people or other beings in this place, imagine that they welcome you. They value you; they're happy you are here. (*Waits twenty to thirty seconds.*) Imagine that this place itself welcomes you. It values your presence, almost as if you complete it. It is happy you are here.

Jenny: (*Breathes peacefully.*)

Therapist: Let's take some time to imagine being in this place, filled with feelings of safeness, peace, and contentment. Imagine all the sensations that come with being in this place.

Jenny: (*Continues to breathe peacefully.*)

Therapist: (*Waits five minutes.*) When you're ready, gently shift your attention to the slow sensation of the breath, and allow your eyes to open.

Jenny: (*Waits twenty seconds or so, then gradually opens her eyes. Smiles.*)

Therapist: How was that?

Jenny: That was really nice. Really peaceful.

Therapist: Did you get a mental experience of this place, and the feelings that go with it?

Jenny: I did. It felt completely comfortable and peaceful.

Therapist: Were you able to imagine that the place and the creatures in it welcomed you?

Jenny: Yeah. It was kind of like one of those children's movies where the animals do funny things. I imagined seagulls flying along beside me, or looking up at me from where they were standing on the beach. It was fun to imagine that.

Therapist: Were there any other people on the beach?

Jenny: Not at first, but after you said that, I imagined a few lying on blankets, higher up on the beach, just lying in the sun and enjoying themselves. It was really peaceful.

Therapist: That's exactly how it's supposed to work. Would you be up for practicing this two or three times over the next week? The idea is to really get used to visiting this place in your mind, activating those parts of your brain that help you feel safe, content, and peaceful.

Jenny: I'd love to.

Therapist: Fantastic. It helps to practice initially when you're already feeling pretty calm, to get good at bringing up the imagery. Once that feels manageable, try using the imagery when your threat system is going and you want to balance things a bit by connecting with feelings of safeness. Does that make sense?

Jenny: Sure does.

Things went really smoothly in the vignette above, as Jenny had identified a likely "safe place" in the previous imagery exercise (an occasional advantage of using a "favorite vacation" prompt in introducing imagery), and she was very good at connecting with the image of the beach. She was also able to quickly move into the imagery and describe it in therapy. It won't always go this smoothly. Some clients won't have a place from memory, so we'll work with them to consider what such a place might be like. Sometimes I start by briefly mentioning a few of my "places"—a walk on a northwestern beach, sitting in a pine forest, even having a pint in a favorite English pub, surrounded by smiling faces and 300-year-old oak, my nose filled with the soothing aroma of a steak-and-ale pie at my table.

For clients who don't transition as easily into imagery as Jenny did, we can provide sensory anchors, using our knowledge of what might be soothing to the client: "Imagine feeling the sun on your face, the smells and sounds of the ocean..." We want to say just enough to facilitate the imagery and feelings of peacefulness and soothing that accompany it, and then gently recede, leaving the client with the imagery. Some clients will need to experiment with a few different "places" before they find one to settle on. Finally, the body work is important—setting the stage with soothing rhythm breathing and prompting a gentle smile can help clients more fully enter into the experience, adding yet another soothing implicit input into the emotional brain.

I really can't say enough about this practice. While no practice works for everyone, I've seen men in prison for violent crimes, who had spent decades struggling with anger, use this practice to soothe themselves when they noticed their anger arising. These men used the imagery to balance their emotions and reengage to deal effectively and assertively with situations that previously would have led to verbal or physical aggression.

THE IDEAL COMPASSIONATE IMAGE PRACTICE

British psychologist Deborah Lee developed a practice called the "perfect nurturer" or "ideal compassionate image" practice (Lee, 2005). This practice was designed to help self-critical clients learn to self-soothe and develop feelings of being accepted and cared for, by imagining an ideal figure who understands them, has compassion for them, and extends kindness, support, and encouragement. In this practice, the therapist works collaboratively with the client to identify characteristics that his ideal nurturer would have—perhaps acceptance, kind concern, and affection—and a deep understanding of what the client is going through. In contrast to experiences that clients may have had with people in their lives, it is emphasized that this nurturer is supportive, nurturing, and encouraging, and is never judgmental, critical, or shaming of the client. The therapist will also help the client develop an image of what this nurturer looks like and sounds like, and how they might interact. As with the safe place exercise above, the idea is to help the client create as vivid a mental experience as possible. If the client has someone in his life who embodies these qualities (or someone he imagines embodies the qualities, such as a spiritual figure), he can use this in his visualization.

Some clients may initially struggle with the exercise, protesting that they've never had anyone like this in their lives. If this happens, we can emphasize that actually, none of us has someone like this—someone who is perfectly understanding, supportive, and nonjudgmental. The idea is to imagine what a being like this would be like, and to imagine that person extending kindness, understanding, and acceptance to us. Let's consider what this practice might look like in a therapy session:

Therapist: Jenny, I'm glad you like the safe place imagery we introduced last session. How did that go over the past week?

Jenny: Really well. It's my favorite piece of homework so far. I did it three times over the past week.

Therapist: Excellent! Repeated practice really is the key. As you've done the practice, have you noticed anything that helps or gets in the way?

Jenny: Well, it helps if I have a quiet place to practice. My dorm can be pretty noisy in the evening, which is when I have time. I ended up putting on headphones to try and make things a little more quiet, and then it occurred to me that I could probably download an mp3 of the sound of the ocean. So I went online and did that, and now when I do the exercise, I listen to the ocean sounds, which makes it seem even more real.

Therapist: Wow! I should have you teaching this stuff! That's a perfect example of compassionate thinking, Jenny—noticing a problem or obstacle, and then instead of getting caught up in it and giving up, asking *What might be helpful in working with this?* When you did that, not only were you able to address the obstacle, but you found a way to make the practice work even better—a way that hadn't even occurred to your therapist.

Jenny: That is pretty cool.

Therapist: It sure is. I'm gonna steal that ocean-mp3 idea, by the way. That's pure gold!

Jenny: (*Laughs.*) Feel free.

Therapist: I thought we might try out another imagery exercise. Does that sound all right?

Jenny: Sure.

Therapist: As we've discussed, self-criticism has been a struggle for you, and you've had experiences of being criticized and picked on by others—really painful experiences.

Jenny: (*Gets a somewhat pained expression; looks down; speaks slowly.*) Yeah.

Therapist: I can tell those memories—those experiences in your mind—still bring a lot of hurt with them. We want to use imagery to help you have very different experiences—experiences of being cared about, accepted, and understood.

Jenny: (*Looks up at the therapist.*)

Therapist: We're going to imagine a perfect nurturer—someone who absolutely cares about you, accepts you, deeply understands you, and wishes the very best for you. Someone who would never judge or ridicule you. How does that sound?

Jenny: It's hard to imagine. I've never had anyone like that.

Therapist: None of us has, really. Real people can't support us perfectly in that way—and your compassionate image doesn't even have to be a person. It could be an animal, or some other type of being. I know people who have used an ancient tree, for example. The idea is to imagine a being that could help you feel safe, accepted, understood, and supported. Let's start by imagining the qualities your nurturer would have. What would this being be like? How would the being relate to you?

Jenny: Well, they'd be nice to me, and would never make me feel stupid. They'd accept me just as I am.

Therapist: That's great. So they'd be kind, and accepting. Anything else?

Jenny: They wouldn't judge or criticize me. They'd just like me.

Therapist: They wouldn't judge you. Maybe along with that, they would completely understand you, understand where you're coming from…really liking you and wanting to help and encourage you when you're struggling.

Jenny: Yeah, that sounds good.

Therapist: Let's start with those qualities: kindness, acceptance, understanding, and encouragement. Let's imagine what this kind being might be like—if it is human or nonhuman, if it has a gender, what it might look like, that sort of thing. What do you think your perfect compassionate image might be like?

Jenny: I don't know… (*Pauses, thinking.*)

Therapist: (*Waits in silence.*)

Jenny: I think it would be a woman. An older woman, who's gone through it and knows what it's like to grow up as a woman and go through all this.

Therapist: Someone who really understands, because she's been through it.

Jenny: Exactly. She could maybe see some of herself in me, and knows how to help me through it, because she's gone through it herself.

Therapist: What might she look like? Sound like? How would she act?

Jenny: She'd have gray hair, and a really kind smile. She'd have a gentle voice, and would laugh a lot. She'd have a good sense of humor.

Therapist: It sounds like she'd be a lot like your compassionate self—kind, wise, and confident. Able to help you handle whatever comes up.

Jenny: Exactly.

Therapist: I think we have a great start, here. Would you like to start the exercise now?

Jenny: Sure. (*Shifts into an upright posture, closes her eyes, and slows her breathing.*)

Therapist: Starting with a minute or so of soothing rhythm breathing… (*Waits twenty to thirty seconds.*) Slowing down the body, slowing down the mind… (*Waits twenty to thirty seconds.*)

Jenny:	(*Breathes quietly.*)
Therapist:	Bringing to mind the image of this kind, wise, confident woman who cares deeply about you, understands you, and is there to support you.
Jenny:	(*Face relaxes a bit; breathes quietly.*)
Therapist:	Imagining her with you, smiling kindly at you. Imagine that she likes you, and wants you to feel understood. Imagine her extending kindness and compassion to you, in whatever way would be most helpful and soothing. Imagine what she might do or say. Imagine being filled with her kindness, understanding, and acceptance.
Jenny:	(*Continues to breathe quietly.*)
Therapist:	(*Waits five minutes.*) If anxiety or other difficult emotions come up for you, imagine her there, understanding and supporting you. Imagine her supporting you as you struggle, believing in you. She understands how hard it can be, and how that isn't your fault. Imagine her extending kindness and support as you face these challenges.
Jenny:	(*Breathes quietly.*)
Therapist:	(*Waits five minutes.*) When you're ready, allow your eyes to gently open, bringing the feelings of being accepted, understood, and supported with you, back into the room.
Jenny:	(*Pauses a few moments, then slowly opens her eyes.*)
Therapist:	How was that?
Jenny:	I really liked it. It was really beautiful, actually.
Therapist:	Can you tell me about it?
Jenny:	I could see her, and she was there with me…and at some point I figured out that this was my future self. And she understood exactly what I'm going through, and… (*Begins crying softly.*)
Therapist:	(*Waits quietly with a kind smile, eyes tearing up a bit.*)
Jenny:	(*still crying*) …and she wanted me to be happy. And she knew that I am going to be okay. That I'm going to make it. (*Smiles softly.*)
Therapist:	(*Leans in, speaking gently.*) You *are* going to make it, Jenny.
Jenny:	(*Smiles.*) I'm starting to believe that.

In the example, we see how powerful this practice can be. There are certain elements demonstrated above that can deepen the experiential aspects of the practice. First, notice that before introducing the exercise, the therapist follows up on other imagery practices to see if there are obstacles to which they should attend. Jenny, like many clients, was able to problem-solve and deepen her practice in working with an obstacle—which the therapist warmly reinforces. Moving into the practice, the therapist speaks to a potential obstacle—that Jenny doesn't have anyone in her life like this—by generalizing it ("None of us really has someone like that"), and elaborating on the nurturer's qualities.

Before moving into the imagery itself, the therapist facilitates a collaborative exploration of qualities Jenny would like her nurturer to have—in terms of both the emotional qualities and orientation she will have toward Jenny, and the physical qualities that will facilitate the imagery. During the practice, the therapist prompts Jenny to first imagine the nurturer supporting her, and then how this might play out should anxiety or other difficulties arise for her. As always, the therapist checks in after the exercise, taking a cue from Jenny's ideal compassionate image about how to support Jenny.

Finally, you'll notice that the therapist is visibly moved upon hearing about Jenny's experience with the imagery. While this is not a planned part of CFT (that would be disingenuous), I included it because I became teary while writing the vignette and recalling such experiences in therapy. Of course, the therapist's emotionality should never play out in a way that intrudes upon or detracts from the therapy, shifting the focus from the client to the therapist. However, I've found it can be a powerful experience for clients to occasionally see that the therapist is genuinely moved by their work in therapy. It's important for the therapist to be a real human being with real feelings, and allowing that to show sometimes can create meaningful moments that deepen the therapy experience. It can also model courageousness and acceptance for clients who may struggle in allowing themselves to experience or express their own emotions.

As you might suspect, the exercise doesn't always go as smoothly as it did with Jenny. As with all of the practices, we don't want to force things if it becomes clear the practice isn't working for the client (although we don't want to give up at the first sign of resistance, either). For example, I had a client for whom this exercise consistently brought up deep pain associated with her experience of never having had anyone who seemed to offer her genuine caring—the act of trying to imagine someone being so kind to her activated her attachment system in very threatening ways. For this client, it was much more helpful to use the Compassionate Self exercise to extend compassion to herself—which didn't trigger the same powerful emotional memories—as well as working to develop real-life relationships that provided her with real-world experiences of acceptance and support.

OTHER IMAGERY EXERCISES

While I've focused on the safe place and ideal compassionate image practices, there are a number of other imagery exercises that are common to CFT. A recurrent theme in these practices is the *flow* of compassion—into the self from outside, from the self to the self (or aspects of the self, like pain), and from the self to others. In each of these practices, there is an emphasis on trying to create experiences of receiving or giving compassion, complete with motivational aspects (to extend or receive compassion), the felt experience of being filled with compassion or the warmth of extending it to others, imagery components (of being filled with compassion or it flowing out of the self to others), and sometimes repeated phrases (for example, *May you have happiness, peace, and ease*). There are a number of resources that detail examples of compassion-focused imagery practices (e.g. Germer, 2009; Kolts & Chodron, 2013). I'll briefly describe a few of these practices.

Compassion for Distress, Threat Feelings, and Pain

In this practice, the client shifts into the kind, wise, confident perspective of the compassionate self, and imagines sending compassion out to parts of the self that are experiencing distress, pain, or threat feelings like anxiety, anger, or sadness (Gilbert, 2009a; Kolts 2012; Gilbert & Choden, 2013). The client imagines feelings of compassion and warmth arising within, and imagines extending that compassion out to the pain or discomfort. It can involve a visualization in which the compassion is pictured as a warm-colored light (the client picks the color) that surrounds, soothes, and kindly envelopes the aspect of the self that is in pain.

Compassion for the Self

In this practice, which is similar to many Buddhist practices, the client imagines being filled with compassion from an external or internal source. One variation involves imagining compassion flowing in from the universe or an external source (such as one's compassionate image) in the form of colored light coming in through the heart or the crown of the head, filling the body, and creating feelings of safeness and ease as it flows in and fills the person.

Another variation of this practice (which we touched on earlier) involves the client shifting into the perspective of the compassionate self and imagining that she is extending compassion to a struggling version of the self. In this practice, after a brief compassionate self induction, the vulnerable version of the self is imagined (anxious self, self-critical self, angry self, and so on), perhaps in a difficult situation. From the perspective of the compassionate self, the client imagines extending warm, compassionate feelings toward the struggling self—moved by how much this vulnerable self is struggling. Perhaps she connects with the feelings and good intentions behind the struggle. (In the case of Jenny, for example, the anxiety may be a reflection of how much she really wants to connect with others). She then imagines extending compassion to this vulnerable version of the self in whatever way would be most helpful, soothing, and reassuring. This practice can also involve repeating phrases out loud or imaginally, in a warm tone of voice, tailored to what would be most helpful. Common phrases used in compassion and loving-kindness meditation (in which compassion is the wish that the being be free from suffering, and loving-kindness is the wish that she has happiness) include things like:

May you be free from suffering, (name).

May you be happy, (name).

May you flourish, (name).

May you find peace, (name). (Gilbert & Choden, 2013, 247)

Variations of these phrases can be designed to focus on extending compassion to versions of the self that are experiencing specific sorts of difficulties, including anxiety (*May you be free of agitation and anxiety. May you feel safe.*), anger (*May you be free of turmoil which stirs your anger and frustration*), or self-criticism (*May you be free of pain that causes this self-criticism*) (Gilbert & Choden, 2013). Statements involving "being free" of difficult affective states should ideally be embedded within an overall practice that involves building up feelings of safeness, peace, and balance.

Compassion for Others

Increasingly, research shows that practices such as loving-kindness and compassion meditation focused on the well-being of others produces measurable benefits for the self in terms of both happiness and behavioral outcomes such as mindfulness, purpose in life, social support, and reductions in illness (e.g. Frederickson, Cohn, Coffey, Pek, & Finkel, 2008). While CFT places a strong focus on the development of self-compassion, I think it's important that the focus really be on developing compassion for *everyone*, with an acknowledgment that the self is included in this. Given that the safeness system is designed by evolution to respond to connection, the social gains that can be produced through development of increased compassion for others are clearly desirable for clients. Additionally, deepening compassion for others can play a primary role in the treatment of clients struggling with behaviors that can actually harm others, such as in problematic anger (Kolts, 2012). A number of practices can be used in cultivating compassion and loving-kindness for others, many of which are adapted from Buddhist sources (e.g. Salzberg, 1995):

- Loving-kindness meditation: Imagine sending compassion out to another person—a loved one, someone who is suffering, or even someone with whom the client is struggling. (It's usually easier to begin with someone the client cares about and wants to help.) Shifting into the perspective of the compassionate self, the client visualizes sending kindness, warmth, and compassionate wishes to the other person. This can involve the client imagining his kindness and compassion extending to the other person in the form of light, filling that person with peace, ease, and happiness. It can also involve saying the phrases described in the "Compassion for the Self" section above, this time directed at the other person. The phrases can be tailored to the specific needs of the recipient, with the emphasis on feelings of warmth, compassion, and the desire to be helpful to the person.

- The client can visualize another person (or actually look at the person), reminding herself that this person, just like everyone else, only wants to be happy and to not suffer. This brief practice can be done while walking, or waiting at a stoplight, or at any other time another person is present. The idea is to repeatedly get into the habit of becoming aware of others in a compassionate way.

- As an extension of the previous practice, the client can visualize another person, with the awareness that just like everyone else, that person has a life that runs just as deep as the client's—just as filled with hopes, dreams, triumphs, tragedies, disappointments, and the full range of human experiences. The other person can be visualized going through the cycle of life from birth to death, being born as a helpless child, growing up and maturing (with all that entails), growing older, and dying, with the meditator imagining extending compassion and loving-kindness to the individual throughout the process. This practice can be punctuated by the reflection, *If I could contribute to this person's life, what sort of life would I want them to have?*, connecting with one's deep wish that others could find happiness and freedom from suffering (Kolts, 2012; Kolts & Chodron, 2013).

There are many other compassion and loving-kindness practices that motivated clients can use to deepen their experience of compassion for themselves and others. In addition to books (e.g. Kolts & Chodron, 2013; Gilbert & Choden, 2013; Germer, 2009; Neff, 2011), a quick Internet search for "compassion and loving-kindness meditation" brings up numerous written and guided audio practices that can be used to cultivate compassion for oneself and others. I'd recommend working collaboratively with individual clients to find specific practices that work for *them*. The key is to find ways to help clients learn to feel moved (warm sympathy rather than harsh criticism) when faced with their suffering and the suffering of others, and to develop feelings of warmth and the kind motivation to help.

SUMMARY

Imagery can be a powerful tool as clients grow in their capacity to work with emotions and extend compassion to themselves and others. In using imagery in therapy, the key is to begin with an idea of the underlying psychological processes we wish to facilitate. Is it helping the client create feelings of safeness in herself? Learn to accept compassion from an external source? Learn to develop and extend compassion toward her own pain and difficult emotions? Learn to develop and extend compassion to other people? With these processes in mind, we can select imagery exercises and structure a practice plan that will help clients gradually deepen their capacity to self-soothe and to feel genuine compassion for themselves and others.

CHAPTER 12

Embodying Compassion: Chair Work in CFT

In helping clients work compassionately with difficult emotions, CFT seeks to make things as experiential as possible. A powerful way to accomplish this is through chair work, including empty-chair, two-chair, and multiple-chair exercises. Chair work brings an immediacy and intensity that allow clients to work compassionately with difficult emotions in real time.

CFT draws heavily from the work of a pioneer of modern chair work, Leslie Greenberg, who along with his colleagues has placed chair work as a central component of emotion-focused therapy (EFT) and applied it extensively with self-critical patients (Greenberg, Rice, & Elliot, 1993; Greenberg & Watson, 2006; Pos & Greenberg, 2012). A recent pilot study demonstrated the usefulness of such chair work for increasing self-compassion and self-reassurance in self-critical clients, in addition to decreasing self-criticism and symptoms of anxiety and depression (Shahar et al., 2012).

CHAIR WORK IN CFT

CFT builds upon the EFT approach to chair work by emphasizing the role of the compassionate self. In CFT, the focus is on the continued development of the compassionate self and the application of this aspect of the self in working with difficult emotions and self-criticism (Gilbert, 2010). In this chapter, I'll present a few variations of how compassion-focused chair work can be applied in therapy.

Empty-Chair Work

When working with self-critical clients who may have a hard time viewing their difficulties from a compassionate perspective, empty-chair work can be a good way to start. Empty-chair work can be brought into the therapy shortly after introducing the Compassionate Self practice as a way to help clients more deeply connect with this compassionate perspective, especially as it applies to themselves. In this practice, we bring in another chair, positioned across from the client's chair. Beginning with a Compassionate Self exercise, we have the client imagine another person, perhaps someone the client cares about, sitting in the chair opposite him. We have him imagine that this person is presenting with a challenge that is very similar to the one the client has been experiencing, and around which he has criticized himself. We have the client imagine how he would feel about and interact with this beloved person from the kind, wise, confident perspective of the compassionate self. Let's consider how this exercise might look:

Therapist: Josh, we've been talking about your struggles with anger, and how you feel a lot of shame around that.

Josh: Yeah…it makes me feel like a piece of shit. This stuff has been helping, but sometimes I come home from work and I just want to have a good time with my wife and the kids. Then some small thing sets me off—the kids whining about their homework or something—and I find myself raising my voice to them instead. You can see them tense up, and they all look at me like I'm the problem. I see them walking on eggshells around me. It makes me sick. I'm trying to get my shit together, but I just keep doing it. I'm a terrible husband and father.

Therapist: That sounds like it feels awful.

Josh: Yeah, but it's my own damn fault.

Therapist: I'm wondering if you'd be willing to try an exercise that would help us bring some compassion to this situation. Something to strengthen that compassionate self we've been building up to help you work with your anger?

Josh: I guess I'm willing to try anything at this point.

Therapist: That's the sort of courage that's really going to help as we go through this process. This is going to be an "empty-chair" exercise, so I'm going to move this chair right here opposite yours, okay?

Josh: Okay… *(somewhat dubiously)*

Therapist: *(Smiles.)* Trust me…there's a reason for the chair. When I first learned about chair techniques, I thought it was a little weird, too. But I'm sold on it, now.

Josh: All right.

Therapist: Let's begin with the Compassionate Self practice we introduced last session. We'll start by doing some soothing rhythm breathing, focusing our attention on slowing down the body, slowing down the mind.

Josh: (*Straightens, closes his eyes, and slows his breathing.*)

Therapist: (*Waits one minute or so.*) Now let's shift into the kind, wise, confident perspective of the compassionate self. Imagining that you're filled with the kind wish to benefit others and yourself. (*Waits thirty seconds.*) Filled with a deep wisdom and the ability to see things from many perspectives. (*Waits thirty seconds.*) And a deep, courageous confidence, knowing that *whatever arises, I can work with this, too.* (*Waits thirty seconds.*) When you're ready, slowly open your eyes, bringing this compassionate perspective with you into the room.

Josh: (*Waits a bit, then slowly opens his eyes.*)

Therapist: Josh, I'd like you to imagine that in this chair is someone you like and care about…maybe a good friend you enjoy hanging out with and would want to help. Do you have someone like that?

Josh: Yeah. My buddy Nathan is like that. We hang out all the time, watching sports and things like that. We also talk a lot—he's about the only person I talk about this stuff with.

Therapist: It's great to hear that you have someone you can talk with. It sounds like you guys are pretty close.

Josh: Nathan gets it. He's like a brother.

Therapist: Perfect. Josh, let's imagine that Nathan is sitting here in this chair, and that he's just been really vulnerable. He's told you that he's struggled with anger his whole life, that he's worked really hard to control it but it seems like nothing works. He's told you that despite his best efforts, he sometimes raises his voice to his wife and kids, and he knows they walk on eggshells around him. He's even getting therapy to try and help with it, which was really difficult for him to do. He tells you he feels like a terrible husband and father. He's really feeling ashamed.

Josh: I think I see where you're going with this…

Therapist: I bet you do. But let's see if we can go with it, shall we? If Nathan were here in this chair, and he had just told you all of this about his struggles with anger, how would you feel about him? Would you condemn him?

Josh: Condemn him? No. I'd tell him I know what it is like.

Therapist: Seeing him struggle with this anger, seeing how hard this is for him, what would you feel?

Josh: I'd feel terrible for him. And I guess I'd look up to him for being so honest about it, and for getting help. That's hard to do.

Therapist: It sure is. From this place of compassion—seeing his struggle and wanting to help—what would you want him to understand? How might you reassure him?

Josh: I'd want him to understand that he isn't the only one…that I feel like that too, sometimes. I'd tell him some of what we've talked about—that it isn't his fault that he learned to get angry, and that he can learn things that will help. I'd tell him the fact that he's concerned about what kind of husband and father he is probably means he's a pretty good one, and that I know for sure he's a damn good friend. And going to therapy—that's tough.

Therapist: Josh, that's wonderful. Your compassionate self has a lot to say to Nathan. How do you think he'd feel if he heard that?

Josh: I think he'd feel better. I know I've felt better when he's said that kind of stuff to me.

Therapist: So he's encouraged you like this in the past?

Josh: Yeah. Like I said, he's like a brother to me.

Therapist: I've noticed that the things you would say to Nathan—and the things he says to you—are very different from the condemning way your self-critic talks to you when you've struggled with anger. Which ways of talking seem to be more helpful—the compassionate reassurance and encouragement, or the condemning self-criticism? Which way of talking to yourself will help you shift out of the angry, threatened self and into the man you want to be?

Josh: I think I get it. Beating myself up only makes it worse.

Therapist: True. But we're not just talking about refraining from beating yourself up. It's about finding ways to compassionately reassure yourself and encourage yourself to do better—to help yourself the way you would want to help someone you cared about, like Nathan. Or the way Nathan would help you. Do you think that would be more helpful than beating yourself up?

Josh: It probably would.

Therapist: When you're home at the end of the day, just wanting things to go well, and one of the kids starts whining, you might even try to take a few breaths, slow things down, and imagine what that compassionate version of you might do. Or even imagine what Nathan might say to help you keep from getting angry.

Josh: I believe that might help. I think I'll try that.

This example is adapted from numerous sessions in which I've used chair work with clients who struggle with anger. It was very helpful that Josh was able to identify a good friend—Nathan—for whom it was easy for Josh to feel and direct compassion. It also helped that Josh and Nathan had a friendship in which they actually talked about things, so it was easier for Josh to connect with a compassionate, encouraging perspective around the anger. This isn't always the case, particularly for people who struggle with anger (and perhaps even more so with men), so sometimes more work is required to set up the imagery of someone the client is likely to relate to in a compassionate versus condemning manner. This is one reason that I often like to do CFT for anger treatment in groups. In groups, we can create a shared camaraderie and compassionate understanding among members who know how hard it is, and can model the sort of compassionate understanding and encouragement to one another that Nathan modeled to Josh in the example above.

Two-Chair Work

The hope is that by the time we get to chair work, previous layers of therapy (the therapeutic relationship, understandings about the evolved brain and social shaping of the self, Compassionate Self work) will have laid the groundwork for self-compassion. If so, we can use two-chair work to deepen the client's experience of self-compassion, bringing it directly into the present moment. There are different ways to set this up. First, we'll explore putting the compassionate self in one chair, and the vulnerable self (anxious, depressed, angry, and so on) in the other, and facilitating a dialogue between them. In the second case, we can assist the client in working with self-criticism by facilitating a dialogue between the compassionate self and the self-critical self. In CFT, all of this work is focused on developing and strengthening the kind, wise, courageous perspective of the compassionate self so that clients can get better and better at applying these qualities in their lives.

FACILITATING DIALOGUE BETWEEN THE COMPASSIONATE AND VULNERABLE SELVES

In this practice, two chairs are set up, and the therapist assists the client in having a dialogue between a version of herself that represents the emotion with which she is struggling (such as anxiety, depression, or anger) and her wise, kind, confident compassionate self. Typically, we'll have the client begin in the vulnerable chair, inviting that version of the self to speak its piece—to really let the fear, sadness, or anger flow. Sometimes more than one of these emotions will show up for the client, in which case we can use the Multiple Selves exercise introduced in chapter 14.

Once the threat-based self has had its say, the client is prompted to shift into the compassionate chair, at which point the therapist guides her in shifting into the perspective of the compassionate self. From this perspective, the client then compassionately addresses the vulnerable self, offering validation, understanding, kindness, and encouragement (with guidance from the therapist if needed). Should the client find herself shifting out of the perspective of the compassionate self and back into threat-based language, it's no problem—the therapist just prompts her to switch chairs until the vulnerable self has had her say. Let's consider how this might look:

Therapist: Jenny, we've been exploring how you can bring compassion to your fears with the Compassionate Self practice and things like the compassionate letter. It's my sense that these have been helpful. Is that right?

Jenny: They really have. It's been nice to see things from that perspective. The letter has really helped—I've read it a lot, and it's helped encourage me to do things that I usually don't.

Therapist: That's great. As we've discussed, a big part of working compassionately with anxiety is to help you to face your fears—to be able to do things, even when you're scared of them, so that you can learn that you *can* do it.

Jenny: Yeah, I've been doing more of that. It seems to be helping, although it isn't fun.

Therapist: I would imagine not—it's tough to face the things that scare us, and you're doing a great job. Today I'd like to introduce another practice we can use to deepen that work and bring compassion and encouragement to that anxious part of you. How does that sound?

Jenny: I'd be up for that.

Therapist: Great! This is a two-chair exercise, so I'll have you moving around a bit. (*Gets up to set up two chairs facing one another in the middle of the room.*) This chair is the "anxious chair." (*Gestures toward the chair.*) We'll put Anxious Jenny in this chair, and let her express all of her fears.

Jenny: (*Nods.*) Okay.

Therapist: (*Gestures toward the other chair.*) In this chair, we'll put Compassionate Jenny, who'll be listening to Anxious Jenny, feeling compassion for her, and offering her compassion, understanding, and encouragement. Does that make sense?

Jenny: I think so. It seems a little weird, though.

Therapist: Initially it *can* seem a little weird. No worries—I'm here to facilitate things. I'll give you prompts for what to think about and do, instructions on when to change chairs, and things like that. If you're ready, how about you sit down over here in the anxious chair?

Jenny: Okay. (*Moves to the anxious chair.*)

Therapist: In this chair, we'll give Anxious Jenny the mic, so that we can really hear her perspective. You've got a lot of things you're working on—this group project, wanting to do more social activities, even to start dating. Does Anxious Jenny have much to say about that stuff?

Jenny: She sure does.

Therapist: Well, here's her chance. Take a few minutes to allow yourself to feel the fears and anxiety about these things you want to do. Notice how the anxiety feels in your body. Imagine yourself working in the group project, going out with friends, going on dates. What fears or anxieties come up? Talk about how you're feeling in real time.

Jenny: (*Closes her eyes for a bit, then opens them.*) There are all these things I want to do, but I'm terrified of doing them.

Therapist: What are you afraid of?

Jenny: I'm afraid that I'll put myself out there, and they'll all hate me. I'll say the wrong thing, and look stupid. I'm afraid that just when I start feeling comfortable, they'll make fun of me, and reject me. (*Becomes tearful.*)

Therapist: You're doing great, Jenny. Let the fears come.

Jenny: If they get to know me, really get to know me, they won't like me. I'm not like them, and they'll see that. (*Cries openly.*) It'll be just like it was before. What's wrong with me? Why won't they like me?

Therapist: (*Leans in kindly; waits silently.*) Does Anxious Jenny have anything more she needs to say?

Jenny: (*Dabs her tears and gently smiles.*) No, I think that's about it.

Therapist: Think you're ready to switch chairs?

Jenny: I think so. (*Gets up and switches chairs.*)

Therapist: Slowing down the breath. (*Waits thirty seconds.*) Bringing up the kind, wise, courageous perspective of the compassionate self. Once again, imagining yourself filled with these qualities: the kind wish to help yourself and others, the wisdom to see deeply from many perspectives, the courage to face the scary things. Imagine yourself filled with compassion.

Jenny: (*Closes her eyes and breathes slowly and quietly.*)

Therapist: When you're ready, opening your eyes and looking at Anxious Jenny, sitting there, sharing her fears with us. She just wants to be accepted—to participate, to have friends, to date. She's doing her best, but she's scared because of the things that have happened to her. From this compassionate perspective—filled with kindness—how do you feel about her?

Jenny: I feel terrible for her. It's so hard for her. She just wants to fit in, wants people to like her. She's so scared she'll be hurt again.

Therapist: It makes sense that she'd feel this way, doesn't it?

Jenny: It does make sense, after what happened to her.

Therapist: From this compassionate perspective, I'd like you to talk with Jenny—validate her, encourage her—offering whatever might be helpful. Talk with Jenny like she's sitting right there in this chair, right now.

Jenny: (*Pauses, thinking.*) Jenny, you've been scared for a long time, and you've tried locking yourself away from the world so you don't get hurt again. But what happened to you wasn't your fault. (*Pauses.*) I don't know why those girls did what they did, but it didn't have anything to do with you. That was a long time ago. You've met lots of people since then who have been nice to you, and who like you. (*Pauses.*)

Therapist: That's great, Jenny. Can you encourage her? What do you want her to understand?

Jenny: Jenny, it makes sense that you're scared, but you're working hard on this, and it's paying off. The other members of your group like you. The girls on your floor invite you out with them, which means they probably like you. It's time to start taking more chances.

Therapist: Jenny, (*gesturing toward the other chair*) she's afraid that if they really get to know her, they'll reject her. What do you want her to know?

Jenny: (*Looks at the other chair.*) You are a good person. You are kind, and you think of others before yourself. You do your best. (*Pauses.*) There's nothing wrong with you. (*Eyes redden.*)

Therapist: Jenny, could you say that again?

Jenny: There's *nothing wrong* with you. (*Cries, smiling gently.*)

As we see above, the power of two-chair work is its ability to translate the understandings of the compassionate self into felt experiential realizations. These can be powerful moments in therapy, as clients learn what it means to really feel and express kindness and compassion toward themselves. The therapist sets the stage for the interchange and uses Socratic dialogue to facilitate it, but creates space so that the dialogue comes directly from the client—helping only as needed to aid the client in connecting with the emotional selves, and to connect with and express compassion. This work is a lot easier (and tends to go more smoothly) when the groundwork has been laid in the ways described in previous chapters.

FACILITATING DIALOGUE BETWEEN THE COMPASSIONATE, VULNERABLE, AND SELF-CRITICAL SELVES

Another way to use two-chair work is to help facilitate a dialogue between the compassionate self, the vulnerable self, and the self-critic. This work is reminiscent of that seen in Emotion-Focused Therapy, in which chair work is used to help the client come face-to-face with the self-critic (Greenberg, Rice, & Elliot, 1993; Greenberg & Watson, 2006; Pos & Greenberg, 2012). As we discussed above, the difference is that in CFT, a strong emphasis is on the development and application of the compassionate self in understanding, relating to, and soothing the vulnerable self and self-critic.

This can play out in different ways, depending upon the motivation of the internalized self-critic. We can get at this by asking Socratic questions like, "What does your self-critic want?" "What is his motivation?" "What are you afraid might happen if your self-critic stopped talking?" For some clients, self-criticism plays a primarily behavioral function and is simply the learned strategy they use to motivate themselves. As we've seen with Jenny, it's a tool that seems to work sometimes, despite its drawbacks (*You're so pathetic. Everyone else can do this. Just get on with it!*). In other clients, the self-critic can be motivated by fear—designed to keep them in line, shutting them down so that they don't engage in behaviors that might be risky (*You're just going to screw this up. There's no point in even trying.*).

For other clients, however, the self-criticism is anchored in a deep sense of self-loathing or self-hatred, often acquired through abusive experiences, trauma, or the experience of having done something that is antithetical to their values. In this case the critic can arise from the internalized voice of an abuser, or from a desire to harm and punish the self (Gilbert, 2010). It can be useful to have a sense of this beforehand, because it gets at the underlying motivation of the self-critic—to help, or to harm. For the client who uses self-criticism to motivate herself, we can frame the dialogue around the compassionate self acknowledging that the self-critic is only trying to help, and stepping in to help by taking over the role of self-motivator. Chair work can also help to explore the motivation behind the self-critic, to identify whether it is an internalized voice of an abuser, and to build mindful awareness of the emotional impact of the self-critical inner voice. The exercise can also help clients learn distress tolerance in the face of self-criticism, as well as the ability to shift perspectives between the critical, vulnerable, and compassionate selves. Let's consider a clinical example in which a number of the self-critical dynamics mentioned above are manifested:

Therapist: Josh, you did a great job with the chair exercise last week. When you imagined your friend Nathan struggling with anger, it seemed like you were able to connect with your compassionate self in understanding and relating to him.

Josh: Yeah, that seemed to go pretty good.

Therapist: It sounds like the compassionate way you related to Nathan in that exercise was very different from how you talk to yourself a lot of the time. Like last session when you called yourself "a terrible father." It sounds like your internal self-critic can get pretty loud sometimes.

Josh: Yeah. I disgust myself. I keep trying to get my shit together, and it seems like it works for a while, and then I just fuck it up again.

Therapist: Sounds like your self-critic has a lot to say. Now that you've had some experience of how the wise, kind, compassionate version of you would relate to Nathan, I was wondering if we could do another chair exercise, in which we explore the different perspectives of self-criticism and compassion in working with these feelings. Up for giving it a go?

Josh: Sure. I don't really know what you want me to do, though.

Therapist: Well, let's see if we can make that clear. I'm going to arrange these three chairs here. (*Sets out three chairs in a triangle-shaped pattern, with each chair pointed inward, toward the others.*) This chair (*pointing*) will be for your self-critic. Anytime you have anything critical to say about yourself, you can let it roll…as long as you're sitting in this chair. This chair (*pointing to the second chair*) is for your vulnerable self—the part of you that the critic is criticizing and attacking. This is the part of you that feels the effects of the criticism. Over here (*pointing to the third chair*) is for your compassionate self. This is the wise, kind, courageous part of you that wants to help both of these other parts of the self—to help the criticized self feel safe and manage his emotions, and help calm the self-critic so that he doesn't have to be so attacking. That make sense so far?

Josh: (*looking a bit skeptical*) I think so…

Therapist: Great. How about you sit in this chair (*pointing to vulnerable-self chair*), and tell me about a recent time when you struggled with anger?

Josh: Okay. (*Moves to the chair.*) Two nights ago I let the dog out in our backyard. My daughter Chloe and her friends had been playing outside, and had left the gate open. So the dog takes off through the open gate and starts running around the neighborhood. I was so pissed. I had to chase him down, and I was yelling at him as I carried him back in the house. When I got back in, I just dropped him and snapped at Chloe for not closing the gate. She and her mother just looked at me like I was a monster, and they both avoided me the rest of the night.

Therapist: What was that like for you?

Josh: I was just so angry when it happened—at the dog, at Chloe. I looked like an idiot chasing the dog around the neighborhood. Why can't she just close the damn gate, you know? But then I made it worse by yelling and snapping at her. I always make it worse.

Therapist: It sounds like your self-critic has something to say about this. Want to shift into this chair over here? (*Points to the critic chair.*)

Josh: (*Switches chairs.*) Okay.

Therapist: So in this chair, you can let the criticism roll. Looking back at this chair (*gesturing toward the chair Josh just vacated*), see that version of yourself...the one that got angry, chased after the dog, yelled, dropped the dog, and snapped at Chloe. The one you said always makes it worse. What does your self-critic have to say to him? Imagine that you're speaking directly to him, just like last week.

Josh: You're screwing everything up. (*Looks at the therapist.*) Like that?

Therapist: (*Nods, gesturing back toward the criticized-self chair.*) Just like that.

Josh: (*Looks back to the chair.*) You're an idiot. You're a terrible father and husband. What the fuck is wrong with you, making a huge deal out of everything? If they had any sense, they'd leave you! Why do you always have to fuck everything up? You disgust me! (*Shakes his head and looks down.*)

Therapist: (*Waits in silence for thirty seconds or so.*) Anything else?

Josh: I think that about covers it.

Therapist: So let's shift back to this chair... (*Gestures toward the vulnerable-self chair.*)

Josh: (*Switches chairs.*)

Therapist: Let yourself receive all those things the self-critic had to say. (*Gestures toward the self-critic chair.*) He called you a terrible father and husband, accused you of always fucking everything up... What's it feel like to hear those things?

Josh: (*Shrinks into the chair and looks down.*) It feels terrible. It feels like it's true. I want to do better, but it seems like I just keep screwing things up.

Therapist: Look at him. (*Gestures toward the self-critic chair.*) How do you feel about him?

Josh:	I'm scared of him. He sounds just like my dad. I just want him to leave me alone.
Therapist:	So your father used to criticize you like that.
Josh:	All the time. I could never do anything right.
Therapist:	That sounds like compassionate wisdom to me—figuring out where part of that self-critical voice and maybe some of the anger you struggle with comes from. How about we give the compassionate chair a try? (*Gestures toward the compassionate-self chair.*)
Josh:	All right. (*Switches to the compassionate-self chair.*)
Therapist:	So let's take a few moments to slow down our breathing, and connect with those qualities of the compassionate self. (*Waits ten seconds.*) Imagine being filled with the kind desire to help both of these guys (*gesturing toward the two empty chairs*) …the wisdom to look deeply and see things from different perspectives…and the courage to work with the really difficult stuff.
Josh:	(*Sits quietly.*)
Therapist:	From this wise, compassionate perspective, how can we understand these two guys? Let's start with this one. (*Gestures toward the vulnerable-self chair.*) He's sitting there, feeling ashamed about what he's done, hearing all this criticism. How does he feel?'
Josh:	He feels terrible. Hopeless. He just wants to be left alone.
Therapist:	He feels like he's always screwing up?
Josh:	Well, he is always screwing up.
Therapist:	That sounds like your self-critic showing back up. Should we switch chairs? (*Gestures toward the critic chair.*)
Josh:	No, I'm good.
Therapist:	So looking at this guy (*pointing back to the vulnerable self*) from this kind, compassionate perspective, what do you understand about him? Is he *trying* to screw everything up? Is that what he wants?
Josh:	No. He's not trying to screw it up. He feels terrible about it. He's not doing it on purpose.
Therapist:	So his motivation is actually to do better, but it's hard for him?
Josh:	Yeah. He wants to do better, but he doesn't know how.

Therapist: (*Gestures toward the self-critic chair.*) What about him? What's his story?

Josh: He just wants that guy (*gesturing toward the vulnerable-self chair*) to quit being such a fuck-up. He's just sick of it.

Therapist: He's pretty harsh… You said he sounds like your father used to sound?

Josh: Yeah. That's just the kind of thing my father used to say to me.

Therapist: So we can understand how the self-critic learned to be this way?

Josh: Oh yeah…

Therapist: So when your self-critic attacks him (*gesturing toward the criticized-self chair*), does it help? Does it help him do better?

Josh: (*Pauses for a moment.*) No. It just makes him feel bad.

Therapist: That sounds like compassionate understanding to me. It sounds like you understand how the self-critic learned to be so harsh—from your father—but you know that the harshness isn't helpful. What would you like to say to him, from this compassionate, understanding perspective? (*Gestures toward the self-critic.*)

Josh: (*Turns toward the self-critic chair.*) Look, I get it. You're tired of it. We're all tired of it. But the attacking and running him down doesn't help. It just makes you mad and makes it harder on him. (*Gestures toward the criticized self.*) You don't want to be like Dad. (*Hangs his head.*)

Therapist: Josh, you're doing really well. That feels really vulnerable. How about switching back to that chair? (*Points to the vulnerable-self chair.*)

Josh: (*Switches chairs.*)

Therapist: It sounds like part of you is really scared of ending up like your father.

Josh: Yeah… I mean, he was a great man. But growing up, I was scared of him a lot of the time. He got so angry at every little thing. I'd just avoid him whenever I could. I don't want my kids to feel that way about me. I don't want them to learn that stuff from me the way I learned it from him.

Therapist: How do you want them to feel about you, Josh?

Josh: (*tearful*) I want them to love me, you know. And to know that I love them. But I keep fucking it up. I need to do better.

Therapist: That's why you're here, isn't it? Because you want to do better? You've been working hard at that, haven't you?

Josh: Yeah. I just wish it worked faster.

Therapist: Josh, would you be willing to switch back to this chair? (*Gestures toward the compassionate-self chair.*)

Josh: Sure. (*Moves.*)

Therapist: From this compassionate perspective, look at Josh here. (*Gestures toward the vulnerable-self chair.*) He's here in therapy, trying to learn to do better, to be a good model for the kids. It's not easy for him, is it?

Josh: No, it's really hard.

Therapist: How do you feel about him?

Josh: I feel bad for him, you know?

Therapist: Do you want to help him?

Josh: I do. I mean, I would if I could.

Therapist: Well, you've seen how hard he's been working. Has he made any progress?

Josh: I guess he has. A couple of times this week, I—I mean, *he*—started to get mad and then calmed down. I don't know if anyone even noticed, but I did. It was one of those times when I would have gotten worked up, and I just breathed for a while instead. I've also been spending more fun time with the kids like we talked about.

Therapist: So you've seen his efforts pay off a bit. But he's sitting there, feeling hopeless and terrible about himself—terrified that he'll make his kids feel just like he felt about his father. What do you want to say to him? What do you want him to understand? (*Gestures toward the vulnerable-self chair.*)

Josh: (*Looks at the chair.*) You're not Dad, at least not the bad parts. He never even saw it as a problem, and he sure as hell didn't seem to care what we thought about it. You care, and you're trying to do better.

Therapist: How might you encourage him to keep going?

Josh: You're working hard, and it's helping. Sure, you still screw up sometimes, but you can't expect to be perfect.

Therapist: That's great…keep going…let him know you see what he's doing right.

Josh: You did a good job calming down and making time to play soccer with the kids. They had a lot of fun. (*Turns to the therapist.*) It really was fun.

Therapist: Sounds like it. Would your compassionate self recommend more of those sorts of activities with the kids?

Josh: Sure would.

Therapist: How about we finish up back in this chair? (*Gestures toward the vulnerable-self chair.*)

Josh: (*Switches chairs.*)

Therapist: Let's take a moment to let those things that Compassionate Josh had to say sink in—noticing how hard you're working to do better, the successes you've had, encouraging you to keep going. How does that feel?

Josh: It feels good. A little weird.

Therapist: A little weird...

Josh: Yeah, I've just never talked to myself like that before.

Therapist: But it feels good?

Josh: Yeah...not so hopeless. Encouraging, I guess.

Therapist: So which of those voices seems more helpful in terms of helping you manage the anger and improve relationships with your family? (*Gestures toward the empty chairs.*)

Josh: That one. (*Points to the compassionate-self chair.*)

Therapist: It sounds like once you let yourself really listen to Compassionate Josh, your self-critic didn't have as much to say.

Josh: No, he didn't, did he?

In the vignette above, we see a number of things happening. The therapist elicits a dialogue between the self-critic and the vulnerable self, to get a sense of the dynamics of Josh's self-criticism. The critic appears to be at least partially an internalized voice of Josh's father, who modeled a lot of anger. The critic also has a flavor of disgust, as well as perhaps the misguided intention to get Josh to do better by attacking him. Note that when the therapist has Josh switch chairs, it's often quickly followed by a prompt to connect him with the affective dynamics of the interaction: "How do you feel about him?" "How does it feel to hear that?" Compassionate understanding is brought to both the perspective of the vulnerable self—who is trying but still struggles—and the perspective of the critic, who is playing out an angry, critical script learned from childhood experiences.

Finally, the compassionate self is prompted to extend understanding, kindness, and encouragement to the vulnerable self (with help and encouragement from the therapist), and then a contrast is drawn between the impact of this compassionate interaction and the previous, critical ones. You'll note that we aren't trying to argue with or conquer the self-critic. Rather, the focus is on the facilitation of compassionate understanding. Space permits only a small sample of what this exercise can involve—consider how you might have continued to facilitate things to help Josh learn more about his internal dialogue, shift among these perspectives, and relate compassionately to different aspects of the self.

SUMMARY

In this chapter, we explored the use of chair work to bring a strong experiential focus to the compassionate self, and to explore and apply compassion to the dynamics of self-criticism. The more we can translate compassion into felt experiences, thoughts, and behaviors in the present moment, the better. In the next chapter, we'll explore the role of case formulation in organizing our understanding of our clients and their challenges.

CHAPTER 13

Compassionate Integration: Case Formulation in CFT

A number of therapies use case formulation as a framework for developing an organized understanding of problem origins, maintaining factors, and treatment interventions that is centered on the individual client (Eells, 2010). Particularly for complex cases, a case formulation gives clinicians a way to organize all the information that clients are giving them in a way that sets the stage for theory-based intervention. In this chapter, we'll explore case formulation in CFT.

KEY COMPONENTS OF A CFT CASE FORMULATION

The focus of case conceptualization and formulation in CFT can be thought of as "unpacking" the threat response, so we can understand how historical and current factors have triggered threat experiences in our clients that have shaped their behavioral responding (and over time, their lifestyles), as well as how they relate to themselves and others. Case formulation in CFT parallels our focus on depathologizing client difficulties, in that it helps us understand their challenges in a developmental context in which they make sense. Gilbert (2010, 69) describes CFT case formulation as developing an understanding of *innate and historical influences* that give rise to *key external and internal threats and fears* that give rise to *externally and internally focused safety strategies* that produce *problematic unintended consequences*, which impact *self-to-self and self-to-other relating*, which themselves shape ongoing safety strategies. The CFT case formulation worksheet below depicts these elements in relationship to one another. (This worksheet is also available for download at http://www.newharbinger .com/33094.) Let's briefly explore each component of the formulation.

CFT CASE FORMULATION WORKSHEET

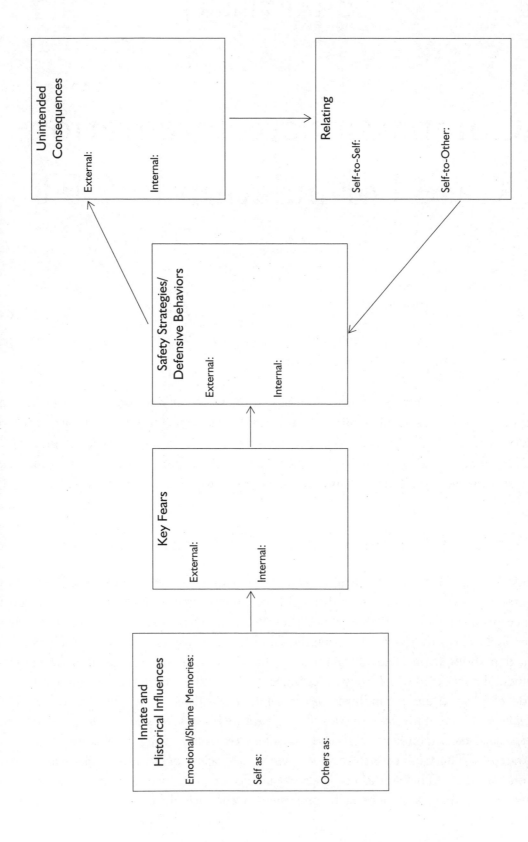

Innate and
Historical Influences

Emotional/Shame Memories:

Self as:

Others as:

Key Fears

External:

Internal:

Safety Strategies/
Defensive Behaviors

External:

Internal:

Unintended
Consequences

External:

Internal:

Relating

Self-to-Self:

Self-to-Other:

Innate and Historical Influences

As we've discussed in previous chapters, a compassionate understanding of our client's problems and behaviors is based on understanding how these challenges make sense within the context of the various biological and social influences that have shaped the client's life. In this section of the formulation, we'll draw upon client memories of significant life events, as well as early attachment experiences and learning history, which we discussed in chapter 6. Emphasis is given to emotional memories of care, threat, neglect, abuse, aloneness, shame, and any other experiences that may have powerfully shaped how the client experiences herself and others (Gilbert, 2010). As you might imagine, this history-taking takes place over time, as relational safeness is established within the therapeutic relationship. With each revelation, we have the opportunity to model compassion, and to help the client learn to relate to her own experiences with compassion, validation, and understanding of how these experiences shaped her life in ongoing ways.

This exploration can help us understand how clients learned to relate to themselves (as competent, vulnerable, flawed, worthy or unworthy of love and care, and so on) and to others (as safe, dangerous, trustworthy or not). Cognitive therapists and schema therapists might call these basic ideas self-schemas (or other-schemas), while attachment-oriented therapists might refer to them as internal working models. In CFT, we emphasize the relationship of these core self- and other-representations to emotional memories of interactions with others, and the felt-sense that they can engender—playing out in terms of powerful emotional and bodily reactions that clients may struggle to understand or verbalize (Gilbert, 2010). We can also consider how such experiences shape our clients' experience of the three circles—relating to themselves and the world in ways that are defined by patterns of threat, drive, and safeness—and whether they will tend to become rigidly stuck within experiences of threat or drive, or are able to fluidly shift among emotions, motives, and perspectives in response to different situations.

Key Fears

In a CFT case formulation, these historical influences can then give rise to key fears, core threats, and unmet needs. These fears often originate in childhood and organize themselves around core themes such as abandonment, rejection, shame, and harm or abuse (Gilbert, 1989, 2010; Beck, Davis, & Freeman, 2014). In CFT, a distinction is made between external threats and internal threats (Gilbert, 2010). External threats are anchored in one's experiences with others and the outside world, and include themes like rejection, exploitation, or being harmed by others. Internal threats can include things like fears of losing control, of being fundamentally flawed or unlovable, or of being overwhelmed by depression, anxiety, or anger. Identifying core threats can be useful in helping clients relate compassionately to their struggles, as they begin to understand relationships between their histories, their basic fears, and troubling experiences they have in the present.

THE DOWNWARD ARROW METHOD

Given the sheer amount of material our clients may present to us, it can sometimes feel tricky to identify a client's core fear schemas. A powerful, straightforward method for doing so is the *downward arrow* method, drawn from David Burns's CBT work (Burns, 1980). In the downward arrow method, the clinician begins by identifying a troubling thought or situation that is bothering the client. Once the situation or thought is identified, the clinician responds with the questions (stated together in a single verbalization), "Why is that upsetting to you? What does it mean?" (The words "about you" can be inserted at the end of the second statement, if appropriate). After the client responds, the statements are repeated until the client and therapist find themselves at the core threat—a moment often marked by a visible shift in the client's nonverbal behavior, as the emotional reality of stating the core threat hits home. Rather than trying to vary the wording of the statements, it can be useful to let the client in on the technique, as demonstrated in the vignette below:

Therapist: Josh, you were saying that you've been really upset lately about your son's behavior in the classroom. Although his report card was good, it sounds like you have concerns about his behavior in class?

Josh: Yeah, I've really been worked up about it. At our conference, the teacher said Aiden had been up out of his seat and was sometimes overly talkative, distracting other students. I've gotten really angry about it—way beyond what was called for, because his grades are good. It just really bothers me.

Therapist: Let's see if we can get to the bottom of this. A lot of times, there are core fears lying underneath troubling thoughts and situations that really bother us. I'd like to try a technique called the *downward arrow*. What we're going to do is that I'm going to ask you about this situation, and then repeat a couple of questions to you over and over when you respond. Don't be annoyed by that—these questions will lead us right to your core fear. Does that sound all right?

Josh: Why not?

Therapist: Good. You mentioned getting really upset about Aiden's behavior in class. Why is that upsetting to you? What does it mean?

Josh: Well, it's a problem. I mean, the teacher identified him as sometimes being disruptive.

Therapist: So she mentioned he's sometimes disruptive. Why is that upsetting? What does it mean?

Josh: Well, in every class, there are a few "problem kids," you know. I'm worried that Aiden will be labeled as one of the problem kids in his class.

Therapist:	Why is that upsetting? What does it mean?
Josh:	You know what people do with those kids. They blame the parents. They always blame the parents.
Therapist:	Why is that upsetting? What does it mean?
Josh:	It means that the teacher or the other parents might think that I'm a bad father.
Therapist:	So they might think that you're a bad father. Why is that upsetting? What does that mean?
Josh:	(*Pauses; looks down.*) Maybe I *am* a bad father.
Therapist:	(*Pauses.*) Do you think that might be your core fear? That you might be a bad father?
Josh:	(*Looks pensive; slowly nods.*) Yeah. I think that's it. I've been worried about that since before Aiden was born.

We see above that Josh's core fear relates to an internal threat—that there is something about him that guarantees he will fail as a father. Depending on their backgrounds, clients may also have core fears related to both external and internal threats. Jenny, for example, presents with the external fear that others ultimately will reject her no matter what she does, and a related internal fear—that perhaps there is something wrong with her that prompts such rejection. Understanding these core fears can often provide a compassionate context for understanding the development of "maladaptive" coping on the part of the client.

Safety Strategies and Defensive Behaviors

Core fears can create great distress in our clients, and many of their problems will be rooted in attempts to avoid this distress. In CFT, these are called *safety strategies*—defensive behaviors designed to minimize threat-related distress. Often rooted in avoidance, these strategies are at work in many of our clients—the PTSD patient who avoids situations that remind him of the trauma, and drinks to cope with memories of it; the depressed or panic-disordered patient who doesn't leave the house; the angry client who blames everyone else for her outbursts; the acutely distressed teen who cuts his arm to cope with powerful emotions. As we use Socratic dialogue to explore our clients' presenting problems, examples of such safety strategies will often become apparent.

The key to recognizing safety strategies—whether they are acute coping behaviors or long-standing lifestyle choices—is that they tend to be *threat-based*, and often involve avoidance. Such strategies are focused on minimizing contact with threatening situations, thoughts, memories, and experience—not on building the sort of lives that clients want to have. Compassion comes from understanding these behaviors in context. As nonsensical or even harmful as they may seem in isolation, in the context of the client's core threats and historical background, we see that they make complete sense. The client is doing whatever he can to cope with the threat, often using strategies that were overtly or covertly taught to him in ways we've discussed. However, as you might imagine, such defensive strategies often have unintended and undesirable consequences—which leads us to the next step of the formulation.

Unintended Consequences

Safety strategies very frequently have unintended and maladaptive consequences which can serve to maintain the client's problems, make them worse, or create other difficulties (Gilbert, 2010; Salkovskis, 1996). They often involve avoidance, as the client tries to limit contact with aversive emotional experiences, thoughts (as in the case of compulsions in OCD), and situations. These unintended consequences can be crippling, as we see in the socially anxious client who avoids social situations and misses out on potentially important life opportunities in order to avoid the anxiety caused by such situations. Clients like Jenny who fear rejection may avoid emotionally honest conversation out of fears of being judged (Gilbert, 2010). These consequences can also be overtly harmful to the client or other people, as we see in those who struggle with self-harm and substance abuse to cope with emotional distress, or who engage in aggression to create feelings of social dominance to ward off feelings of vulnerability.

Socratic dialogue can be used to assist clients in compassionately exploring both how their safety strategies relate to their backgrounds and core fears, and how these strategies produce undesirable consequences in their own lives. As we've seen in previous vignettes, Jenny has been able to observe that her strategies of avoiding and withdrawing from social situations made sense in light of the traumatic rejection experiences she had when she was younger. At the same time, her strategies prevent her from having the potentially nurturing social contacts that she ultimately desires (and which would help her learn to feel safe in relation to others).

Josh presents with a more nuanced safety strategy—his tendency to blame his wife and child for "making me angry" after an outburst. While space precludes including the interchange here, through Socratic dialogue, Josh could be helped to recognize that almost immediately following his anger outbursts, there is a powerful rush of emotional pain and shame (likely related to activation of his core fears of being a bad father and husband). Questions might include: "How do these situations usually play out?" "What does it feel like to see that your wife or son has been hurt by something you've said?" and "What happens next?" To escape this pain, Josh would move almost immediately to blaming his family—relieving himself of the responsibility of how he had treated them. As we can imagine, this behavior creates more problems for Josh, as his family responds to his volatility and blaming by distancing from him and "walking on eggshells" when he is near. Josh then observes this pulling back, reinforcing his sense of himself as a flawed parent and partner.

The unintended consequences of these threat-based safety strategies can continually shape patterns of self-to-self and self-to-other relating that keep clients stuck in their threat circles. While they play out scripts that ever more deeply entrench them in shame-based self-schemas, those scripts prevent them from engaging in nurturing connections with others.

Relating to Self and Others

In the final component of a CFT case formulation, we consider how the unintended consequences described above can shape and reinforce how our clients experience and relate to themselves and to others. There's nothing cold or formulaic about CFT case formulation—at each stage, we're linking back to the core affective experiences of the client. These affective experiences are particularly important in terms of how clients' implicit feelings about themselves and others are shaped over time by the elaboration and consequences of safety strategies. Avoiding others out of fear of rejection produces distance and the withering of social contacts, reinforcing our clients' self-perceptions of being unlikeable and of others as cold and rejecting. Substance abuse to cope with traumatic memories can lead to relationship problems and decreased effectiveness, shaping and reinforcing a shame-based view of themselves as broken and incompetent. As clients observe (or simply *feel*) the consequences of their safety strategies, their experience of themselves and others can be elaborated in ways that seem overwhelming and inescapable.

Like core fears, these patterns of relating to self and others (and related distress) can lead to the development of more safety strategies that produce even more problematic unintended consequences. Over time, clients can find themselves feeling trapped in a cycle in which everything they try—each effort making complete sense in light of the preceding experiences—seems to deepen their problems. By exploring the linkages between the different components of the formulation, we can help our clients compassionately understand the factors that maintain their "stuckness." Having developed that understanding, we can then work collaboratively to help them replace safety strategies with effective, compassionate coping and relating that will yield positive consequences in their lives and build positive self-experiences of being compassionate and competent. Let's look at a completed case formulation worksheet for Josh.

CFT CASE FORMULATION WORKSHEET: JOSH

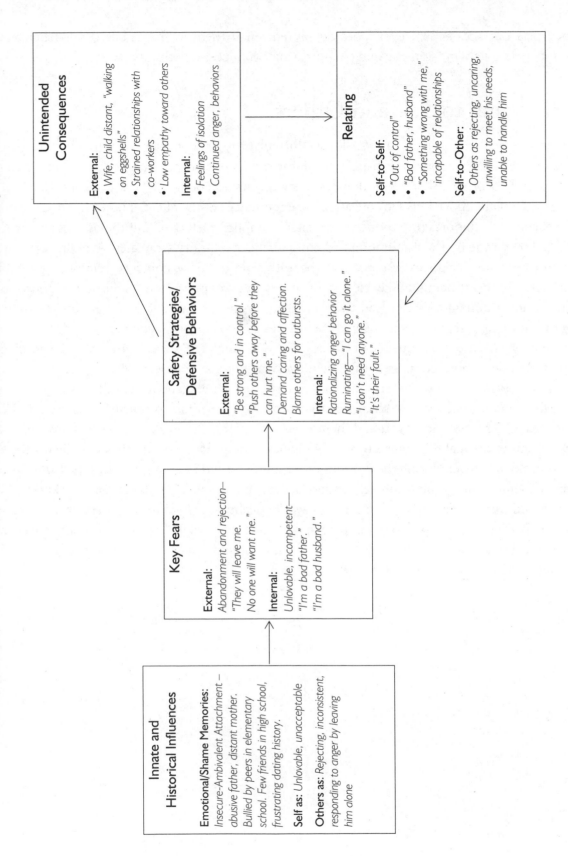

Innate and Historical Influences

Emotional/Shame Memories:
Insecure-Ambivalent Attachment — abusive father, distant mother. Bullied by peers in elementary school. Few friends in high school, frustrating dating history.

Self as: *Unlovable, unacceptable*

Others as: *Rejecting, inconsistent, responding to anger by leaving him alone*

Key Fears

External:
Abandonment and rejection—
"They will leave me."
No one will want me."

Internal:
Unlovable, incompetent—
"I'm a bad father."
"'I'm a bad husband."

Safety Strategies/ Defensive Behaviors

External:
"Be strong and in control."
"Push others away before they can hurt me."
Demand caring and affection. Blame others for outbursts.

Internal:
Rationalizing anger behavior Ruminating—"I can go it alone."
"I don't need anyone."
"It's their fault."

Unintended Consequences

External:
• *Wife, child distant, "walking on eggshells"*
• *Strained relationships with co-workers*
• *Low empathy toward others*

Internal:
• *Feelings of isolation*
• *Continued anger, behaviors*

Relating

Self-to-Self:
• *"Out of control"*
• *"Bad father, husband"*
• *"Something wrong with me," incapable of relationships*

Self-to-Other:
• *Others as rejecting, uncaring, unwilling to meet his needs, unable to handle him*

A good case formulation frequently leads us straight into treatment planning. Considering the formulation above, we can consider that Josh would likely benefit from Socratic dialogue to help him compassionately understand how his anger and problems make sense in the context of his temperament and social shaping. Mindfulness training would help him learn to recognize the arising of anger and irritability as well as thoughts of rejection, unlovability, and negative ruminations about himself and others. Strategies such as soothing rhythm breathing, safe place imagery, and compassionate letter-writing would help him soothe himself in such situations, enabling him to shift into a more compassionate perspective and avoid his previous cycle of outbursts, blaming, and self-shaming. Josh would also likely benefit from compassionate self work, which emphasizes the development of specific skills such as mentalizing and empathy for others and himself. This work would be aimed at developing compassionate self-talk and adaptive ways of relating to his family and coworkers, such as assertiveness training.

SUMMARY

Some of our clients will present with a dizzying array of challenges that can make it difficult to know where to begin treatment. Case formulation helps to organize our observations about clients and to plan effective treatment strategies. As you might imagine, the process of developing a formulation and exploring it with the client can be an emotional one. It can be heartbreaking for clients to realize how their lives have been shaped in ways that have created terrible suffering for them over time—suffering that may have been exacerbated by their own attempts to cope. In CFT, this process is continuously rooted in compassionate understanding and in connecting our exploration to the client's affective experience. In the next chapter, we'll explore a powerful way of helping clients explore their emotions through the process of chair work (introduced in the previous chapter): the Multiple Selves exercise.

CHAPTER 14

Exploring Affect: The Multiple Selves Practice

A primary goal of CFT involves helping clients bring compassion to their emotional experiences. We've discussed how different affects and motivations can organize our clients' experience in very different ways, and we've proposed Compassionate Self work as an organizing framework for developing an adaptive, warm, confident version of the self. In this chapter, we'll introduce a chair exercise that will tie all of this together: the Multiple Selves practice (Kolts, 2012).

MULTIPLE VERSIONS OF THE SELF

In the Multiple Selves practice, developed by Paul Gilbert, clients are guided through an exploration of how various affects and motives shape their experience. We'll prompt clients to identify a situation they've been struggling with, and help them explore their response to the situation in terms of the feelings, thoughts, and motivations associated with different emotional states, guiding clients into and back out of these different emotional "selves." The Multiple Selves exercise commonly focuses on anger ("angry self"), anxiety ("anxious self") and sadness ("sad self"), but different "selves" can be substituted, depending upon a client's presenting concerns. After exploring the perspectives of these different selves, the client is guided to shift into the perspective of the compassionate self, and prompted to consider both the situation and the perspective of the other emotional selves from this compassionate perspective. This works well as a chair exercise, in which a different chair is used for each emotional self, but clients can also complete the exercise in writing as homework, or even in group settings, using a piece of paper divided into four sections—one for each self.

While the Multiple Selves exercise is fairly straightforward, there is a lot going on. My friend and colleague Tobyn Bell, who is conducting research on the Multiple Selves exercise, highlights a number of potential objectives we can keep in mind for the practice—these are just a few (personal communication, 2015):

- Increasing awareness of, and exposure to, threat emotions that may be avoided

- Exploring how different emotional perspectives organize the mind and body

- Providing a window into the emotional dynamics of self-criticism ("What does your angry self think about your anxious self?")

- Learning to shift in and out of different emotional experiences and perspectives, and developing confidence around being able to do this

- Developing and expressing compassion for these different emotional selves

- Compassion-in-action: practice putting the compassionate self in the driver's seat

- Developing tolerance and compassion for avoided aspects of the self, so that they can be integrated into a positive self-identity

Exploring the Selves

In exploring the perspectives of different emotional selves, the therapist begins by prompting the client to "invite in" this aspect of the self, giving herself permission to dive deeply into emotions she may commonly tend to avoid. This can be challenging, as clients may have learned that certain emotions shouldn't even be acknowledged, much less experienced. Some clients may need to engage in the exercise multiple times before they can connect with avoided aspects of the self. Here are some tips for facilitating the practice:

- Provide reassurance that you'll be there to guide the client into and out of the exercise.

- Start by prompting the client to connect with how the emotion is felt in the body, and instruct her to imagine these sensations building within her.

- Then prompt her to consider the mental experiences associated with the emotion: thoughts, imagery, and motivation. If this emotion could speak, what would it say? What would it want to do? If the (angry/anxious/sad) self had complete control and unlimited power, what would it do? What does this emotional self *want*?

- Perhaps begin with an emotion to which the client has an easier time connecting, then proceed to less familiar emotions.

- When shifting from one self to another, have the client do some soothing rhythm breathing. I also sometimes like to offer a mental "palate cleanser," tossing out a few random—often silly—things for the client to visualize or think about, to aid the shift out of an emotion and to lighten the experience a bit.

- Let clients know that it is all right if they find an emotion to be "sticky" and have trouble shifting out of it. Reassure them that this is normal, and encourage them to honor this aspect of themselves, and to keep going.

The Captain of the Ship

One goal of the Multiple Selves exercise is to help clients relate compassionately to the various threat-based versions of the self. The idea is to shift their relationship with these emotions from *something that is wrong with me* to *understandable responses to perceived threats*. Our evolved threat emotions aren't *bad*; they just aren't always the most useful responses to modern stressors.

I've found that clients often have an easier time relating compassionately to these threat-based emotional selves if we set the stage for the exercise by using a metaphor, which I'll call the "captain of the ship" (Kolts & Chodron, 2013). In this metaphor, we have the client imagine a ship at sea, with various passengers on board, including the various emotional selves. When the ship eventually encounters a storm (as we all will face emotional "storms" in life), we imagine the emotional passengers doing what they always do: the angry self rages and criticizes; the anxious self worries and cowers; the sad self shrinks and becomes mournful. We then set up the compassionate self as the captain of the ship. Kind, wise, and confident, this captain understands that storms are just a part of sailing, and has the wisdom and experience to guide the ship to safety. The captain also understands that such storms can be very scary for the passengers, so instead of becoming upset with them, the captain comforts them, reassures them, and offers to take care of things.

This metaphor sets the stage for clients to relate compassionately to the understandable reactions produced by various threat emotions, while understanding that we don't want to give these emotional selves control of the ship. Instead, we set up the compassionate self as a superordinate aspect of the self and apply this perspective in working with both the situation and the emotions produced by it.

Let's consider an example of how this might play out in a session:

Therapist: Josh, we've spent some time discussing your anger, but in doing the case formulation, it sounds like there might be some other emotions worth looking at as well. I was wondering if you'd be up to trying another chair exercise to explore these different feelings.

Josh: I'm not sure I understand the point of it. The anger is really the problem.

Therapist: Interestingly, anger can sometimes act as a secondary emotion—this means that it can arise in response to other feelings. If we look deeply at our anger, we often find that there are other, more vulnerable feelings behind it—like fear, sadness, or anxiety. Sometimes we can even use anger to try and avoid those feelings. Does that make sense?

Josh: It makes a lot of sense. I do that.

Therapist: Could you tell me more about that?

Josh: I feel anger so I don't have to feel that stuff. I don't go there.

Therapist: Ahh... I've heard that a lot. A lot of us tend to use anger in that way. Do you think you might be willing to go there if I were there to help?

Josh: (*reluctantly*) I guess so.

Therapist: Remember when we talked about compassion being about having the courage to face the stuff that scares us? This is exactly what we were talking about. In this practice, we'll consider a recent situation that triggered your anger, and explore how different emotions relate to that situation. We'll visit the perspective of your angry self, your anxious self, and your sad self, and finish up with the compassionate self, which you're familiar with.

Josh: Mmm-hmm.

Therapist: While I set up the chairs for the exercise, could you bring to mind a recent time when you struggled with anger? (*Gets up and arranges four chairs positioned a few feet apart as corners of a square, pointed inward.*)

Josh: That's easy. My wife and I got in a fight last night.

Therapist: (*sitting back down*) Could you tell me a little more about that?

Josh: Sure. I got home from work, and the moment I walked in the house, she started in on me. A couple of weeks ago, our lawn mower had stopped working. I'd told her that I'd fix it as soon as I could—even though I don't know what's wrong with it. Well, I'd planned to try and fix it over the weekend, but we got busy with other things. Last night, the moment I walked in the door, she points out that it's still not working—(*in a nagging voice*) "Is the lawn mower fixed yet?" She knew it wasn't! I just blew up at her, and told her that if she wanted the damn thing fixed, maybe she should fix it herself. After that, she just shut down. She and the kids avoided me for the rest of the night, and I just spent the evening stewing over it.

It's like I'm always the problem…I mean, I'd just walked in the door from work. But I feel terrible about it. I thought I'd been doing better at this…

Therapist: This sounds like a perfect experience for this exercise, Josh. It sounds like you have a lot of feelings about this situation. Ready to start?

Josh: I guess so.

Therapist: Great. To start, how about you move over into this chair? (*Points to the chair.*)

Josh: (*Moves to the chair and sits.*)

Therapist: This is where your angry self is going to sit. Remember when we discussed that different emotions can organize our minds and bodies in different ways? Our attention, thoughts, feelings—that sort of thing? We're going to explore that. I'd like you to invite your angry self into the room. Thinking of this situation, allow any anger you feel about it to come to the surface. If you were to feel that anger rising in you, how would you feel it in your body?

Josh: I feel it as tension—in my jaw, my forehead, my gut. I tighten up all over.

Therapist: Imagine that tension filling your body, building and building…your angry self completely in control. Imagine being completely being taken over by the anger. We want to give that angry version of you a voice—to hear what it has to say. Imagining yourself filled with anger, how do you feel?

Josh: Furious! Furious at her, and furious at me.

Therapist: You're doing great. From this perspective of your angry self, what are you thinking? What does this angry version of you have to say?

Josh: That she doesn't appreciate any damn thing I do. I had just walked in from work! All I wanted was to relax and unwind a little bit, and she starts nagging me about the lawn mower. Why doesn't *she* fix the fucking lawn mower? Why do I have to be the one that does everything? She always says, "We need to do this…" or "We need to do that…" Well, I know what that means—that *I* need to do it! I get sick of it, you know?

Therapist: It sounds like your angry self has a lot to say. If your angry self were in complete control in this situation, what would he want to do? What would you do?

Josh: I know exactly what I'd do. I'd tell her where she could stick her lawn mower. I'd tell her that I'm sick of being taken for granted, and then I'd pack up my shit, get in my car, drive away, and never come back. (*Begins breathing more quickly, and shakes his head back and forth.*)

Therapist: Josh, you mentioned feeling angry at Karen, but also at yourself. Could you talk about that, from the perspective of your angry self? How does your angry self feel about you?

Josh: My angry self hates me. Why do I keep screwing it up? What the fuck is wrong with me? And then, after...I wanted to apologize to her, to try and talk to her, but I couldn't do it. What the hell is wrong with me?

Therapist: So it sounds like there is some anger with yourself for how you handled things, both during the situation and after, but also maybe some other feelings—like some fear or anxiety that kept you from apologizing, or some disappointment with yourself.

Josh: (*Nods, hangs his head, and looks down.*)

Therapist: This seems like it might be a good time to shift to another chair. Before we do, does your angry self have anything else to say?

Josh: (*Shakes his head to indicate "no."*)

Therapist: In that case, how about you move to this chair over here? (*Points to the adjacent chair.*)

Josh: (*Moves to other chair and sits.*)

Therapist: Before we move on, let's do some soothing rhythm breathing—slowing down the breath...slowing down the body...slowing down the mind. (*Waits for thirty seconds to one minute.*)

Josh: (*Slows his breathing.*)

Therapist: Looking over to the angry chair, let's thank your angry self for sharing his perspective with us. He did a good job of helping us to understand the perspective of your anger.

Josh: (*Looks at the anger chair with a neutral expression on his face.*)

Therapist: Let's have some mental "palate cleansers." I'll say a few things, and you think of them, okay?

Josh: Okay.

Therapist: Tater tots! (*Waits five seconds.*) Dancing pandas! (*Waits five seconds.*) Your favorite sports team! (*Waits five seconds.*) What is your favorite sports team, anyway?

Josh: I like the Oakland Raiders.

Therapist: Well, that explains the anger. (*Smiles.*) Just joking—I'm a Chargers fan.

Josh: (*Smiles.*) I get you. Too bad they've never won a Super Bowl.

Therapist: Ouch—well played! That was just a way to focus our attention on something else, to transition from the anger. I find a little silliness can sometimes help with that. Ready to keep going?

Josh: Why not?

Therapist: Good. This chair we're in now is the "anxious chair." In this chair, we're going to invite your anxious, fearful self to share his perspective. Bringing up the situation last night with Karen, is there any anxiety or fear that comes up? Any worries about how things happened?

Josh: Yeah. Yeah, there are.

Therapist: Like we did before, let's give your anxious self the floor. Imagine the anxiety building in your body. How would you feel it in your body?

Josh: Restless, and jittery, like I can't relax. And an unsettled feeling in my stomach… a little nauseous.

Therapist: Imagining that anxiety building and building, how does your anxious self feel about this situation?

Josh: Scared, and worried.

Therapist: Scared?

Josh: Scared that I'll never be good enough. That I'll keep coming to these sessions but nothing will change. Worried that they'll finally get sick of it, and leave me. Scared that I'll push them away, and I'll be alone. Hell, I'm even worried that I can't fix the lawn mower, and that Karen will decide that I'm not good for anything.

Therapist: It sounds like there's a lot of anxiety in there with the anger. If this anxious version of you were in complete control, what would he do? From this perspective of your anxious self, what would you do?

Josh: Pretty much what I did last night—nothing. Just sit there and think about it over and over, scared to do anything. (*Pauses, becomes tearful, looks down, then up at therapist.*) I wanted to apologize, you know. I wanted to tell her I was sorry for snapping at her, that I'd meant to fix the lawn mower but wasn't sure how to do it. But I was scared that she wouldn't care—that she'd tell me if I was really sorry, I wouldn't talk to her like that. Maybe she'd be right. I'm scared that she doesn't love me anymore, and that the kids just see me as this raging lunatic.

Therapist:	It sounds like your anxious self is really scared that there's no making things better, that maybe there's no way to control the anger and repair your relationship with your family.
Josh:	(*Looks down.*) Yeah.
Therapist:	It also sounds like there's some real sadness coming up about this situation as well. Rather than resisting it, why don't we invite your sad self into the room? Would you mind shifting over to this chair? (*Points to the next adjacent chair to the right.*)
Josh:	(*Quietly moves to the next chair.*)
Therapist:	This is the "sad self" chair. It seems to me that there is some sadness coming up in you about this situation. Is that right?
Josh:	(*Nods.*)
Therapist:	Let's go with the sadness, then…inviting your sad self to share his perspective. What does the sadness feel like in your body?
Josh:	Heavy, like a sinking feeling, right here. (*Motions toward his gut.*)
Therapist:	Imagine if that sad, heavy, sinking feeling were to build and build in you. What feelings would come up?
Josh:	This is the worst. I don't do this.
Therapist:	I'm here to help, Josh. You can do this. How does that sad version of you feel?
Josh:	(*crying*) I just feel hopeless. Look at me, sitting here crying like a baby. I feel helpless, like there's nothing I can do.
Therapist:	There's a lot of sadness in there, isn't there? Sadness, and feelings of hopelessness. What does your sad self think about all this? What thoughts come up?
Josh:	(*crying*) That I'm losing my family, and it's my fault. That they don't love me, and they'd be better off without me. That my daughter and son are ashamed of me.
Therapist:	(*nodding quietly*) Mmm-hmm.
Josh:	I feel like I'm a terrible father. Like I'm teaching them all the wrong stuff. That they're ashamed of me, and ashamed to be with me.
Therapist:	If this sad self were in complete control, what would he want to do? What would he do?
Josh:	Just give up. Just lay down and die. Maybe then they could just forget about me and go on with their lives.

Therapist: (*Pauses.*)

Josh: (*Pauses, wipes his eyes, and sighs.*)

Therapist: You did it, Josh. You let yourself feel it.

Josh: For whatever it's worth...

Therapist: I think it's worth a lot. That took a lot of courage. That's what we've been talking about—the courage of compassion. (*Pauses.*) Would you mind moving to this last chair? (*Gestures.*)

Josh: Sure.

Therapist: This chair is where your kind, wise, courageous, compassionate self sits. In a minute, we'll slow down our breathing, and invite the compassionate self into the room. But first, let's look around at these other emotional selves (*gesturing*)— the angry self, the anxious self, the sad self—and thank them for sharing their perspectives. They've done a good job helping us understand your anger, anxiety, and sadness. (*Pauses.*)

Josh: (*Slows his breathing; looks around at the chairs.*)

Therapist: Now this self will be more familiar, as we've been practicing here and in your homework. Let's take a bit of time to do some soothing rhythm breathing— slowing things down, and paving the way for compassion to arise. (*Pauses for one minute.*)

Josh: (*Closes his eyes; slows his breathing.*)

Therapist: Now allowing yourself to feel those compassionate qualities rising in you...the kind motivation to work with the suffering, to help yourself and others... (*Pauses.*) The wisdom to look deeply, and understand things from different perspectives... (*Pauses.*) The confidence and courage to work with whatever comes up... (*Pauses.*) And when you're ready, opening your eyes, bringing these compassionate qualities with you.

Josh: (*Opens his eyes.*)

Therapist: Now, we're going to hear from the compassionate self, but I want to set things up a bit. We all have these different versions of us—angry, anxious, sad—but the idea is that we can choose which part of ourselves we want to put in charge. Imagine that we're out at sea, on a ship. Imagine that there is a big storm—just like we'll all face stormy times in life—and that there's thunder, and rain, and water sloshing over the side of the ship. These emotional selves (*gesturing toward the chairs*) are passengers on the ship. It's scary, and they're freaking out—doing the only things they know how to do. Your angry self is raging and blaming. Your anxious self is shaking and worrying. Your sad self shrinks into a corner, hopeless. They're doing their best, but they don't have what it takes to steer us to safety. And here you are—the compassionate self. Imagine that the compassionate self—this kind, wise, confident version of you—is captain of the ship. You've spent a lot of time on ships, and you know that storms just happen sometimes. More than that, you know what to do. You know how to get the ship through safely, and how to rely on your crew when you need help. This compassionate captain is also kind. You understand how scary this can be for the passengers (*gesturing*), and that they're doing the best they can.

Josh: (*Nods.*)

Therapist: Looking at the other passengers—the other versions of you in this stormy situation—does it make sense that they'd be freaking out?

Josh: It sure does.

Therapist: How do you feel about them?

Josh: I feel bad for them. They're scared and they don't know what to do—and what they do know how to do doesn't help.

Therapist: So as this kind, wise, courageous captain, what would you do? How would you reassure them? What would you say?

Josh: I'd tell them it's going to be okay. I'd tell them not to worry—that I'm going to handle it.

Therapist: How do you think they'd feel, hearing that?

Josh: Maybe a little better.

Therapist: Now let's think about your current situation. You've had this argument with Karen. Your angry self is raging—at her, and at you—and wants to just storm off. Your anxious self wants to apologize, but is scared to do so, and scared to be rejected if he does. Your sad self is ready to give up, feeling like a terrible husband and father, like nothing is working. What do you have to say to them? How would you reassure them?

Josh: I'd tell them that this isn't the end of the world. Deep down, I know that I want to be with Karen, Chloe, and Aiden, and that they want to be with me—they've told me so. While we still go at each other sometimes, it happens a lot less than it used to. Even last night, I let it drop rather than keeping at it. Karen knows I'm trying, and she appreciates it. She told me last week that she was proud of me for going to these sessions, and for keeping at it.

Therapist: So you'd reassure them that all isn't lost, and that things are getting better?

Josh: (*Nods.*) They *are* getting better. We had a really good weekend—went to the lake, went swimming and fishing. It was the best time we'd had in a while, and I didn't get angry once.

Therapist: Do you normally get angry at the lake?

Josh: Well, Aiden's a little kid, and so he's always getting his fishing line tangled, or losing lures. In the past I've gotten irritated and lectured him about how he needs to be more careful, which always shuts things down. This time, I didn't even mind. I reminded myself that even I get tangles sometimes, and he's just a little kid. He doesn't do it on purpose.

Therapist: That's great, Josh. That's just what compassion looks like—trying to understand what's going on from the other person's perspective, and to be helpful.

Josh: Well, it worked a lot better than getting all worked up about it.

Therapist: If you could go back to the situation last night and work with it from the perspective of your compassionate self, would you do anything differently?

Josh: I would. First, I'd try not to get worked up in the first place, and try to remind myself that she wasn't purposefully trying to criticize me—she's probably just noticing the grass getting longer and wondering when she might be able to mow it.

Therapist: What if you had gotten worked up, and had the conflict. Would your compassionate self have handled things differently afterward?

Josh: Yeah. I'd apologize, tell her I'll get to it as soon as I can, and ask her to be patient with me. I think she could do that, as long as she sees that I really am trying.

The vignette above demonstrates several characteristic aspects of the Multiple Selves exercise. The therapist guides the client into the perspective of various affective "selves," beginning with physical sensations, and then prompting the client to explore feelings, thoughts, and motivations associated with these emotions. Transitions are eased via the use of breathing exercises, and making things a bit lighter through a bit of banter about football. Although a mental "palate cleanser" was used once, the therapist was able to find easy transition points the rest of the time, taking advantage of natural shifts in the client's dialogue to move fluidly from one emotional self to the other.

Sometimes our clients will be reluctant to explore an emotional "self" that feels particularly threatening or unfamiliar. When Josh became hesitant to enter the perspective of the sad self, the therapist offered encouragement, providing reassurance to the client that he had support. The therapist followed up on this later, reinforcing the client for his willingness to enter these vulnerable perspectives, and linking to the ongoing work ("That's the courage of compassion."). You may have also noticed the therapist beginning to explore the dynamics of self-criticism through considering the interactions between different selves ("How does your angry self feel about you?"). This exploration could be deepened when time allows ("How do your sad and anxious selves feel about your angry self?").

Finally, the therapist spent a fair bit of time paving the way for the transition to the compassionate self via the "captain of the ship" metaphor, and through various suggestions ("How would you reassure them?"). Depending on how deeply the client has been able to connect with the perspective of the compassionate self through previous therapeutic work, the therapist will be more or less active in facilitating this perspective—not "feeding him lines," so much as suggesting particular affective orientations ("Can you understand how they'd be scared? How would you reassure them?"). If things go well, by the time the transition is made to the client's problematic situation, he'll be ready to offer a compassionate perspective, as Josh did—bringing compassion both to his own feelings about the situation and to how he might handle similar situations more helpfully in the future. One thing the therapist could have done (but in this case didn't) was to have the compassionate self speak directly to the other selves, reassuring them and offering to help.

Debriefing the Exercise

It's important to follow this (and all such exercises) with a debriefing. We want to explore what the experience was like for the client, and what he learned from it. If a client struggled with entering the perspective of a particular self, or has any other problems, we can offer validation and encouragement—this is tough stuff! This is a good time for the therapist to draw upon the perspective of her own compassionate self, connecting with sympathy and empathy around the difficulty of what she's asking the client to do in exploring these feelings, and considering what might be most helpful in helping him make sense of the experience. Here are a few questions that can be useful in the debriefing:

- What was that like for you?

- Were you able to connect with the emotional selves? Which were easier, or more difficult?

- Did you find yourself able to shift from one self to another? What challenges showed up as we did that?

- What was it like looking at these emotions from the perspective of your compassionate self?

- Were you able to see how each of these reactions makes sense?

- What did we learn from this that we can take forward into our work?

When it comes to the Compassionate Self work in the exercise, we want to focus on reinforcing the effort—validating the challenges, and acknowledging the triumphs. The key is to try and help the client consider how he might bring compassion to both aspects of the experience: the feelings he has, and the situation itself.

SUMMARY

I've placed the Multiple Selves exercise toward the end of the book because it allows us to tie together many of the themes that run through a course of CFT. Rather than avoiding uncomfortable emotions and situations, clients are helped to compassionately turn toward these scary experiences—with warmth rather than judgment—so that they can really understand them. Clients can develop the confidence that comes from learning they *can* feel these emotions without getting trapped in them, and consider how it makes sense that these feelings might arise in them. Emotional conflicts can be explored, and clients can be guided to see how different emotions can serve as triggers for other emotions—for example, how they might shift to anger in the effort to avoid sadness, or experience anxiety when faced with their own rage, sadness, or fears. They can learn to relate to these emotions as valuable parts of themselves that nonetheless aren't equipped to "steer the ship." Finally, the exercise can help clients learn to empower the compassionate self as a helpful perspective for working effectively with challenging emotions and the situations that trigger them.

CHAPTER 15

Riding the Third Wave: Integrating CFT into Your Therapy

This is an exciting time to be a mental health professional. Recent decades have proven revolutionary in terms of how quickly we're learning new things about how human beings work. Even as we've only explored the tip of the iceberg, the rapidly growing bodies of research in neuroscience, behavioral science, and emotion are allowing the beginnings of a truly integrative understanding of human functioning. CFT seeks to represent this evolved, integrated understanding of what it means to be a human being, and to translate this science into powerful, practical methods for helping people turn toward their struggles with warmth and acceptance, and work with these struggles effectively.

WHAT DOES A CFT THERAPIST LOOK LIKE?

In approaching this book, I've attempted to emphasize the aspects of CFT that distinguish it from other therapies. Particularly in a "Made Simple" book, space prohibits me from exploring much more than the basic elements of the therapy. This is why I've generally chosen not to cover even compassion interventions that, while entirely CFT-consistent, are well covered in other places (such as in Kristin Neff and Chris Germer's excellent Mindful Self-Compassion program; Neff & Germer, 2013). While reading the various case vignettes in the book, you may have had questions like, "Would a CFT therapist use exposure therapy with this patient?" "What about social skills training, activity scheduling, and behavior activation?" "Would a CFT therapist prompt a client to explore her values?" The answer to all of these questions is a resounding "Yes!"

A core value CFT therapists hold is that we don't ignore good science. What this means is that CFT is constantly evolving from both a theoretical and a practice perspective. For example, over the past few years, we've placed increasing emphasis on breath and body work in consideration of Stephen Porges' excellent work on polyvagal theory (e.g. Porges, 2011) and other research demonstrating the power of engaging the parasympathetic nervous system. Applications of CFT have been developed that consider the new science of memory reconsolidation (Monfils, Cowansage, Klann, & LeDoux, 2009; Schiller et al., 2010) in applying Compassionate Self work within exposure therapy (Kolts, Parker, & Johnson, 2013). My friends and colleagues Dennis Tirch, Benji Schoendorff, and Laura Silberstein have worked to integrate the compassion focus of CFT with the theoretical perspective of acceptance and commitment therapy, or ACT (Tirch, Schoendorff, & Silberstein, 2014). And I'm increasingly intrigued by the implications of relational frame theory (Hayes, Barnes-Holmes, & Roche, 2001) for understanding the nuances of threat system processing in CFT.

When one hears the word "compassion," one doesn't necessarily think *empiricism*. But from the perspective of CFT, one of the most compassionate things we can do is to get better and better at really understanding the sources and dynamics of human suffering, and do a better and better job at researching and refining powerful ways to help alleviate and prevent it. Compassion is about helping *effectively*, not just about feeling helpful. In this way, science is core to compassion, and the CFT therapist is likely to draw upon any tools that have good science behind them. So if you want to do CFT, you don't have to give up any of the things you already do that work.

What may change, however, is how you do them. Because CFT is rooted in *compassion*. This emphasis should be present in all aspects of the therapy—the way the therapist relates to the client, and how we help clients relate to themselves, and to others. Rooted in our understanding of underlying affective systems, this means that CFT will always contain warmth (expressed in ways that work for the client), an emphasis on assisting clients to relate to their experiences with understanding and kindness rather than shame, a focus on helping clients learn to create feelings of safeness in themselves, and the development of the emotional courage to approach and work with the things that really scare them. Like ACT, CFT isn't about moving away from feelings and experiences that make us uncomfortable. It's about moving *toward* effective, compassionate ways of being in our minds and in the world, and even moving toward the things that bother us, so that we can compassionately work with them. So whatever we're doing in CFT, there is always an emphasis on warmth, understanding, safeness, and courage.

CFT AND OTHER MODELS

In writing this book, it wasn't my intention to convert therapists to CFT, but to provide you with compassionate perspectives, understandings, and tools that you can use to further develop your effectiveness as a therapist, regardless of your existing modality. As you may have noticed, CFT has a good deal in common with some other therapy approaches. While I've discussed some of the common ground between CFT and approaches such as ACT, DBT, and EFT, those of you with different therapeutic backgrounds may notice similarities with other models as well—attachment therapy approaches, schema therapy, and even newer psychodynamic approaches spring to mind, for example. It's my hope that practitioners from many other traditions will find something here to deepen their existing therapy practices, particularly in helping clients relate warmly and compassionately to themselves, to their problems, and to other people.

In considering where CFT interfaces theoretically with other approaches, I see it falling within the "third wave" of behavior therapies, with an emphasis on changing one's relationship to uncomfortable thoughts and emotions (rather than trying to get rid of them), the cultivation of mindfulness, and a priority placed on helping people build adaptive, meaningful lives (versus simply reducing symptoms). While it's a bit more of a stretch, I also see CFT generally fitting alongside therapies like ACT and functional analytic psychotherapy (FAP) within the realm of contextual behavioral science (CBS). The philosophical core of CBS—functional contextualism—involves understanding that the function of a behavior (which can include thoughts and perhaps even emotions and motives) must be understood within the context in which it occurs. In understanding human functioning, CFT expands the meaning of "context" from strict behavioral terms to include the neurological contexts that influence affect, cognition, and behavior, as well as the evolutionary contexts that have shaped how emotions, motivations, and their behavioral manifestations play out in our lives.

This is both a strength and a weakness of the CFT approach, depending upon one's perspective. It's certainly a trade-off. I think that considering the evolved functions of emotions and motives and having a neuroscience-based understanding of the ways emotions operate in our brains and bodies has tremendous power in helping to deshame the challenges faced by our clients. Understanding why and how our emotions play out the way they do—and that this is not our fault (as we didn't design these processes)—can be quite powerful in helping people stop beating themselves up for their own experiences and learn to work with these experiences effectively.

However, the intellectually honest CFT practitioner must admit that drawing upon such explanations comes with sacrifices, from the standpoint of strict empiricism. Behaviorists would note that ontological statements about the evolutionary origins and evolved functions of emotions and motives in large part defy empirical observation, and they'd be right. It's fair criticism.

In weighing these issues for myself, I've concluded that the trade-off is worth it. I think the benefits of considering the functions and dynamics of our emotions and motives within evolutionary and neurological, as well as behavioral, contexts (as best we understand them), justify this compromise—*if* we keep a steady eye to the science. The Dalai Lama is well known for having said, "If science disproves some aspect of Buddhism, then Buddhism must change." The same can and should be said for CFT, or, I would argue, for any approach that aspires to be empirically based. To the extent that an approach extends beyond tenets that have been established through solid, observable science, that approach must be amenable to change based on new data. (Of course, the hope is that *all* approaches would be amenable to change based on new data.) Dogmatism benefits no one—our patients least of all. Humility, on the other hand, offers the promise of approaches which can be continually refined in the service of doing an ever-better job at eliminating and preventing human suffering.

BRINGING CFT INTO YOUR THERAPY ROOM

It's my hope that you've found something useful in CFT, and want to begin bringing what you've learned into your therapy practice. One way to do this would be to select a clinical case and try to follow the progression I've attempted to lay out in this book—incorporating the various layers of relationship, understanding, mindful awareness, and purposeful cultivation of compassion. If that feels like a lot, perhaps simply try to incorporate one or more of the elements you've found here that falls outside the things you normally do in therapy. Below, I've included a few suggestions about how you might begin to do this.

Consider the Roles You Are Inhabiting as the Therapist

We've discussed the various roles served by the CFT therapist—teacher, facilitator of a process of guided discovery, secure attachment base, and model of the compassionate self. As we do therapy, we can consider the roles we are inhabiting, and how best to do that. What function are we serving within the context of the therapeutic relationship, and how can we use our presence to facilitate the goals and direction of the therapy? Perhaps try to pay a bit more attention to these roles, and consider whether doing so helps clarify questions in the therapy such as *What should I do now?* In this way, we can borrow from the Compassionate Self practice as we reflect on the therapeutic work outside the session: when our clients throw us a curveball, we can consider—from the perspective of the teacher, facilitator, secure base, or compassionate model—*How would I understand what is happening here? How might I respond?*

Occasionally Bring in the Evolutionary Model

We don't have to go into deep discussions of evolution—in fact, those generally aren't helpful. But helping people recognize the different things that happen to their minds and bodies when they feel threatened or driven versus when they feel safe can be helpful. Considering threat emotions as having evolved to help us protect ourselves can help clients understand why they get so "stuck" in these emotions. It's no accident that these emotions narrow our attention, thinking, and mental imagery onto perceived sources of threat, and it's certainly not the client's fault that this happens. Learning that helping themselves feel safe reverses this process (facilitating more flexible attention and reasoning, reflective thinking, and prosocial tendencies) can improve client motivation around working with these emotions. Helping clients understand what to do and why or how it will be helpful can be very powerful in building their willingness to do something new.

Use Socratic Dialogue to Undermine Self-Attacking

With or without going into the evolutionary model, we can use Socratic dialogue to help clients shift from shaming themselves for their internal experience to the awareness that there are many aspects of their lives that they neither chose nor designed—things which are quite literally not their fault.

- "What was your experience of that emotion? Did you *choose* to get angry/afraid/resentful there, or did those feelings just arise in your mind and body?"

- "When did you learn that you _____? What experiences taught you that?"

- "Given what we know about your/her/his background, does it make sense that you/she/he would feel/think/experience things in this way?"

- "When your self-critic attacks you for _____, how do you feel? What does it motivate you to do? What do you end up doing?"

Questions like these can help clients begin to let go of the tendency to attack themselves for things they didn't choose or design, and to understand their experiences and behaviors in the context of their lives. In other words, the questions set the stage for them to compassionately take responsibility for making their lives better.

Use the Three Circles as a Facilitator for Mindfulness

Clients who initially struggle with mindfully observing and accepting their thoughts and emotions can sometimes be helped by the simplicity of the three circles. I've had numerous clients who had great difficulty observing thoughts or labeling specific emotions, but who were able to consider which of those three circles was active at any given time. Combined with an understanding of how those circles organize our minds and bodies (for example, that threat emotions tend to narrow and focus attention and thinking, and safeness emotions lead to reflectiveness, flexibility, and pro-sociality), it can be a powerful thing for a client to learn to notice *what circle am I in?* As I've mentioned, a former student of mine who was also a cheerleading coach came up with a pithy way to remember this: "When in doubt, circle out!"

Use the Three Circles in Considering Your Interactions with the Client

We can also "circle out" in the therapy room. I've found it can be useful to consider the three circles both in my treatment planning and in working with challenges that arise in therapy. For example, I roughly shoot for around a 3-2-2 safeness-drive-threat ratio in therapy: three parts safeness, two parts drive, two parts threat. My goal for the therapeutic environment is to create an experience of safeness for my clients that grows as they learn to create these experiences in themselves. Good therapy also gets the drive system going—inspiring and motivating clients to work for change in their lives. Finally, there will be a good bit of threat in the therapy if we're working with real issues—but the key is that there is a balance, with threat experiences evoked in an intentional manner so that they can be compassionately worked with. It's not just about safeness—we're striving for a flexible, fluid balance in which different affective experiences and motivations can arise and be evoked as they serve the situation at hand. Together, we want to appropriately work with perceived threats, activate and maintain motivation around pursuing therapeutic goals, and create a context of safeness in which comfort can be experienced and questions of meaning and values can be reflected upon.

Considering the three circles can also be helpful when we're struggling in therapy or the relationship doesn't seem to be going as well as we'd like. Sometimes we'll find that we've inadvertently become a threat cue for the client. We can think of countertransference in this way—considering that perhaps our own threat or drive systems have been triggered by the client's behavior, or something about that client that triggers our own previous conditioning. We may observe that we've been so much in drive—excited by our wonderful new treatment plan—that we've left our client behind. When therapy seems to have hit a sticking point or there's a rupture in the therapeutic relationship, considering the situation in terms of the three circles either on our own or together with the client can sometimes shed light on the challenge and provide direction:

- *Which circle am I triggering in my client? Which do I want to be triggering?*

- *Which circle has been running the show for me?*

- *What would help to bring balance to both me and the client as we work with this situation?*

Sometimes, simply naming the situation and slowing things down to have a process-level discussion of how things have been playing out in the session can be a great help. The three circles can help us do this in a compassionate way: "Looks like our threat circles have been bouncing off of one another. This happens sometimes when dealing with real-life issues. Let's take a minute to do some soothing rhythm breathing and consider how we want to proceed."

Use the Perspective of the Compassionate Self

One nice thing about the Compassionate Self practice is that once this kind, wise, courageous perspective has been established, we can use it as an anchor-point to facilitate other aspects of the therapy. Let's consider just a couple of examples:

THE COMPASSIONATE SELF AS AN ANCHOR-POINT

There's a growing appreciation of the value of behavioral activation in creating emotional change. Simply getting clients moving in the direction of value-based goals (a major focus of ACT) can be tremendously powerful, and most good treatment protocols for problems of anxiety and depression involve mobilizing client behavior to help them address life areas they may have been avoiding. This can be challenging with clients who struggle with motivation, perhaps because they are deeply entrenched in avoidance, habitually procrastinate, or are very depressed. Therapists who take it upon themselves to be "motivator in chief" can inadvertently set up a coercive environment in therapy that can disempower clients or even invite them to resist the therapist's efforts to get them moving. However, once such clients have connected with the perspective of the compassionate self, this perspective can be useful in shifting the role of motivator from the therapist to the client. "What does your compassionate self know that you need to do?" "If that kind, wise, courageous version of you were here, what home practice would she assign?" Questions like these can help clients shift from a perspective of avoidance and resistance to one that is driven by intuitive wisdom about what they really need to work on—in a way that also helps them empower themselves by shifting into the perspective of the compassionate self, and acting from that perspective.

THE COMPASSIONATE SELF IN EXPOSURE THERAPY

Exposure therapy is historically one of the most effective treatment methods we have at our disposal, as well as one of the most avoided by clinicians. Because coming into contact with feared memories and situations can be quite an aversive experience for the client, it can be challenging for clinicians to motivate their clients and themselves to engage with exposure practices. However, there's quite a lot of literature supporting exposure as a core component in the treatment of many different problems.

In CFT, the compassionate self can be used both as a motivator to engage with exposure and as a means to make it more palatable to clients and therapists alike. First, the question "What does your compassionate self know that we need to do?" can be helpful in building motivation for the exposure. Many clients intuitively know (or can come to realize through Socratic exploration) that facing their fears is something they need to do to progress toward their goals.

Additionally, some preliminary work has been done to incorporate Compassionate Self work into exposure therapy itself, with promising (albeit unpublished) preliminary results (Kolts, Parker, & Johnson, 2013). Over the years, various theorists have utilized the addition of imaginal elements to exposure therapy protocols. Recently, exciting new research on memory reconsolidation (e.g. Monfils, Cowansage, Klann, & LeDoux, 2009; Schiller et al., 2010) has demonstrated that exposure can be done in a way that not only adds new learning, but can produce *alterations in original fear memories* by considering certain time constraints, and adding in new, nonfearful elements during the exposure process. These researchers have observed that a "reconsolidation window" appears to open approximately ten minutes following an initial imaginal reexposure to a fear memory, during which time the fear memory itself becomes somewhat malleable. During this time, new elements can be introduced, allowing the "rewriting" of memories so that fear is no longer expressed (Schiller et al., 2010).

In CFT, this can be done by having the client initially bring up a fear memory—for example, an acute trauma memory or "hot spot" (particularly fearful piece of a longer trauma memory). The reconsolidation literature indicates that a period of ten minutes or so needs to pass between the initial recall of the fear memory and the point at which it becomes malleable to updating via new information. We can spend this time assisting the client to shift into the perspective of the compassionate self, say, by doing one minute of soothing rhythm breathing, five minutes of mindful breathing, and a five- to seven-minute Compassionate Self exercise (Kolts, Parker, & Johnson, 2013). Then, the client is instructed to return to the fear memory in standard fashion, keying into both the sensory aspects of the memory and the feelings and thoughts that are present. Once the memory is vivid, we can prompt clients to slow down their breathing, shift into the perspective of the compassionate self, and imagine that they are in the situation as their current, compassionate self—observing the vulnerable version of themselves in the memory, feeling compassion for that scared version of themselves, and offering support and reassurance in whatever way would be experienced as most helpful. Focus is placed on creating feelings of warmth, kindness, and a desire to help the suffering self, and on offering support and encouragement to this vulnerable self. "How would you support that vulnerable version of you?" "What would you want that vulnerable self to understand?" "How might you be there for her and encourage her?"

Then the client can be prompted to shift back and forth between the perspective of the compassionate self (now placed into the context of the memory) and the perspective of the vulnerable version of the self that experienced the event. The client imagines himself back in the situation, with all of the scary aspects of the event still present, but also having the future kind, wise, courageous version of the self there as well—offering kindness, encouragement, support, and perhaps the certainty that *you will make it through this*, to become this future self. The therapy then progresses, shifting back and forth between these two versions of the self, using subjective distress ratings as anchor-points for tracking the client's distress.

While the efficacy of this variant of exposure therapy needs to be systematically evaluated through research, it is consistent with recent science on memory reconsolidation, and preliminary observations seem to indicate that it can significantly reduce client distress and avoidance while producing similar gains to traditional exposure therapies. These few cases have also demonstrated anecdotal evidence consistent with the reconsolidation studies, with clients saying things like, "The memory is still there, but instead of the fear that used to be there, there is an experience of being supported—of not being alone" (Kolts, Parker, & Johnson, 2013).

Conclusion

Whether you picked up this book in the hope of learning to formally practice CFT as a cohesive therapy approach, or simply wanted to add some new tools and perspectives to your existing treatment approach, I hope you've found something of use. Compassion offers powerful tools for helping clients to overcome shame, and relate to their struggles with warmth, courage, encouragement, and the commitment to build better lives.

I've attempted to organize and present CFT as a collection of layered processes and practices: the roles embodied in the therapeutic relationship; a compassionate understanding of the human condition based in an understanding of evolution, affective neuroscience, attachment, and behavioral science; the cultivation of a mindful awareness; and the purposeful development of compassion and compassionate strengths. When CFT is at its best, these various layers deepen, strengthen, and reinforce one another. While we can choose to select certain practices and techniques and use them in isolation, I'd encourage you to consider all of these layers, and how you might weave them into the therapy process.

As we began, let's end by reminding ourselves of the price of admission: if we're going to have human lives, we're going to face pain and suffering. We'll all face difficulties, disappointments, challenges, and grief. It's understandable that we (and our clients) wouldn't *want* to face these things—we'd often prefer to turn away and avoid the things that make us uncomfortable. But that doesn't work, because in organizing our lives around minimizing discomfort, we shut ourselves off from many of the things that can make them deeply meaningful. We can build our lives around endless efforts to stay comfortable, or we can make them about pursuing goals and relationships that are deeply important to us and imbue us with meaning, safeness, fulfillment, and joy. But we can't do both.

Compassion gives us a way to turn *toward* the things that scare us—with kindness, wisdom, and courage—and to work with them. When we stop trying to avoid discomfort, we can turn toward suffering and look deeply into it, so we can come to understand the causes and conditions that create it—perhaps even learning enough to help make things better.

Perhaps most of all, compassion involves courage: the courage to let our hearts break. But here's the thing: *our hearts are going to break anyway.* Bad things sometimes happen in life, and we all have to find ways to work with them. Remember, it's the price of admission to have a human life. The question is this: *What are we going to do when that happens?* Will we close ourselves off, or open ourselves up?

What if we accept this pain and occasional heartbreak as simply part of what it costs to have an amazing life? What if we consider what that kind, wise, courageous, compassionate version of us would do? What if we let ourselves *care*, connecting with likeminded others to support one another in the courageous work of making positive change in our lives, and in the world? Let's keep ourselves pointed toward the things that are important to us, help our clients do the same, and keep going. *This is compassion.*

Afterword:
Unpacking the
Compassionate Mind

This book is a wonderful beginning guide to compassion-focused therapy (CFT). CFT is part of a family of contextual forms of cognitive and behavioral therapy that are concerned with issues such as self-kindness, compassion for others, mindfulness, and values-based actions. The specific theories and techniques that are part of these new methods vary, but they are clearly interconnected. Thus, even though I am not an expert in CFT, I am honored to have been asked to write a short afterword to this book, and it is those interconnections that I would like to focus on.

I predict that evidence-based therapies in general, and cognitive behavioral therapy (CBT) in particular, will soon be thought of more as comprising evidence-based processes and procedures for solving problems and for promoting human prosperity, than as named packages of therapeutic techniques linked to syndromes and the elimination of symptoms. As that transition occurs, I expect that process-oriented forms of contextual treatment will increasingly link a portion of their evidence-based change principles to compassion as it's considered from the point of view of more basic scientific areas including evolution, learning, emotion, cognition, and culture. Thus the core vision of CFT, in my opinion, is likely to have a very long life indeed.

Through books like this, therapists can quickly see for themselves how central these issues are in therapy. They are central in part because of the modern world itself. The human mind did not evolve for the present day. Modern technology, gushing a constant stream of images and sound, has created a fire hose of human language. Everything imaginable is there in the stream, but the biases of commerce and media mean that messages conveying courage, love, and connection are simply being overwhelmed by those spreading pain, horror, criticism, and judgment. If it bleeds, it leads. Pain sells.

There is, in effect, no place that the cacophony cannot reach. I am a few feet from a television remote, my iPhone is inches away, I'm typing on my laptop, and the newspaper sits on the floor next to my chair. Without so much as lifting my rear end from this chair I can tell you that the man who long represented Subway sandwich shops is going to jail for molesting children; that it has been one year since news correspondent James Foley was beheaded; that a baby boy died after his father was seen beating him in a car while driving; that July was the hottest month in recorded history; that a talk-show host wants to house undocumented immigrants in tents and rent them out as slaves; and that a fifty-eight-year-old homeless Latino person was beaten and urinated on by men who said Donald Trump was right about immigrants.

That is just one day, and I've hardly gotten started.

Human beings are cooperative primates, and both the desire to be included and the effects of mentally including others are built into our bones, into our language systems, and into our cultures. Our ability to cooperate and to care about others is why we have a civilized society. It is why we even have television, or iPhones, or laptops, or newspapers.

We should neither romanticize these abilities nor take them for granted. In order to have compassion for others, we need to take their perspective and not run away when it is emotionally hard. At the same time, multilevel selection theory teaches us that we evolved to be cooperative in part because of between-group competition. In the modern interconnected world, we can no longer rely on that mechanism—being "for" our in-group and "against" outsiders—to foster compassion and concern. We need now to care about that much larger group called "humanity." That can be a challenge to us all.

If the core vision of CFT is here to stay, then it is up to evidence-based therapists across the board to take that vision seriously. This means digging into the more specific predictions about processes of change, and their linkage to specific methods relevant to compassion, made by the contextual forms of CBT. We need to know, and soon, not just that compassion is important in a general sense, but how and why it is important in specific areas, and how best to target those areas. It will take a lot of cooperation and effort from a very large group to acquire that knowledge in detail and in a reasonable time frame. Those interested in compassion as a clinical issue and those practicing CFT will need to take part.

For all of these reasons, a book like this is invaluable. It opens up CFT ideas to the larger therapeutic community so that the involvement and interest in these issues and methods can continue to broaden and grow. In the modern world, compassion is too crucial for us to do anything else.

—Steven C. Hayes
Foundation Professor, University of Nevada, Reno
Cofounder of ACT and author of
Get Out of Your Mind and Into Your Life

Acknowledgments

First, sincere appreciation goes to my wife, Lisa Koch, and my son, Dylan Kolts, who never grumbled when I snuck away to write on a weekend morning. Also to my parents, John and Mary Kolts, who offered continuous support and encouragement for this book as for all things.

Thanks to all at New Harbinger who nurtured this book and me while I was writing it, including Tesilya Hanauer, Catharine Meyers, Nicola Skidmore, and Jess Beebe. Sincere thanks also to Susan LaCroix, whose copyediting made this a much better book.

Paul Gilbert is the reason this book exists—Paul, I hope I haven't butchered your model too much! To credit Paul as he deserves would make for an impossibly cumbersome text, as virtually every page contains something I learned from Paul—if not from his written works, then from evenings spent chatting about CFT over glasses of red wine and the occasional interlude to play guitar. Thanks also to my dear friends in the CFT community: Dennis Tirch, Laura Silberstein, Jean and the entire Gilbert family, Chris Irons, Korina Ioannou, Christine Braehler, Deborah Lee, Tobyn Bell, Fiona Ashworth, Michelle Cree, Kate Lucre, Corinne Gale, Mary Welford, Neil Clapton, Ken Goss, Ian Lowens, and many others.

Sincere thanks also go to Matthieu Villatte for his valuable feedback on the sections regarding relational frame theory, and to the many others who contributed directly or indirectly to this book, including Susanne Regnier, Jason Luoma, Melissa Ranucci-Soll, Kelly Koerner, Amy Wagner, Sandy Bushberg, and Kelly Wilson.

I also want to acknowledge my wonderful colleagues and students at Eastern Washington University, who have supported and nurtured my career for going-on two decades now. In particular, I'd like to recognize my department chair, Nick Jackson; my dean, Vickie Shields; and my dear friends and colleagues Phil Watkins, Amani El-Alayli, and Kurt Stellwagen. I also want to acknowledge the fantastic students in my research team, including Amy Frers, Leah Parker, Elijah Johnson, Ahva Mozafari, and Blaine Bart.

Appendix: Reproducible Forms

The following forms are also available for download at http://www.newharbinger.com/33094.

CFT CASE FORMULATION WORKSHEET

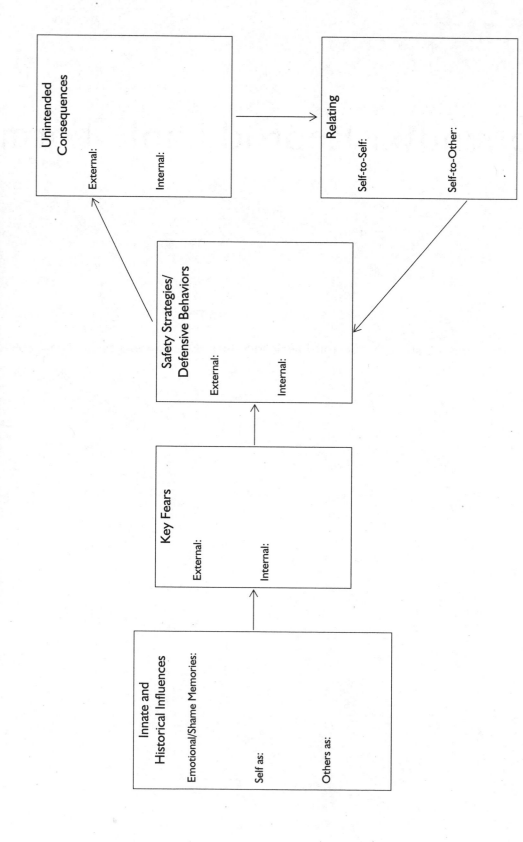

Innate and Historical Influences

Emotional/Shame Memories:

Self as:

Others as:

Key Fears

External:

Internal:

Safety Strategies/ Defensive Behaviors

External:

Internal:

Unintended Consequences

External:

Internal:

Relating

Self-to-Self:

Self-to-Other:

THREAT EMOTION MONITORING FORM

The purpose of this homework is to help you become familiar with the situations that tend to provoke your anger and the ways in which you tend to respond, and to learn to generate compassionate alternatives. Pick one time during the week when you experienced a threat emotion, such as anger or anxiety.

Situation/Trigger: _____

_____

_____

_____

_____

Emotions: _____

_____

_____

_____

_____

Thoughts: _____

_____

_____

_____

_____

Behaviors (What did I do?): _____

_____

_____

_____

_____

Outcome (How did the situation turn out?): _____

_____

_____

_____

_____

What does my compassionate self say? _____

_____

_____

_____

_____

What would my compassionate self have done? _____

_____

_____

_____

_____

FILLING OUT THE THREAT EMOTION MONITORING FORM

Situation/Trigger: Briefly describe what happened—the situation that provoked your threat response. What threat was involved? Describe the context as well (*I was late, and the people in front of me were...*). Often, there are fairly consistent "triggers" that tend to activate us. It is important to identify what our specific triggers are—what sorts of experiences tend to make us feel threatened—so we can learn to work skillfully when faced with them.

Emotions: What feelings came up in the situation? Use specific terms (*anger, irritation, anxiety, loneliness, embarrassment, shame, fear, sadness, excitement*).

Thoughts: What words and images came up in your mind? (For example: *She can't treat me like that!* or *I can't handle this.*) Did your thoughts fuel or calm your threat system?

Behaviors: What did you do? What actions did you take?

Outcome: How did it turn out? What helped in this situation? What did you do that worked? What got in the way of your handling the situation the best way you could?

What does my compassionate self say? How would your wise, kind, confident, compassionate self understand and approach this situation?

What would my compassionate self have done? How would your compassionate self behave in this situation?

INSTRUCTIONS FOR COMPASSIONATE LETTER-WRITING

This exercise is designed to help us develop the compassionate self. We want to build and strengthen mental patterns that will help us find the courage to work with difficult experiences, to accept ourselves, and to build a sense of peace within ourselves that we can share with others. Learning to think and behave compassionately can sometimes be helped by writing a letter to ourselves. In this exercise, you're going to write about difficulties, but from the perspective of your compassionate self. You can write a general letter to yourself, or you can tailor the letter to support yourself around a particularly challenging situation.

- First, get out a pen and paper. You might even pick out a special journal or notebook.

- Spend a few moments doing soothing rhythm breathing. Allow yourself to slow down and settle into your experience.

- Now try to shift into the perspective of your compassionate self. Connect with your compassionate self, imagining yourself at your best—your calmest, your wisest, your most caring, your most confident and courageous. Feel yourself filled with feelings of kindness, strength, and confidence. Imagine yourself as this compassionate person who is wise, understanding, and committed to helping. Imagine your manner, your tone of voice, and how you feel as this compassionate being.

- When we are in a compassionate frame of mind, even slightly, we try to use our personal life experiences wisely. We know that life can be hard. We can look deeply into the perspectives of ourselves and other people involved in difficult situations, and try to understand how it makes sense that they might feel and act this way. We offer strength and support, and try to be warm, nonjudgmental, and noncondemning. Take a few breaths and feel that wise, understanding, confident, compassionate part of you arise—this is the part of you that will write the letter.

- If thoughts of self-doubt, like *Am I doing it right?* or *I'm not really feeling it* arise, note these thoughts as normal comments our minds make, and observe what you are experiencing as you write the best that you can. There is no right or wrong...you're just practicing, working with your compassionate self. As you write, try to create as much emotional warmth and understanding as you can.

- As you write your letter, try to allow yourself to understand and accept your distress. For example, you might start with, *I am sad, and I feel distress. My distress is understandable because...*

- Note the reasons—realize that your distress makes sense. Then continue... *I would like myself to know that...*

- The idea is to communicate understanding, caring, and warmth while helping ourselves work on the things we need to address.

When you have written your first few compassionate letters, go through them with an open mind and see whether they actually capture compassion for you. If they do, see if you can spot the following qualities in your letter:

- It expresses concern, genuine caring, and encouragement.

- It is sensitive to your distress and needs.

- It helps you face your feelings and become more tolerant of them.

- It helps you become more understanding of your feelings, difficulties, and dilemmas.

- It is nonjudgmental and noncondemning, helping you to feel safe and accepted.

- A genuine sense of warmth, understanding, and caring fills the letter.

- It helps you think about behavior you may need to adopt in order to get better.

- It reminds you why you are making efforts to improve.

This handout was developed for the book *CFT Made Simple*, by Russell Kolts. Permission is granted for the free reproduction and dissemination of this form for clinical or training purposes.

COMPASSION PRACTICE JOURNAL

Day	Type of Practice and How Long	Comments—What Was Helpful?
Monday		
Tuesday		
Wednesday		
Thursday		
Friday		
Saturday		
Sunday		

This worksheet was developed for the book *CFT Made Simple*, by Russell Kolts. Permission is granted for the free reproduction and dissemination of this form for clinical or training purposes.

References

Ainsworth, M. D. S. (1963). The development of infant-mother interaction among the Ganda. In B. M. Foss (Ed.), *Determinants of Infant Behavior, Vol. 2*, 67–112. New York: Wiley.

Andrews, B., Brewin, C. R., Rose, S., & Kirk, M. (2000). Predicting PTSD symptoms in victims of violent crime: the role of shame, anger, and childhood abuse. *Journal of Abnormal Psychology, 109*, 69–73.

Andrews, B., & Hunter, E. (1997). Shame, early abuse, and course of depression in a clinical sample: a preliminary study. *Cognition and Emotion, 11*, 373–381.

Andrews, B., Quian, M., & Valentine, J. (2002). Predicting depressive symptoms with a new measure of shame: the Experiences of Shame Scale. *British Journal of Clinical Psychology, 41*, 29–33.

Ashworth, F., Gracey, F., & Gilbert, P. (2011). Compassion focused therapy after traumatic brain injury: theoretical foundations and a case illustration. *Brain Impairment, 12*, 128–139.

Baumeister, R. F., Bratslavsky, E., Finkenauer, C., & Vohs, K. D. (2001). Bad is stronger than good. *Review of General Psychology, 5*, 323–370. doi:10.1037//1089–2680.5.4.323.

Beaumont, E., & Hollins Martin, C. J. (2013). Using compassionate mind training as a resource in EMDR: a case study. *Journal of EMDR Practice and Research, 7*, 186–199.

Beck, A. T. (1976). *Cognitive Therapy and the Emotional Disorders*. New York: International Universities Press.

Beck, A. T., Davis, D. D., & Freeman, A. (2014). *Cognitive Therapy of Personality Disorders* (3rd ed.). New York: Guilford Press.

Bowlby, J. (1988). *A secure base: clinical applications of attachment theory*. London: Routledge.

Bowlby, J. (1982). *Attachment and loss: Vol.1. Attachment*. London: Hogarth Press and the Institute of Psycho-Analysis. (Original work published 1969.)

Bowlby, J. (1973). *Attachment and loss: Vol.2. Separation: anxiety and anger*. New York: Basic Books.

Braehler, C., Gumley, A., Harper, J., Wallace, S., Norrie, J., & Gilbert, P. (2013). Exploring change processes in compassion focused therapy in psychosis: results of a feasibility randomized controlled trial. *British Journal of Clinical Psychology, 52*, 199–214.

Burns, D. D. (1980) *Feeling good: the new mood therapy*. New York: New American Library.

Carvalho, S., Dinis, A., Pinto-Gouveia, J., & Estanqueiro, C. (2013). Memories of shame experiences with others and depression symptoms: the mediating role of experiential avoidance. *Clinical Psychology and Psychotherapy*, doi: 10.1002/cpp.1862. [epub ahead of print].

Cozolino, L. J. (2010). *The Neuroscience of Psychotherapy: Healing the Social Brain*. New York, NY: Norton.

Depue, R. A., & Morrone-Strupinsky, J. V. (2005). A neurobehavioral model of affiliative bonding: implications for conceptualizing a human trait of affiliation. *Behavioral and Brain Sciences, 28*, 313–349.

Eells, T. D. (2010). *Handbook of Psychotherapy Case Formulation* (2nd ed.). New York: Guilford Press.

Feeney, B. C., & Thrush, R. L. (2010). Relationship influences upon exploration in adulthood: the characteristics and function of a secure base. *Journal of Personality and Social Psychology, 98,* 57–76. doi: 10.1037/a00169691

Fonagy, P., & Luyten, P. (2009). A developmental, mentalization-based approach to the understanding and treatment of borderline personality disorder. *Development and Psychopathology, 21,* 1355–81.

Frederickson, B. L., Cohn, M. A., Coffey, K. A., Pek, J., & Finkel, S. (2008). Open hearts build lives: positive emotions, induced through loving-kindness meditation, build consequential resources. *Journal of Personality and Social Psychology, 95,* 1045–1062.

Fung, K. M., Tsang, H. W., & Corrigan, P. W. (2008). Self-stigma of people with schizophrenia as predictor of their adherence to psychological treatment. *Psychiatric Rehabilitation Journal, 32,* 95–104.

Gale, C., Gilbert, P., Read, N., & Goss, K. (2014). An evaluation of the impact of introducing compassion-focused therapy to a standard treatment programme for people with eating disorders. *Clinical Psychology and Psychotherapy, 21,* 1–12.

Germer, C. K. (2009). *The Mindful Path to Self-Compassion.* New York: Guilford Press.

Gilbert, P. (2014). The origins and nature of compassion focused therapy. *British Journal of Clinical Psychology, 53,* 6–41.

Gilbert, P. (2010). *Compassion Focused Therapy: The CBT Distinctive Features Series.* London: Routledge.

Gilbert, P. (2009a). *The Compassionate Mind.* London, UK: Constable & Robinson; Oakland, CA: New Harbinger.

Gilbert, P. (2009b). *Overcoming Depression: A Self-Help Guide to Using Cognitive Behavioral Techniques* (3rd ed.). New York: Basic Books.

Gilbert, P. (2002). Body shame: a biopsychosocial conceptualization and overview, with treatment implications. In P. Gilbert & J. Miles (Eds.), *Body Shame: Conceptualisation, Research, and Treatment,* 3–54. London: Brunner.

Gilbert, P. (2000). The relationship of shame, social anxiety, and depression: the role of the evaluation of social rank. *Clinical Psychology and Psychotherapy, 1,* 174–189.

Gilbert, P. (1998). What is shame? Some core issues and controversies. In P. Gilbert & B. Andrews (Eds.), *Shame: Interpersonal Behavior, Psychopathology, and Culture,* 3–36. New York: Oxford University Press.

Gilbert, P. (1989). *Human Nature and Suffering.* Hove: Lawrence Erlbaum Associates.

Gilbert, P., & Choden. (2013). *Mindful Compassion.* London: Constable & Robinson.

Gilbert, P., & Irons, C. (2005). Focused therapies and compassionate mind training for shame and self-attacking. In P. Gilbert (Ed.), *Compassion: Conceptualisations, Research, and Use in Psychotherapy,* 263–325. London: Routledge.

Gilbert, P., McEwan, K., Catarino, F., Baiao, R., & Palmeira, L. (2013). Fears of happiness and compassion in relationship with depression, alexithymia, and attachment security in a depressed sample. *British Journal of Clinical Psychology, 53,* 228–244.

Gilbert, P., McEwan, K., Matos, M., & Rivas, A. (2011). Fears of compassion: development of three self-report measures. *Psychology and Psychotherapy: Theory, Research, and Practice, 84,* 239–255.

Gilbert, P., & Proctor, S. (2006). Compassionate mind training for people with high shame and self-criticism: overview and pilot study of a group therapy approach. *Clinical Psychology and Psychotherapy, 13,* 353–379.

Gillath, O., Shaver, P. R., & Mikulincer, M. (2005). An attachment-theoretical approach to compassion and altruism. In P. Gilbert (Ed.), *Compassion: Conceptualisations, Research, and Use in Psychotherapy.* London: Routledge.

Goss, K. (2011). *The Compassionate-Mind Guide to Ending Overeating: Using Compassion-Focused Therapy to Overcome Bingeing and Disordered Eating.* Oakland, CA: New Harbinger; London: Constable & Robinson.

Goss, K., & Allan, S. (2009). Shame, pride, and eating disorders. *Clinical Psychology and Psychotherapy, 16,* 303–316.

Greenberg, L. S., Rice, L. N., & Elliot, R. (1993). *Facilitating Emotional Change: The Moment-by-Moment Process.* New York: Guilford Press.

Greenberg, L. S., & Watson, J. C. (2006). *Emotion-Focused Therapy for Depression.* Washington, D.C.: American Psychological Association.

Hackmann, A., Bennett-Levy, J., & Holmes, E. A. (2011). *Oxford Guide to Imagery in Cognitive Therapy* (Oxford Guides in Cognitive Behavioural Therapy). Oxford: Oxford University Press.

Harris, R. (2013). *Getting Unstuck in ACT: A Clinician's Guide to Overcoming Common Obstacles in Acceptance and Commitment Therapy.* Oakland, CA: New Harbinger.

Hayes, S. C., Barnes-Holmes, D., & Roche, B. (Eds.) (2001). *Relational Frame Theory: A Post-Skinnerian Account of Human Language and Cognition.* New York, NY: Kluwer Academic/Plenum Publishers.

Hayes, S. C., Strosahl, K. D., & Wilson, K. G. (1999). *Acceptance and Commitment Therapy: An Experiential Approach to Behavior Change* (1st ed.). New York, NY: Guilford Press.

Henderson, L. (2010). *The Compassionate-Mind Guide to Building Social Confidence: Using Compassion-Focused Therapy to Overcome Shyness and Social Anxiety.* Oakland, CA: New Harbinger; London: Constable & Robinson.

Hofmann, S. G., Grossman, P., & Hinton, D. E. (2011). Lovingkindness and compassion meditation: potential for psychological interventions. *Clinical Psychology Review, 31,* 1126–1132.

Hofmann, S. G., Sawyer, A. T., Witt, A. A., & Oh, D. (2010). The effect of mindfulness-based therapy on anxiety and depression: a meta-analytic review. *The Journal of Consulting and Clinical Psychology, 78,* 169–83.

Holman, G., Kanter, J., Tsai, M., & Kohlenberg, R. J. (2016). *Functional Analytic Psychotherapy Made Simple.* Oakland, CA: New Harbinger.

Hoyt, W. T. (1996). Antecedents and effects of perceived therapist credibility: a meta-analysis. *Journal of Counseling Psychology,* 430–447.

Judge, L., Cleghorn, A., McEwan, K., & Gilbert, P. (2012). An exploration of group-based compassion focused therapy for a heterogeneous range of clients presenting to a community mental health team. *International Journal of Cognitive Therapy, 5,* 420–429.

Kabat-Zinn, J. (1994). *Wherever You Go, There You Are: Mindfulness Meditation in Everyday Life.* New York: Hyperion.

Kaleem, J. (2013). Surprising number of Americans don't believe in evolution. *The Huffington Post.* Retrieved from http://www.huffingtonpost.com/2013/12/30/evolution-survey_n_4519441.html

Kannan, D., & Levitt, H. M. (2013). A review of client self-criticism in psychotherapy. *Journal of Psychotherapy Integration, 23,* 166–178.

Kelly, A. C., & Carter, J. C. (2014). Self compassion training for binge eating disorder: a pilot randomized controlled trial. *Psychology and Psychotherapy: Theory, Research, and Practice.* doi:10.1111/papt.12044.

Kim, S., Thibodeau, R., & Jorgenson, R. S. (2011). Shame, guilt, and depressive symptoms: a meta-analytic review. *Psychological Bulletin, 137*(1), 68–96.

Knox, J. (2010). *Self-Agency in Psychotherapy: Attachment, Autonomy, and Intimacy* (Norton Series in Interpersonal Neurobiology). New York: Norton.

Kohlenberg, R. J., & Tsai, M. (1991). *Functional Analytic Psychotherapy: A Guide for Creating Intense and Curative Therapeutic Relationships.* New York: Plenum.

Kolts, R. L. (2012). *The Compassionate-Mind Guide to Managing Your Anger: Using Compassion-Focused Therapy to Calm Your Rage and Heal Your Relationships.* Oakland, CA: New Harbinger; London: Constable & Robinson.

Kolts, R. L. (2013, December). *Applying CFT in Working with Problematic Anger: The 'True Strength' Prison Program.* Paper presented at the 2nd Annual Conference on Compassion-Focused Therapy, London.

Kolts, R. L., & Chodron, T. (2013). *Living with an Open Heart: How to Cultivate Compassion in Everyday Life.* (US title: *An Open-Hearted Life: Transformative Lessons on Compassionate Living from a Clinical Psychologist and a Buddhist Nun*). London: Constable and Robinson; Boston: Shambhala.

Kolts, R. L., Parker, L., & Johnson, E. (2013, December). *Initial Exploration of Compassion-Focused Exposure: Making Use of Reconsolidation.* Poster presented at the 2nd Annual Conference on Compassion-Focused Therapy, London.

Laithwaite, H., O'Hanlon, M., Collins, P., Doyle, P., Abraham, L., Porter, S., & Gumley, A. (2009). Recovery after psychosis (RAP): a compassion focused programme for individuals residing in high security settings. *Behavioral and Cognitive Psychotherapy, 37,* 511–526.

Leahy, R.L. (Ed.). (2006). *Roadblocks in cognitive-behavioral therapy: Transforming challenges into opportunities for change.* New York: Guilford Press.

Leaviss, J., & Uttley, I. (2014). Psychotherapeutic benefits of compassion-focused therapy: an early systematic review. *Psychological Medicine,* doi:10.1017/S0033291714002141.

LeDoux, J. (1998). *The Emotional Brain.* London: Weidenfeld and Nicolson.

Lee, D. A. (2005). The perfect nurturer: a model to develop a compassionate mind within the context of cognitive therapy. In P. Gilbert (Ed.), *Compassion: Conceptualisations, Research, and Use in Psychotherapy,* 263–325. London: Routledge.

Lee, D. A., & James, S. (2011). *The Compassionate-Mind Guide to Recovering from Trauma and PTSD: Using Compassion-Focused Therapy to Overcome Flashbacks, Shame, Guilt, and Fear.* Oakland, CA: New Harbinger; London: Constable & Robinson.

Liotti, G., & Gilbert, P. (2011). Mentalizing, motivation, and social mentalities: theoretical considerations and implications for psychotherapy. *Psychology and Psychotherapy: Theory, Research, and Practice, 84,* 9–25.

Linehan, M. M. (1993). *Cognitive-Behavioral Treatment of Borderline Personality Disorder.* New York: Guilford Press.

Lucre, K. M., & Corten, N. (2013). An exploration of group compassion-focused therapy for personality disorder. *Psychology and Psychotherapy: Theory, Research, and Practice, 86,* 387–400.

Luoma, J. B., Kulesza, M., Hayes, S. C., Kohlenberg, B., & Larimer, M. (2014). Stigma predicts residential treatment length for substance use disorder. *The American Journal of Drug and Alcohol Abuse, 40,* 206–212. doi:10.3109/00952990.2014.901337.

Maclean, P. D. (1990). *The Triune Brain in Evolution: Role of Paleocerebral Functions.* New York: Plenum Press.

Martin, D. J., Garske, J. P., & Davis, K. M. (2000). Relation of the therapeutic alliance with outcome and other variables: a meta-analytic review. *Journal of Consulting and Clinical Psychology, 68,* 438–450.

Mascaro, J. S., Rilling, J. K., Negi, L. T., & Raison, C. L. (2013). Compassion meditation enhances empathic accuracy and related neural activity. *SCAN, 8,* 48–55.

Mikulincer, M. & Shaver, P. R. (2007). *Attachment in Adulthood: Structure, Dynamics, and Change.* New York: Guilford Press.

Mikulincer, M. & Shaver, P. R. (2005). Attachment security, compassion, and altruism. *Current Directions in Psychological Science, 14,* 34–38.

Mikulincer, M., Gillath, O., Halevy, V., Avihou, N., Avidan, S., & Eshkoli, N. (2001). Attachment theory and reactions to others' needs: evidence that activation of the sense of attachment security promotes empathic responses. *Journal of Personality and Social Psychology, 81,* 1205–1224.

Monfils, M-H., Cowansage, K. K., Klann, E., LeDoux, J. E. (2009). Extinction-reconsolidation boundaries: key to persistent attenuation of fear memories. *Science, 324,* 951–955, doi:10.1126/science.1167975.

Neff, K. D. (2011). *Self-Compassion: Stop Beating Yourself Up and Leave Insecurity Behind.* New York: William Morrow.

Neff, K. D. (2003). The development and validation of a scale to measure self-compassion. *Self and Identity, 2,* 223–250.

Neff, K. D., & Germer, C. K. (2013). A pilot study and randomized controlled trial of the mindful self-compassion program. *Journal of Clinical Psychology, 69,* 28–44.

Panksepp, J. (1998). *Affective Neuroscience: The Foundations of Human and Animal Emotions.* New York: Oxford University Press.

Panksepp, J., & Biven, L. (2012). *The Archaeology of Mind: Neuroevolutionary Origins of Human Emotions.* New York: Norton.

Pepping, C. A., Davis, P. J., O'Donovan, A., & Pal, J. (2014). Individual differences in self-compassion: the role of attachment and experiences of parenting in childhood. *Self and Identity, 14,* 104–117. doi:10.1080/15298868.2014.955050.

Persons, J. B., Davidson, J., & Tompkins, M. A. (2000). *Essential Components of Cognitive-Behavior Therapy for Depression.* Washington, D.C.: American Psychological Association.

Pinto-Gouveia, J., & Matos, M. (2011). Can shame memories become a key to identity? The centrality of shame memories predicts psychopathology. *Applied Cognitive Psychology, 25,* 281–290.

Porges, S. W. (2011). *The Polyvagal Theory: Neurophysiological Foundations of Emotions, Attachment, Communication, and Self-Regulation.* New York: Norton.

Pos, A. E., & Greenberg, L. S. (2012). Organizing awareness and increasing emotion regulation: revising chairwork in emotion-focused therapy for borderline personality disorder. *Journal of Personality Disorders, 26*, 84–107.

Ramnerö, J., & Törneke, N. (2008). *The ABCs of Human Behavior: Behavioral Principles for the Practicing Clinician.* Oakland, CA: New Harbinger; Reno, NV: Context Press.

Rector, N.A., Bagby, R. M., Segal, Z. V., Joffe, R. T., & Levitt, A. (2000). Self-criticism and dependency in depressed patients treated with cognitive therapy or pharmacotherapy. *Cognitive Therapy and Research, 24*, 571–584.

Rüsch, N., Corrigan, P. W., Wassel, A., Michaels, P., Larson, J. E., Olschewski, M., Wilkniss, S., & Batia, K. (2009). Self-stigma, group identification, perceived legitimacy of discrimination and mental health service use. *British Journal of Psychiatry, 195*, 551–552.

Rüsch, N., Lieb, K., Göttler, I., Hermann, C., Schramm, E., & Richter, H. (2007). Shame and implicit self-concept in women with borderline personality disorder. *American Journal of Psychiatry, 164*, 500–508.

Salkovskis, P. M. (1996). The cognitive approach to anxiety: threat beliefs, safety-seeking behavior, and the special case of health anxiety and related obsessions. In P. M. Sarkovskis (Ed.), *Frontiers of Cognitive Therapy*, 48–74. New York: Guilford Press.

Salzberg, S. (1995). *Lovingkindness: The Revolutionary Art of Happiness.* Boston: Shambhala.

Schiller, D., Monfils, M-H., Raio, C. M, Johnson, D. C., LeDoux, J. E., & Phelps, E. A. (2010). Preventing the return of fear in humans using reconsolidation update mechanisms. *Nature, 463*, doi:10.1038/ nature08637.

Schore, A. N. (1999). *Affect Regulation and the Origin of the Self: The Neurobiology of Emotional Development.* Hillsdale, NJ: Lawrence Erlbaum & Associates, Inc.

Segal, Z. V., Williams, J. M. G., & Teasdale, J. D . (2001). *Mindfulness-Based Cognitive Therapy for Depression: A New Approach to Preventing Relapse.* New York: Guilford Press.

Shahar, B., Carlin, E. R., Engle, D. E., Hegde, J., Szepsenwol, O., & Arkowitz, H. (2012). A pilot investigation of emotion-focused two-chair dialogue intervention for self-criticism. *Clinical Psychology and Psychotherapy, 19*, 496–507. doi:10.1002/cpp.762.

Siegel, D. J. (2012). *The Developing Mind: How Relationships and the Brain Interact to Shape Who We Are* (2nd ed.). New York: Guilford Press.

Sirey, J. A., Bruce, M. L., Alexopoulas, G. S., Perlick, D., Friedman, S. J., & Meyers, B. S. (2001). Stigma as a barrier to recovery: perceived stigma and patient-rated severity of illness as predictors of antidepressant drug adherence. *Psychiatric Services, 52*, 1615–1620.

Skinner, B. F. (1953). *Science and Human Behavior.* New York: Macmillan.

Sroufe, L. A., & Waters, E. (1977). Attachment as an organizational construct. *Child Development, 48*, 1184–1199.

Tangney, J. P., Wagner, P., & Gramzow, R. (1992). Proneness to shame, proneness to guilt, and psychopathology. *Journal of Abnormal Psychology, 101*, 469–478.

Teasdale, J. D., & Barnard, P. J. (1993). *Affect, Cognition and Change: Remodelling Depressive Affect.* Hove, UK: Psychology Press.

Teyber, E., & McClure, F. H. (2011). *Interpersonal Process in Therapy* (6th ed.). Belmont, CA: Brooks/Cole.

Tirch, D. (2012). *The Compassionate-Mind Guide to Overcoming Anxiety: Using Compassion-Focused Therapy to Calm Worry, Panic, and Fear.* Oakland, CA: New Harbinger; London: Constable & Robinson.

Tirch, D., Schoendorff, B., & Silberstein, L. R. (2014). *The ACT Practitioner's Guide to the Science of Compassion: Tools for Fostering Psychological Flexibility.* Oakland, CA: New Harbinger.

Törneke, N. (2010). *Learning RFT: An Introduction to Relational Frame Theory and Its Clinical Application.* Oakland, CA: New Harbinger; Reno, NV: Context Press.

Tsai, M., Kohlenberg, R. J., Kanter, J., Kohlenberg, B., Follette, W., & Callaghan, G. (2009). *A Guide to Functional Analytic Psychotherapy: Awareness, Courage, Love and Behaviorism.* New York: Springer.

Wallin, D. J. (2007). *Attachment in Psychotherapy.* New York: Guilford Press.

About the author

Russell L. Kolts, PhD, is a licensed clinical psychologist and professor of psychology at Eastern Washington University, where he has taught for the past seventeen years. Kolts has authored or coauthored numerous books and scholarly articles, including *The Compassionate-Mind Guide to Managing Your Anger*, and has pioneered the application of compassion-focused therapy (CFT) to the treatment of problematic anger. An internationally recognized expert in CFT, he regularly conducts trainings and workshops on compassion and CFT, and has appeared in his own TEDx Talk.

Foreword writer **Paul Gilbert, PhD**, is world-renowned for his work on depression, shame, and self-criticism, and is the developer of CFT. He is head of the mental health research unit at the University of Derby, and has authored or coauthored numerous scholarly articles and books, including *The Compassionate Mind*, *Mindful Compassion*, and *Overcoming Depression*.

Afterword writer **Steven C. Hayes, PhD**, is Nevada Foundation Professor and director of clinical training in the department of psychology at the University of Nevada. An author of forty-one books and nearly 600 scientific articles, his career has focused on analysis of the nature of human language and cognition, and its application to the understanding and alleviation of human suffering and promotion of human prosperity. Among other associations, Hayes has been president of the Association for Behavioral and Cognitive Therapy, and the Association for Contextual Behavioral Science. His work has received several awards, including the Impact of Science on Application Award from the Society for the Advancement of Behavior Analysis, and the Lifetime Achievement Award from the Association for Behavioral and Cognitive Therapy.

Index

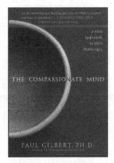
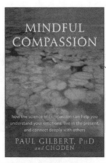
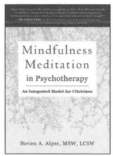

Register your **new harbinger** titles for additional benefits!

When you register your **new harbinger** title—purchased in any format, from any source—you get access to benefits like the following:

- Downloadable accessories like printable worksheets and extra content

- Instructional videos and audio files

- Information about updates, corrections, and new editions

Not every title has accessories, but we're adding new material all the time.

Access free accessories in 3 easy steps:

1. Sign in at NewHarbinger.com (or **register** to create an account).

2. Click on **register a book**. Search for your title and click the **register** button when it appears.

3. Click on the **book cover or title** to go to its details page. Click on **accessories** to view and access files.

That's all there is to it!

If you need help, visit:

NewHarbinger.com/accessories

new harbinger
CELEBRATING
40 YEARS